NAKED AIRPORT

Alastair Gordon

Metropolitan Books   Henry Holt and Company · New York

NAKED AIRPORT

A Cultural History of the World's Most Revolutionary Structure

m

Metropolitan Books
Henry Holt and Company, LLC
Publishers since 1866
115 West 18th Street
New York, New York 10011

Metropolitan Books™ is a registered
trademark of Henry Holt and Company, LLC.

Library of Congress Cataloging-in-Publication Data
Gordon, Alastair.
    Naked airport: a cultural history of the world's most revolutionary structure/Alastair
    Gordon. — 1st ed.
        p.   cm.
    Includes bibliographical references and index.
    ISBN 0-8050-6518-0
        1. Airports — History. I. Title.
    TL725.G647 2004
    387.7'36 — dc22   2003067612

Henry Holt books are available for special promotions and
premiums. For details contact: Director, Special Markets.

Please see www.nakedairport.com for additional material, discussion, and links.

First Edition 2004
Designed by Fritz Metsch
Printed in the United States of America
10 9 8 7   6   5   4   3   2   1

For Barbara

"In the main passenger terminal, chaos predominated."   —Arthur Hailey

Contents

NAKED AIRPORT

Prologue

Any technology gradually creates a totally new human environment.
—Marshall McLuhan

It was my cousin's last day in the United States—August 26, 1964—and he wanted to see the world's fair before flying back to London. My father drove us in his Buick to Flushing Meadow. The sky over Long Island was tempered blue and streaked with contrails. We bought tickets for General Motors's Futurama exhibit and rode around a miniature landscape that showed what life would be like in the future. My cousin and I were disappointed. There was something hokey about the whole fair, and the so-called future seemed shabby.

We then drove south a few miles on the Van Wyck Expressway and reached the periphery of Idlewild, which is what my father still called the airport, although it had been renamed John F. Kennedy International the year before. We glided along freshly paved overpasses and beneath the signs bearing candy-colored numbers. The terminals were strung out like pavilions around the looping roadway, and it felt as if we were back at the fair. There was the flashy stained-glass entry to American Airlines, the flying-saucer roof of Pan Am, and the endless glass facade of the arrivals building. Then we parked in front of the TWA terminal and walked inside.

I had seen photographs of the birdlike structure, but none had done it justice. The interior was a continuously flowing surface of cast concrete. There were no sharp corners, no right angles, no dull flat ceilings. The building was topsy-turvy—in some places the walls swooped down to become floor, while other parts curved above our heads like ocean waves that were about to break yet were somehow frozen in place. Between the vaults were gaping ellipses of glass through which you might see a tail fin or a passing cloud. I was only twelve and knew nothing about architecture, but the pavilions at the world's fair seemed stodgy in comparison. This wasn't pretending to be the future; this *was* the future. Those were real Boeing 707s sitting on the tarmac.

The air was charged with anticipation. Pilots stepped through pools of milky light. Beautiful stewardesses trailed behind them wearing trim red outfits and perfectly straight stocking seams. The ambient lighting, the flirtatious smiles, the lipstick-red carpet and uniforms, the cushioned benches and steel railings curving around the mezzanine—all conspired on the senses. Even the clock that hung from the ceiling had a suggestive globular shape. We sat in an oversize conversation pit, beneath a panoramic screen of glass, and watched the service vehicles scoot between the planes. "This is unbelievably cool," said my cousin in a hushed, almost reverential tone.

When his flight was announced, he walked up the long umbilical departure tube, turned once to wave, like an astronaut, and then disappeared into the satellite at the far end of the tube. There was an otherworldly, *Twilight Zone* quality to this moment—as if my cousin were flying not to London but to Mars. Perhaps it was the recessed lighting or the curved walls that made for the slow-motion, spacy feeling. Perhaps it was the subtle rise of floor that made the boarding tube seem hyperextended, much longer than it actually was. All I knew was that I didn't want to leave just then. I wanted to savor the moment.

Still, my father and I headed back onto the Belt Parkway and drove east into the slanting afternoon light. I was unsettled for the rest of the drive: my cousin's departure had been dreamlike and

Departure tube at the TWA terminal, Idlewild/Kennedy Airport, circa 1962.

elusive but, at the same time, very real—the essential modern moment—when technology seemed perfectly in tune with human aspiration, before hijackings and air rage, before jumbo jets, before deregulation, dysfunctional baggage carousels, and electromagnetic scanners.

Over the next few years I flew frequently but never on TWA until I took a student year abroad. My flight had been booked on another airline, but it was canceled because of a bomb threat at JFK. It was Black September, 1970. There were bombs going off everywhere. The only available flight to Paris was on TWA, and I was able to transfer my ticket, pleased to get the chance to return to that inspiring terminal and walk up its mysterious boarding tube.

I pushed my way through a mob of angry German tourists—their flight had been canceled as well—and noticed how some of the openings had been boarded over with ugly sheets of plywood. The glacial panes of glass were grimy. The too-bright lighting cast garish shadows on the concrete walls that now looked cracked and dry—the texture of old chewing gum. The bright red carpeting was now faded and curling at the edges. The stewardesses looked haggard.

My plane was almost empty except for a group of plucky dames from Dallas who were heading to Paris on a shopping spree and weren't going to let any terrorists ruin their fun. Drinks were free, and when the plane touched down at Charles de Gaulle, everyone stood and cheered. My next few flights across the Atlantic were on cheap charter planes, and I learned to lower my expectations. Air travel had become an ordeal to be endured, not enjoyed. But I always wondered what had happened in that brief interval between the perfect airport moment of 1964 and the disappointments of later years.

As air travelers, we remove ourselves from the experience by thinking about something else, but we are never altogether comfortable with the airport process. Instead of being thrilled—as I was at twelve—we are more often than not horrified or bored by the reality. We check our bags and pass through security. We stand on the moving sidewalk and learn the status of our flight from a computer screen. We are both repelled and attracted at the same time. Some react with air rage, incensed by the impersonal nature of the setting. Others feel oddly light-headed, disembodied, or experience, as Joan Didion once wrote, a "certain weightlessness." Most of us just want to reach our destination as quickly and safely as possible.

A sign at an airport construction site today reads: EXCUSE OUR APPEARANCES. WE ARE TEARING DOWN YESTERDAY TO MAKE ROOM FOR TOMORROW. But the idealized "tomorrow" never comes. The airport is at once a place, a system, a cultural artifact that brings us face-to-face with the advantages as well as the frustrations of modernity. The sprawling, hybrid nature of the subject challenges easy assumptions. Its history has been a recurrent cycle of anticipation and disappointment, success and failure, innovation and obsolescence. This book traces that history through mutations of technology, design, and marketing—showing how the airport was gradually shaped into a new kind of human environment, while, in turn, shaping the rest of the modern world.

CHAPTER 1

Prototypes: 1924–1930

"Yes, it's definitely an airport . . ."
    —*Charles Lindbergh, 1927*

Paris, May 21, 1927. At first he was confused. It didn't look like
an airport. Charles Lindbergh could see a faintly illuminated
perimeter, but there were no approach lights or revolving beacons
like the ones they used in the United States, just some floodlights
revealing the edge of a field with hardly enough space to land a
plane. He wondered if he hadn't overshot his mark, so he circled
round to have a closer look. Were those hangars or the buildings of a
factory complex? Then there was the odd twinkling along the eastern edge of the darkness. Could that be factory windows? He'd been
in the air for over thirty hours. Maybe his eyes were playing tricks.
He tried signaling down with his flashlight, but there was no
response. He began a slow descent, leaving the line of unidentified
lights well to his right. He didn't want to end his 3,610-mile flight
by crashing into a smokestack. Then he saw outlines of the hangars.
"Yes, it's definitely an airport," he wrote. "I see part of a concrete
apron in front of a large half open door. . . . It's a huge airport. The
floodlights show only a small corner. It must be Le Bourget."[1]
    Meanwhile, on the ground there was a mood of delirious expec-
tation not seen in Paris since the end of the Great War. Lindbergh's
plane had been spotted over Ireland, and then again over the fields
of Normandy. Word of his approach was passed on to Paris by tele-

graph. A crowd of 150,000 people waited impatiently at the aerodrome. More than ten thousand cars pressed down the narrow roads leading to Bourget. Traffic was backed up all the way to the city. The twinkling reflections that Lindbergh had mistaken for factory windows were the headlamps of the cars.

He circled again and came in low to learn the lay of the field. "After the plane stopped rolling I turned it around and started to taxi back. . . ." Thousands of spectators broke through the barriers. They surrounded the plane and pressed their bodies against the fuselage as if it were a holy relic. The mob dragged him from the cockpit and carried him aloft for nearly half an hour. "Speaking was impossible," recalled Lindbergh, "no words could be heard in the uproar."

With his landing at Bourget, the airport became a place of ritualistic transformation. Charles Lindbergh went from an unknown mail pilot to a twentieth-century deity during that eerie night scene. While not the first to fly across the Atlantic, Lindbergh's singular achievement was to do it alone, nonstop, between the new world and the old. His journey marked the beginning of a modern global consciousness, delivered by the mechanical integrity of his Wright Whirlwind engine, by the Pathé cameras positioned on the terminal roof, the radio telegraph, and the other marvels of the age. Lindbergh was made world famous the instant his plane touched down. The lights that had so confused him were, in fact, confirmation of his celebrity.

As early as 1907, Rudyard Kipling, the English author and world traveler, had written about the airplane with remarkable prescience: "The time is near when men will receive their normal impressions of a new country suddenly and in plan, not slowly and in perspective; when the most extreme distances will be brought within the compass of one week's—one hundred and sixty-eight hours'—travel; when the word 'inaccessible,' as applied to any given spot on the surface of the globe, will cease to have any meaning."[2]

Lindbergh realized Kipling's prophecy: he not only linked two

Retouched news photograph of Lindbergh's night landing at Le Bourget, Paris, 10:22
P.M., May 21, 1927.

hemispheres, he redefined the concept of "arrival." Destinations
would no longer be approached in the traditional perspective of
Renaissance space, nor from the gradual, ground view of trains,
buses, or ships, but rapidly, from the air, with the city appearing
oddly splayed in abstraction. The gateways would no longer be
harbors and railroad stations. Now it was the airport, a place of
blinding lights and unexpected urgency.

European Skyways

If the twentieth century was still in search of allegories, aviation provided them in abundance. Pilots like Lindbergh and

Amelia Earhart became heroes for the young. Airline companies provided models of business innovation and the airplanes themselves, with their aerodynamic functionalism, became a source of inspiration for modern designers. At some point in the 1920s, a new kind of public place was beginning to take shape. Depending on where you landed, it might be referred to as an airport, air station, air depot, *aerogare, flughafen, stazioni aeroplani,* or *aeroporto.* In some countries it was called an aerodrome, an adaptation of velodrome from the Greek *dromos,* meaning speed, since many early fields were built as sporting venues. Pilots flew their planes around oval courses as if they were racing automobiles, hoping to set new speed records.

In Britain, early air meets were held at the Hendon Aerodrome outside of London. "On those days when a programme of contests is carried out and racing craft are 'banking' round the pylons," wrote one Hendon enthusiast, "there is so much to be seen that a

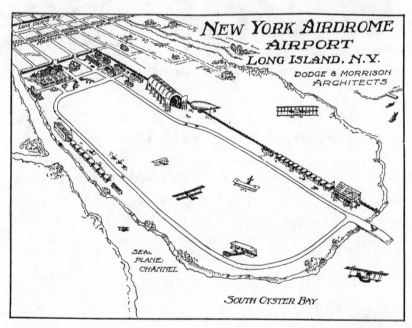

New York Airdrome airport, Long Island, New York. Dodge & Morrison Architects, 1920. Buildings were placed around the perimeter of early airfields as if on the banks of a lake.

spectator becomes almost bewildered."[3] The course at Rheims, France, had elaborate grandstands built specially for La Grande Semaine de l'Aviation de la Champagne in 1909. Spectators sat in elegantly appointed seats sipping champagne and watching the action.

After watching Wilbur Wright give a demonstration of his flying machine in Paris in 1908, an eyewitness imagined a moment in the near future when every town would possess a port for flying machines. "These ports," he wrote, "will be squares erected in the forms of cones and surrounded by hangars."[4] Soon, visionary planners and modernists began to see the airport as the key to the city of the future. In 1912, the Italian futurist Antonio Sant'Elia proposed a giant airplane station for the center of Milan. His plan was a bold foreshadowing of what an airport might actually look like one day, but Sant'Elia would never see it realized. He joined the Italian army in 1915 and was killed in action a year later.

On the opposite side of the trenches, Erich Mendelsohn huddled in a bunker and, between mortar rounds, sketched a kind of dream city. Among his drawings were plans for a large-scale airport to be built from cast concrete with rounded corners and flowing surfaces over a skeletal steel frame.[5] That same year, Wenzel Hablik, another German visionary, proposed a utopian community that would hover in the sky. His drawings for a "flying settlement" depicted a cylindrical airship encircled by propellers. Within its core were workshops, baths, and storerooms. The upper level contained residential spaces, the lower level a landing platform for smaller planes: "The settlement and a smaller satellite hover high in the clouds above a distant city in the mountains." In "Das Karussell," Bruno Taut proposed a giant aerial theater, a "cosmic-comical aerial amusement in silver," that would be carried aloft by airplanes and rotated by propellers in the wind, while planes disguised as comets would zoom around it.[6]

In the United States, the public imagination was stimulated by science-fiction magazines and movies. Air-minded designers were intoxicated by visions of airplanes and skyscrapers. Cities like New

York and Chicago would soon be sprouting glass towers with high-level landing pads. Planes and "autogyros" would flit between towers like bees buzzing around a hive. In 1908, illustrator Moses King depicted airships docking at Manhattan skyscrapers. Hollywood would convey the same suspension of disbelief in films like *Metropolis, Just Imagine*, and *Things to Come*.[7] These vertical fantasies were regarded with skepticism from the start. The journal *Aerial Age Weekly* published a satirical cartoon in 1921 that showed a New York skyscraper hung with a giant net: "The . . . net enables the aviator to land upon the roof without the slightest fear of falling off the other side."[8] Meanwhile, real airplanes were landing in muddy cow pastures.

Satirical cartoon, 1921.

Airport construction was given a boost after World War I when aviation drew a new kind of political map. European borders became more fluid as planes flew directly between capital cities. Airports thus became symbols of progressive thinking and utopian planning. WWI bombers like the Farman Goliath and the Blériot Mammoth were converted for civilian use and fitted out with upholstered chairs. Stripped of its bombing apparatus, the Mammoth could carry twenty-six passengers. Airfields built during the war, like Bourget and Croydon, were converted into civilian aerodromes. The first international service in Europe began on August 25, 1919, at Hounslow Aerodrome in London when Aircraft Transport and Travel Ltd. began regularly scheduled flights to Paris. A one-way fare cost £21. Hounslow had been a training depot during the war, and one of the old air corps hangars was refitted as a customs and passenger shed.9

By the time of Lindbergh's flight in 1927, there was a fully established network of airlines flying to all the major capitals of Europe. Air travel was now fashionable, and hundreds of thousands of Europeans had already been aloft. It was also something of the vogue for progressive Americans to come to Europe to fly, a daring and modern thing to do. The American journalist Lowell Thomas and his wife, Frances, set out on an "aëreal jaunt" through Europe in the summer of 1927; the idea was to travel without using train or ship. By the end of the trip, the couple had covered more than twenty-five thousand air miles, crisscrossing the continent and going as far east as Istanbul. With the exception of Moscow, Thomas had nothing but praise for European airports, especially compared to the "cow-pasture aerodromes" he knew in the States, where the entire fleet of airliners consisted of thirty or so passenger planes, and you were lucky to get a seat on a mail sack.10 Service on the European airlines was courteous and efficient: "The planes in which we have flown," wrote Thomas, "have moved off to the dot more often than the trains we used on previous jaunts . . . Instead of arriving late, we have more often been a few minutes ahead of time . . ."11

Thomas kept notes and published his impressions in *European Skyways: The Story of a Tour of Europe by Airplane,* which was dedicated to "All Who Have Missed the Joys of Flight." Unabashed propaganda for the airline business, *European Skyways* makes little mention of bad weather, air sickness, forced landings, or engine failures. But it gives an authentic account of the passenger's perspective at this early stage. "A new visionary world unfolds before the eye of the modern traveler who hurries from cloud to cloud," writes Thomas. "We spiral down past cliffs of glistening mist, turning shell-pink on their edges as they are touched by the setting sun." Between airports, the narrative digresses into mythology, ancient history, and the author's own memories of the Great War, with anecdotes about Dedalus, Hannibal, trench warfare, and flying ace Eddie Rickenbacker. "As I speed across the sky, the whole history of the region below me comes rushing to mind," he writes at one point. "I really see a double panorama—one with my eyes, the other with my imagination."

The Thomases began their air odyssey at the Croydon Aerodrome, aerial gateway of the British Empire. Covering more than 330 acres, Croydon was the largest airport in the world at the time. Thomas, an anglophile, had already mythologized another monument to empire, scholar/soldier T. E. Lawrence, in his book *With Lawrence in Arabia* (1924), and understood the marketing potential of tradition even better than the British: "All earthly roads may lead to Rome," he wrote, "but all celestial roads meet at Croydon, the Liverpool of Britannia's air."[12] The Royal Flying Corps field had been expanded to include new hangars, a fifty-room hotel, and an imposing terminal.

The Handley Page Aircraft Company started a flying service from London to Paris in 1922 using HP-42s that seated twelve to fourteen passengers. The company motto was: "Once you have flown to Paris, you will never go by boat again," but the early flights were still quite primitive. The cabins were chilly, and the engines were deafeningly loud. Passengers were provided with earplugs, lap rugs, and foot muffs. There were also frequent mechanical problems and forced landings due to inclement weather. Conditions improved when the British government sponsored a national airline system. Imperial Airways was formed in 1924 under the chairmanship of Sir Eric Geddes. It was a consolidation of several different companies and was subsidized by the government as an "instrument of Empire."[13]

At Croydon Lowell and Frances Thomas passed through a grandiose passenger station hailed by the British press as a symbol of the new air age.[14] The building was imperious in scale with high windows and a crenelated lookout. It might have been the county seat of an English lord except that the rusticated stone facing was in fact concrete block and the four-story tower contained a modern control room.

The logic of Croydon's terminal lay in its symmetrical plan.

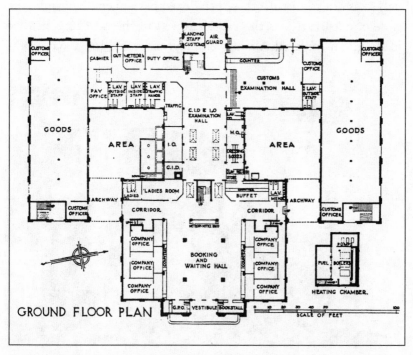

GROUND FLOOR PLAN

Beginnings of an airport vernacular: the ground-floor plan of the passenger station at the Croydon Aerodrome, London, 1928. The logic lay in its symmetrical separation of arriving and departing passengers. The outer wings were designated for freight.

Arrivals moved through one part of the terminal while departures moved through the other. Here were the conceptual beginnings of airport circulation. The outer wings of the building were designated for freight. The cavernous Booking and Waiting Hall received natural light through a domed skylight. Check-in counters lined both sides of the hall, and there was a bookshop, a restaurant, a reading lounge, and a buffet ⸱counter for fast lunch service. At the center was a "time-kiosk" raised on an octagonal plinth where a series of clocks displayed the times of different world cities. At one end of the hall an attendant ran back and forth on a raised platform updating weather and arrival information on a giant map of Europe.

Thomas took note of the people waiting in the lounge and was reassured that they came from the "best classes." The plane's three mighty Jaguar engines were warmed, at a distance from the terminal, so as not to disturb these privileged passengers. Not until the time of departure was the HP-42 towed to the boarding area for loading. An Imperial Airways employee, dressed like a naval offi-

Booking hall at the Croydon Aerodrome, London, circa 1928. At the center was a "time-kiosk" where a series of clocks displayed the times of cities around the world. An attendant stood on a raised platform and updated flight information.

cer, called out the flight number and led the group up a corridor and out to the apron.

But who were the people willing to pay the extra price and take the risk of flying? It was true, some were the affluent, titled type—the "best classes" admired by Thomas—but there were also movie stars, journalists on deadline, statesmen, businessmen, many of them American, as well as the occasional jazz-age flapper looking for a thrill. You had to have money to fly. Airfares were anywhere from 25 percent to 50 percent more expensive than first-class travel by train or ship. One aviation journal profiled the new breed of passengers as: "exceptional businessmen, clever tourists, romantic honeymoon couples, fast-moving directors, modern lawyers, anxious motorists, attractive mannequins, fresh oysters and crabs. . . ."

Imperial Airways carried one such group of "exceptional businessmen" on a junket across the continent in 1928, flying them to Paris, Cologne, Hannover, Berlin, Prague, Vienna, Budapest, Basel, and London—"all in fourteen days," according to the airline, "a trip impossible by any other form of transport." Thomas had an easy time picking out the Americans by their "ubiquitous horn-rimmed glasses" and the patronizing tone they used when addressing airline staff.

Thomas had covered the battles of World War I from the backseat of a biplane and was an experienced flier, but his wife was a novice. So it was with trepidation that Frances boarded Imperial's "City of New York." "The wind created by the whirling propellers almost blows my hatbox out of my hand," Thomas wrote, switching to his wife's point of view. Once aboard, a man known as a "rigger" came down the aisle rearranging passengers and baggage so that the plane would be evenly balanced during take-off. They were advised to fasten their safety belts, "a wide strip of leather attached to the chair," noted Frances, which only made her more anxious. "Mentally I review all the horrid smash-ups that might happen between Croydon and Amsterdam," she observed, but she seemed even more concerned about her attire: "If I ever live through this day, I am wondering if the little silk dress and lone evening gown in our joint suit-case will stand the wear and tear of every capital in Europe."[15]

A traffic controller in Croydon's tower waved a red signal flag and soon the Handley Page lumbered onto the runway. Frances held her breath as the plane climbed "like a crinolined circus lady on a tight-rope. Then up and up . . . I am at last astride Mother Goose's broom. . . . My nerves are at the snapping point," she confessed, but looking back to earth, Frances felt surprisingly empowered: "a giantess flying over pygmy villages."[16]

The plane crossed the English Channel and skirted the coast above Dunkirk, Ostend, and Zeebrugge, cities that appeared "in kaleidoscopic bird's eye views." Soon they were in Holland, which, Thomas observed, looked Dutch even from the sky—a "gigantic garden laid out by landscape artists with a passion for geometrical designs." At Schiphol Airport outside of Amsterdam they were greeted by a cheery stationmaster who handed each of them a glass of Schiedam gin to relax their nerves after the turbulent flight. As the stationmaster explained, Schiphol was built thirteen feet below sea level on land reclaimed from the Haarlemermeer Lake. "As the freak aerodrome of the world, it takes the blue ribbon," noted Thomas. The name "Schiphol" means "hole of ships," and the airport stands over the ruins of a famous naval battle fought between the Dutch and Spanish in 1573. Automatic pumps were installed, and over 150 miles of drainage structures were built under the landing area. Royal Dutch Airlines, KLM (Koninklijke Luchtvaart Maatschappij) began scheduled flights out of Schiphol in 1920. Under the farsighted leadership of Albert Plesman, KLM's director, the airport became one of Europe's most important aerial crossroads.

On their flight to Paris a few days later, the Thomases crossed the war-scarred landscape of Belgium and France before their plane banked over Le Bourget, an oddly V-shaped site with the Moirée Stream running to the north and a group of military buildings to the west. By 1921, ten different airlines were flying out of Paris to such distant cities as Dakar and Casablanca. Franco Roumaine airline, for example, flew the first transcontinental route from Paris to Prague, Vienna, Bucharest, and Ankara.

At the time of the Thomases' visit, the Aerogare de Paris was already a sprawling complex. The industrial-looking hangars that had confused Lindbergh were strung in a row along the eastern boundary. Right in their midst was a complex of neoclassical brick pavilions: Bourget's administrative center with a passenger terminal, airline offices, weather bureau, police station, customs, and the Paul-Bert Pavilion, where pilots received medical exams. The grounds were neatly landscaped, with gravel walkways and lines of pollarded trees; it all looked more like a corner of the Tuilleries Gardens than an airport.

The Thomases continued from Bourget to Constantinople. After refueling in Basel, and a quick cup of Swiss chocolate, their plane crossed the Alps, and Thomas pointed out that it took three hours to cross the same mountain range that took Hannibal and his elephants three weeks to cross. On their way back from Constantinople, they stopped in Berlin, where they attended a performance of *Lohengrin* at the opera house.

The Treaty of Versailles had decreed the destruction of all German aircraft and airfields after World War I. When the Allies finally lifted restrictions on aviation in 1925, the Germans wasted no time in catching up. Within three years, Lufthansa, the national airline, was logging more miles than all other European airlines combined.[17] In some ways, Versailles helped push Germany ahead of other nations. Since the country was not allowed to build for war, its energy and resources went toward the development of civil aviation. Lacking the colonial outposts that gave Britain and France their global reach, Germany used the airplane to extend its influence. After the humiliation of Versailles, every new air route, every new airport, was seen as a small victory, as was the production of new aircraft, like the F-13 Junkers, one of the first truly modern airliners. The all-metal plane could carry five passengers in relative comfort and cruise at a speed of 106 miles per hour.

"My wife and I wing our way from Berlin to Paris to catch a plane for Africa." Illustration from Lowell Thomas's *European Skyways*, 1927.

Berlin's airport, Tempelhof, was considered "the finest commercial aerodrome in the world," reported Thomas. It had an oval-shaped landing field, a hard surface apron, and a passenger terminal designed in clean Bauhaus lines by the architects Heinrich Kosina and Paul Mahlberg. Two miles from the center of Berlin, it was built on the site of the parade grounds where Hussars used to goose-step before Kaiser Wilhelm. Tempelhof had become the hub of an airline network that radiated out to Amsterdam and London in the west, Paris to the south, Vienna and Warsaw to the east, and Moscow and Copenhagen to the north.

Steadman Hanks, a lieutenant colonel in the U.S. Air Corps Reserve, believed that air travel promoted a new kind of international fellowship. When he crossed Europe in 1928, he was astonished by the level of cooperation that existed between different governments and competing airline companies. "Perhaps we in America do not fully realize the political and economic aspects of air transportation lines in Europe," wrote Hanks. "For example, Dutch airplanes flying from England to Holland, pass over France and Belgium. These international barriers appear to be easily swept aside. What other frontiers," wrote Hanks, "are also going to be disregarded by the plane?"[18] One such frontier was created by postwar partitioning when East Prussia was ceded to Poland and effectively isolated from the rest of Germany by what was known as the Polish corridor. Out of political necessity, an airport—"a bright green aerodrome as level as a billiard table"—was built in Königsberg to bridge this rupture in German sovereignty and maintain a sense of connection to the old province, even if only by air. A terminal with Jugendstil decoration was designed by Hans Hoppe and built in 1922.[19]

When Lowell Thomas reaches the Soviet Union, the narrative loses its tone of exuberance. After a bumpy, thirteen-hour flight from Berlin, the plane lands in Moscow, but there are no porters. "This was our introduction to the capital of the country where every man is as good as every other, according to the official doctrine, and where not many, apparently, are keen to wait on others." Lowell and Frances have to carry their own bags to a gloomy hangar, where a stone-faced customs officer cross-examines them. The Soviet officer is "gruff and rude, with none of the urbane courtesy for which the Russian upper classes were renowned." He turns the contents of their bags inside out and confiscates their magazines and books.

After Moscow, the Thomases' enthusiasm is diminished. They grow weary, spending as much time reading as gazing at the clouds. What had previously seemed miraculous is now everyday. "My wife is becoming so blasé at this ultra-modern way of traveling that instead of seeing Hungary through her own eyes she is seeing it through the Irish spectacles of George Birmingham, the novelist and clergyman, whose 'A Wayfarer in Hungary' she finds more interesting." To Thomas, this lack of sensation is proof that flying has become so safe and convenient that it is almost boring.

Lindbergh's Tour

When Lindbergh returned from Europe on June 10, 1927, he dedicated himself to the improvement of American aviation. "All Europe," he said, "is covered with a network of lines carrying passengers between all the big cities. Now it is up to us to create and develop passenger lines that compare with our mail routes." Lindbergh and fellow boosters appealed to national pride. After all, two American brothers, Orville and Wilbur Wright, had been the first to fly. Unlike in Europe, U.S. commercial airlines remained in private hands, while airport building was usually left up to municipal initiatives. The federal government made a concerted effort to stay clear of commercial aviation. The U.S. Airmail Service had been established in 1918 with a chain of modest airfields strung across the country, but there was no comprehensively planned system. Secretary of Commerce and future president Herbert Hoover believed that airports were too great a financial burden. He compared them to "harbors of the air"; like commercial waterfronts, they should be controlled by private enterprise or city governments. Yet organizations like the National Advisory Committee for Aeronautics (NACA) urged the government to intervene and assist in the building of safer landing fields.

Congress passed the Air Commerce Act in 1926 and federal controls were established for the licensing of pilots, the registering of aircraft, and the creation of civil airways. However, the new act specifically prohibited direct government sponsorship of airports. William P. McCracken Jr., first head of the Aeronautics Branch of the Commerce Department, declared it to be the "duty" of every city in America to build and operate its own facility. While most felt there were more pressing issues on the public agenda, a handful of city councils saw the light and made long-range plans.

Even before the Air Commerce Act, Boston's chamber of commerce purchased 189 acres of muddy land called Commonwealth Flats in East Boston and turned it into one of the first municipally owned airports in the country, being formally dedicated on September 8, 1923. Thirty houses were demolished to make way for a landing area made from silt pumped out of Boston harbor. Washington-Hoover, the first aerial gateway to the nation's capital, was built across the Potomac in Virginia on a field where the Pentagon now stands.

Buffalo, New York, developed an exemplary airport that was the result of eight years of planning on the part of farsighted officials who understood the economic benefits of aviation. Buffalo had been the birthplace of the Curtiss Aeroplane and Motor Company, which manufactured many of the planes flown by Allied pilots during World War I. City fathers selected a 518-acre site in Cheektowaga Township, ten miles east of Buffalo, that was well drained and free of obstacles. It was also adjacent to the Lehigh Valley Railroad. One million dollars were spent on the first phase of airport construction, which included two hard-packed runways, hangars, and a terminal. Henry Ford donated the use of several tractors for grading the airfield since it was in his interest to see Buffalo's airport completed as soon as possible. Ford was inaugurating his own transport company out of Dearborn, Michigan, and needed destinations.

Cleveland, Ohio, was another city that understood the importance of aviation and, on the advice of flying ace Eddie Rickenbacker, the city council paid $1.4 million for two hundred acres. Out in California, the city of Oakland claimed 845 acres on the eastern shore of San Francisco Bay, and built a freestanding terminal, several hangars, and the first airport hotel in America. But these early examples were exceptions to the rule. Most cities in the U.S. were reluctant to spend taxpayer money, but that would soon change.

Forty days after returning from Paris, Lindbergh set out on an air tour of the continental United States that was sponsored by the Daniel Guggenheim Fund for the Promotion of Aeronautics, one of its missions being the improvement of ground facilities. Indeed, the evolution of the early American airport can be traced to the influence of this event. The now-famous pilot flew his *Spirit of Saint*

Louis from airfield to airfield, visiting more than eighty cities in forty-eight states. He officiated at the dedication of several new airports, marched in parades, gave speeches, and attended honorary banquets. In smaller cities like Sioux Falls, South Dakota, and Abilene, Texas, he touched down for only a brief ceremony and then dashed away. The airport had never been considered much of a public place, but Lindbergh's tour gave it meaning. Throngs of onlookers rushed toward his plane at every stop and threw flowers. Minor incidents—a fog delay in Maine, say—made headlines.

At the Ford Airport in Dearborn, Michigan, he was invited to test-fly a small, experimental prototype. Lindbergh, in turn, invited Henry Ford to take a spin in the *Spirit of Saint Louis*. The automobile magnate understood the significance of such a gesture, folded his scrawny frame into the cockpit, and took the first airplane ride of his life.

In Grand Rapids, Michigan, Lindbergh took his mother for a twenty-minute flight. The next day he made a triumphal return to St. Louis, the city that had sponsored his transatlantic quest. Wichita, Kansas, followed and then Milwaukee, Wisconsin; Denver, Colorado; Salt Lake City, Utah; Seattle, Washington; and Portland, Oregon, where he dedicated a new airport at Swan Island. After a seven-hour flight down the coast, Lindbergh banked over San Francisco Bay and made his approach to Mills Field. As always, there were thousands on hand, but upon landing, the wheels of his plane sank into a mud hole. While no damage was done, it was a humiliating moment for city officials and became known locally as the "Lindbergh Incident."

More than two hundred thousand people came out to Vail Field in Los Angeles, where Lindbergh was greeted by Mary Pickford and Douglas Fairbanks. In San Diego, where the *Spirit of Saint Louis* had been built in a dilapidated old fish cannery, Lindbergh made a break in his routine, piloting the inaugural flight of Maddux Airlines from San Diego to Los Angeles with comedian Will Rogers riding beside him in the cockpit.

Lindbergh traveled twenty-two thousand miles and was seen by more than 30 million people. But what he witnessed wasn't very inspiring. American airfields were an embarrassment, and, more often than not, the buildings were shabby hangars or shacks for servicing mail planes. A few had tiny waiting rooms for the handful of passengers who dared to fly, but certainly nothing compared to the great air stations of Europe. Even Roosevelt Field, considered one of the best in the country, was little more than a grass field with a few hangars and sheds scattered around its periphery. Still, Lindbergh, the aerial Johnny Appleseed, set off a wave of airport construction. Municipalities began to compete to build the best and biggest.

Just as his transatlantic flight had symbolically connected the old and new worlds, Lindbergh's cross-country tour fostered a new kind of awareness, linking the entire country in a modern, air-age union, east to west, north to south. Within a year of his tour, passenger figures quadrupled, and more than 425 municipally owned airports were in operation. Hundreds more were in the planning stages, while older, preexisting fields were refurbished and expanded. Local airfields, which had previously been considered the domain of reckless pilots, had a new identity: they would be seen as gateways to a prosperous future. "Since Lindbergh's flight everything that happens in aviation appears to the public to be extraordinary," noted one magazine. Politicians who had shunned the airplane as a passing fad now embraced it as a patriotic symbol of the American way of life. Between 1927 and 1928, more than $30 million were spent on new construction.

Despite so much enthusiasm, the building of an airport still posed a Herculean challenge. The most difficult part of the process was finding a large tract of level land in relatively close proximity to a city's business district. Sites needed to have good drainage and be free of dangerous obstructions. Industrial areas were undesirable because of high smokestacks. Low-lying areas that experienced frequent fog were also unsuitable. The city of Newark transformed 420 acres of New Jersey marshland into a thriving airport by dumping tons of refuse, including seven thousand Christmas trees and two hundred bank safes donated by a junk dealer. Philadelphia reclaimed shipyards that lay along the Delaware River, and for its new airport, the city of New Orleans, Louisiana, built a spade-shaped peninsula out into Lake Pontchartrain.

Once a site was cleared, drained, and leveled, a landing surface was prepared. Early planes needed to take off and land into the wind, so airfields were designed to be omnidirectional and open. Planning manuals resembled children's picture books with airfield configurations shaped like squares, octagons, and stars. Lines for landing were drawn in relation to prevailing winds. Buildings were placed along one edge of the site, as if on the banks of a lake, while the field remained inviolate and open—a peripheral arrangement that posed one of the inherent challenges of airport design.[20]

Boston Municipal Airport was an exception to the open-field approach. Since it was built on reclaimed land in the harbor there wasn't enough room to have a wide, "all-way" field. Instead, two cinder runways were laid out in accordance with prevailing winds, each measuring approximately fifteen hundred feet long and two hundred feet wide.[21] Buffalo and Milwaukee also built long narrow cinder runways. Chicago laid out eight different runways that crisscrossed like the lines of a Union Jack. Unidirectional runways allowed more freedom in planning, making it possible to move terminals closer to the center of action. As planes became heavier they needed harder landing surfaces like reinforced concrete. Long narrow runways were laid in crisscrossing "X," "L," or "T" configurations, creating a kind of airport alphabet when seen from the air.

Besides investing in costly construction, city governments were also required to pass new forms of aerial legislation, rezone peripheral areas, and establish rights-of-way. Once an airport was completed, municipalities were obliged to maintain and manage what was almost certainly a money-losing proposition and target for fis-

(Opposite) Flagman at Newark Airport, circa 1929.

cally conservative crusaders like Reverend "Fighting Bob" Shuler, a California evangelist who preached that it was a sin for governments to own or operate an airport. One reactionary journal opposed all "little airport wasters" and promised to leave "no stone unturned to the end that the real needs of Aviation are adequately served with the least possible waste of public funds."[22]

Some cities boosted revenue by charging general admission, adding restaurants and gift shops, or holding air shows. "Air races, air circuses, and even everyday aeronautical activity find eager throngs at every airport," wrote William E. Arthur, an airport designer.[23] The airport in Glendale, California, built permanent grandstands adjacent to the field. The Wayne Airport in Detroit had rooftop terraces that provided a 360-degree view of the field. A platform on the Curtiss terminal in Chicago could hold two thousand spectators at a time. Washington-Hoover added a public swimming pool that was twice as big as its terminal and more profitable. Cleveland held national air races and the airport in Camden, New Jersey, built a dog-racing track right on airport grounds.

The most dangerous combination of flying and leisure was surely the airport proposed for Enterprise, Alabama, where three different runways cut through the heart of a nine-hole golf course. There was a long drive across runway #2 to the second green. The seventh hole called for a tricky approach shot across runway #3. The terminal itself was disguised as a country club, with barnlike gables, gambrel roof, and cedar shingles. It had a dancing terrace overlooking a swimming pool, and a hangar that could double as a community theater and basketball court. "By including recreational items in the Airport . . . the town will derive an income from the property sufficient to solve the ever-present problem of upkeep, as well as to attract the general public," wrote one promoter. "In this way it becomes a self-liquidating community asset."[24] But even with swimming pools and reckless golf courses, municipalities found it impossible to keep their airports in the black. The future of American air travel would depend on private investment.

Boom

One of the clichés of the Roaring Twenties—along with jazz-age flappers and bathtub gin—was footage of an aerial daredevil, often a scantily clad showgirl, hanging acrobatically from the wing of a biplane. It was a fitting metaphor for the wild speculation of the times. Aviation was both sexy and dangerous and seemed to appeal to financial risk takers. Aeronautical investments, along with Florida real estate and Texas oil, soared. Again, Lindbergh was the catalyst. As *Forbes* magazine reported in 1927: "Lindbergh's significance to business seems greater than that of any mercantile or financial magnate on either side of the Atlantic."[25] The period after his flight, from 1927 to 1929, was a boom time and close to a billion dollars were invested in aviation. New companies sprang up overnight. By 1929, there were more than sixty different passenger lines operating in the United States. Older, preexisting companies that had started as airmail carriers quickly switched over to passenger service. Bigger, faster, and more comfortable passenger planes were designed and rushed into production. American airports began to catch up with their European counterparts.

Aviation futures soared on Wall Street. Pan American Airways stock, which had been issued at $15 a share, went as high as $90 during the peak of the boom. Despite the Sherman Anti-Trust Act, corporate combines were formed and absorbed smaller airline concerns or put them out of business altogether. Before new antitrust restrictions came into effect, many of the companies that manufactured airplanes would also run airlines and build their own airports. These kinds of unregulated monopolies were allowed by the laissez-faire administration of Herbert Hoover. His postmaster general, Walter Folger Brown, displayed unabashed favoritism in awarding the most lucrative government contracts to Wall Street insiders, including the likes of Frederick Rentschler of United Aircraft and Transport and Clement Keys of Transcontinental Air Transport (TAT).

The temptation was irresistible. Just as an earlier generation had made fortunes monopolizing the railroads, aviation offered a similar incentive to a new generation of entrepreneurs. Juan Trippe was only twenty-six years old when he took control of Pan American Airways and confessed to friends that his aspiration was to become the J. P. Morgan of aviation. The initial group of investors in American Airways (later to become American Airlines) included Robert Lehman, of Lehman Brothers investment firm, and Averell Harriman, heir to the Union Pacific Railroad fortune, who hoped to profit from the airplane the way his father, E. H. Harriman, had from the railroads. The American Airways holding company raised $38 million and purchased eighty different aviation properties, including plane manufacturing plants, airline companies, and several airfields.

Then in 1928, the Guggenheim Fund for the Promotion of Aeronautics invested $180,000 to sponsor Western Air Express in creating a "model airway" between Los Angeles and San Francisco. The idea was to show that a commercial airline could be run exclusively for passengers without relying on postal contracts. Western's president, Harris Hanshue, was hoping to attract the most affluent clients with a new level of service and in-flight luxury. A publicity photograph for Western's airway showed a beautiful young woman dressed in a skimpy satin robe, lying on a divan in a luxuriously appointed cabin—an early example of blatant sex being used to attract customers.

Another significant development was the creation of the Curtiss-Wright Airports Corporation, a national network of private airports operated under "unified ownership and standardized management." Strategic locations were selected and architects hired to draw up plans. While space would be leased to different companies, all commercial transport would be reserved for the Curtiss-Wright Flying Service to be flown in planes that were manufactured in Curtiss-Wright factories. Twelve full-fledged Curtiss-Wright airports went into operation, in New York, Baltimore, St. Louis, San Francisco, and Pittsburgh. There were also thirty-five lesser bases and many more in the planning stages.[26]

The first cross-country service between New York and Los Angeles followed on July 7, 1929, inaugurated by Transcontinental Air Transport. The idea was to cross the continent in forty-eight hours, saving a full day over the fastest train service. President Clement Keys invested millions of his own money to develop a deluxe service that would attract wealthy clients who needed to cross the country in a hurry. It was a bold gamble, since without mail contracts, TAT (like Western's Model Airway) would have to rely entirely on passenger income. At first, TAT flew its planes only during daylight hours, and the service was run in conjunction with the Pennsylvania Railroad. A passenger starting in New York would board a sleeper train—the Airway Limited—that left Pennsylvania Station at six P.M. and arrived in Columbus, Ohio, the next morning. From there, passengers transferred to a TAT plane and continued on by air, making several refueling stops before arriving in Los Angeles. (The flying range of early passenger planes was only about five hundred miles.) As TAT's technical adviser, Lindbergh selected airport sites along the route, and encouraged the company to spend over $1.5 million on ground facilities. On July 8, 1929, Lindbergh piloted the first leg of TAT's inaugural service to New York. A crowd of several thousand gathered at the Grand Central Air Terminal in Glendale to watch as movie stars Gloria Swanson and Mary Pickford christened the plane with a bottle of Prohibition grape juice.

Model-T Airport

It made sense that a capitalist of Henry Ford's stature would understand that aviation called for a unified approach and, in the Ford manner, he proceeded to consolidate all aspects of production and passenger services into a single entity. When advised by an aide that 719 acres of his land in Dearborn had been allocated for housing, Ford said: "Maybe it was a subdivision yesterday, but today it is a landing field." Within days tractors were leveling the site for a runway.[27] Ford had entered the aviation business and would show the rest of America how it should be done.

The father of assembly-line production decreed that "flying is now 90% man and 10% machine . . . Our undertaking is to make it 90% machine and 10% man."[28] Testing and production of the Trimotor passenger plane began in 1926 and, by 1929, Ford's airplane factory was manufacturing twenty-five of the sturdy, all-metal planes per month under the same system the company used to manufacture cars. No matter how many planes were produced, however, they were meaningless without reliable airlines, airports—and passengers. Thus Ford's first task was winning over a hesitant public: "Safety—First, Last and Always" became his motto, and everything about his aircraft, airline, and airport was intended to instill confidence in the otherwise anxious traveler.

The company ran a steady stream of advertisements in popular magazines, reassuring people that Ford planes were the safest in the world, flown by the most experienced pilots. "The Ford Motor Company expects as startling a development in the air as the present generation has witnessed along the highways . . ." ran one ad.[29] But Ford knew that the best advertising was firsthand experience. To win the public over, you had to get people out to the airport and show them that flying was as safe as driving a car. The more they saw with their own eyes, the more likely they were to take a plane trip on their own.

A sense of doom hovered over early airports: hundreds had been killed in commercial flying accidents. Of the fourteen hundred American passengers who flew in 1928, fourteen died: one in a hundred, a sobering statistic that would make anyone hesitate. "When the crucial moment comes to board the plane," wrote one passenger, "I have visions of flags at half-mast and a brass band playing. . . ."[30] Some airlines printed brochures to help calm the nerves of first-time fliers. "Don't worry. Relax, settle back and enjoy life," read one of these early in-flight magazines. "If there's any worrying to be done, let the pilot do it;

that's what he's hired for." Considering the statistics, there was plenty to worry about.

As in Europe, most passengers were high-level businessmen, politicians, and entertainment types—what the *Saturday Evening Post* referred to as "the great and the near-great." (TAT's first official passenger was an oilman from Los Angeles.) Business executives were starting to feel that the risks were worth the edge that flying gave them over rivals who were still traveling by train. "When the occasion comes for your first time up," read one advertisement, "it will not be to 'joyride' in an antiquated and hazardous machine; but far more probably it will be to reach some distant meeting-place in advance of business competition!"[31]

It was reported that some U.S. corporations encouraged their executives to fly after 1927 and authorized them to submit airfares as reimbursable expenses. This was a significant change, since a short time before most companies had seen air travel as too danger-ous and had put clauses in their contracts that forbade executives to fly. But to many, the railroad continued to seem like a superior means of transportation, even if it was slower. As one pilot put it: "It's a lot easier to put your passengers on a train than on an ambu-lance."[32]

In *Dodsworth,* Sinclair Lewis's novel of 1929, the eponymous protagonist, Samuel Dodsworth, is a midwestern automobile mag-nate—not unlike Henry Ford—the millionaire president of the Revelation Motor Company. He has never flown before and decides to try it, but on his way to the airport he has second thoughts. The urge to be modern and forward thinking goes against his better instincts. Flying seems unnatural. His doubts are relieved, how-ever, as soon as he arrives at the airport: "[Dodsworth] dismounted at the flying field, when he saw the great plane, its metal body and thick crimped metal wings as solid-looking as a steamer, when he saw how casually the pilot took his place in front and the atten-dants loaded luggage, all nervousness vanished in exultation."[33] Reassured, Dodsworth overcomes his fears and climbs aboard.

This was the idea Henry Ford had in mind: to appeal to the sensible judgment of the American businessmen—those no-nonsense Babbitts and Dodsworths that Sinclair Lewis chronicled in his novels. If they could be convinced, then others would soon follow. Ford's airport in Dearborn was probably the first in America to be designed explicitly for propaganda purposes to convert a wary public through the logic of its plan and the efficiency of its service. The airport featured paved runways and floodlights for night landings. A sky sign was laid out in white crushed stone spelling out F-O-R-D like a giant advertisement in two-hundred-foot-high letters. A Sperry beacon flashed from the roof of the hangar, and one of the first radio systems was put into service for all-weather flying. There was a mooring mast for dirigibles as well as a freestanding terminal, one of the earliest. Ford even built a one-hundred-room hotel, called the Dearborn Inn, across the street from his airport. He inaugurated his own air transport service, and Ford Trimotors began to fly regularly from Dearborn to Chicago, Cleveland, and Buffalo. The airport was closed on Sundays, however, since Ford's wife, Clara, complained about landings on the Sabbath. Teetotaling Clara also heard that alcohol was consumed by passengers, so Ford declared it to be, forever after, a "dry" airport.

As a publicity event, all the parts of a Model-T were packed aboard one of the Ford planes and shipped to Buffalo, where the car was reassembled—in twenty-eight minutes—and driven away. Ford also sponsored air shows and "Reliability Air Tours," in which planes competed in city-to-city races. In 1927, more than nineteen thousand people visited the airport and took short plane trips over Detroit. Every one of them came back alive to tell the tale and spread the word.[34]

Ford Airport, Dearborn, Michigan: one of the first comprehensively planned airports in America.

Experiment in the Caribbean

Flying wasn't just about safety and efficiency. It was a modern adventure, and Juan Terry Trippe, chief of Pan American Airways (PAA), understood this better than anyone in the aviation business. If Henry Ford imagined the airport in terms of assembly-line order, Trippe saw it as an exclusive kind of country club. He was catering to a more refined kind of client than the Babbitt business-man. Trippe understood his passengers' needs because he himself came from an affluent background. Born on June 27, 1899, he was the only son of Charles White Trippe and Lucy Terry Trippe, both descendants of early English settlers. His father was a successful Wall Street broker, and Juan grew up splitting his time between a fashionable neighborhood in Manhattan and a country home in East Hampton. Trippe's father took him to a country fair, where they watched a stunt flier hang from the wings of a plane. As soon as he got home, young Juan began fabricating a model airplane of his own design. At Yale, he organized the college's first flying club. During World War I, he served as a pilot in the Naval Reserve Flying Corps. After a short stint on Wall Street, Trippe grew restless. Along with wealthy Yale friends John Hambleton, Cornelius Vanderbilt ("Sonny") Whitney, and William H. Vanderbilt, he bought several surplus warplanes and founded Long Island Airways, a small outfit that ferried wealthy New Yorkers out to their summer retreats in the Hamptons.

While his first venture failed, Trippe would not be deterred; he soon bought into another airline company, Colonial Air Transport, that flew between New York and Boston.[35] Trippe was only twenty-six years old, but Colonial wasn't big enough for his ambitions. In 1927, he invested in a small upstart called Pan American Airways.

On October 19, 1927, PAA flew ninety miles from Key West, Florida, to Havana, Cuba, and inaugurated the first international mail route outside the United States. A few months later PAA started a daily passenger service using two new Fokker F-10 Trimotors. The fare was $100 round-trip. Trippe and Hambleton flew to Havana themselves in June 1928 and, after lengthy negotiations, managed to extract a twenty-five-year exclusive flying concession from President Gerardo Machado y Morales, the Wall Street–backed dictator of Cuba. The agreement froze out competitive airlines. In honor of the deal, one of PAA's new planes was named after Machado, but a few months later, when the plane

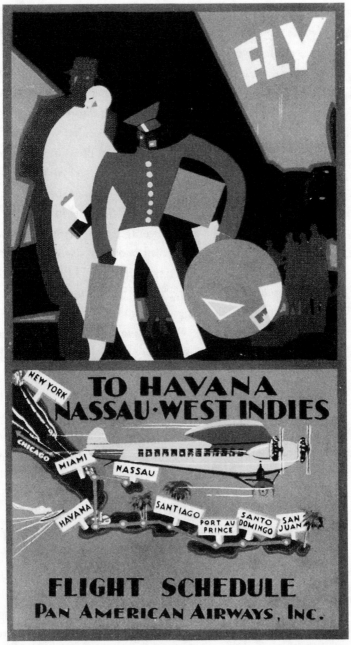

A brochure for Pan American Airways, which began regular flights to the Caribbean in 1928 and offered escape from U.S. prohibition laws: "Fly to Havana and you can bathe in Bacardi Rum two hours from now," cried PAA agents on the streets of Miami.

crashed into the sea, the general grew sick with worry—that the crash was a premonition of his own death. In fact, Machado would be deposed a few years later, in August 1933, during a revolutionary coup led by Fulgencio Batista. At the request of the U.S. State Department, PAA flew the deposed dictator out of Havana to Miami, only minutes before an angry mob stormed the airfield to kill him. This was the first of many occasions when the airline found itself meddling directly in the affairs of a foreign state.[36]

When the company's operations were moved from Key West up to Miami, Trippe built an elegant new airport near Thirty-sixth Street on the future site of the Miami International Airport. PAA was still dependent on mail revenue, but Trippe saw ways to expand the passenger trade. Prohibition laws were in effect, thus many were willing to take the risk of flying to Havana just to enjoy the booze, legal gambling, and unrestricted nightlife. PAA agents would stand outside the company's ticket office on Biscayne Boulevard to lure in passengers: "Fly to Havana and you can bathe in Bacardi rum two hours from now," they barked to the passing tourists.[37]

Business increased, and PAA's passenger list began to include wealthy socialites and debutantes going on winter holidays. There were also professional polo players, oilmen, and bankers heading south to speculate, as well as the occasional mobster, since organized crime had moved into Havana's hotel and nightclub business. On one occasion, an air-sick Al Capone and four of his bodyguards were seen on a PAA flight to Havana.

Cuba was just the opening act of Trippe's "experiment in the Caribbean," as he liked to call it. During the booming 1920s, a wave of economic speculation descended onto Latin America. Between 1921 and 1927, Yankee investments multiplied fortyfold. (Some $1.5 billion of Latin American government bonds were floated on Wall Street.) Trippe's vision for PAA extended to a farreaching network that would island-hop across the Caribbean and stretch another two thousand miles to Central and South America. Beyond Havana, it would split into two paths, one heading east toward Brazil, leapfrogging through Trinidad and the Guianas; the other leading west to the Yucatán Peninsula and down into Panama.

PAA representatives forged their way through the "green hell" of Latin America, negotiating deals and seeking permission to develop air routes and build airports along the way.[38] "It was a piece of real, creative pioneering," said Trippe of these early efforts. Technically it was against the law for a U.S. citizen or corporation to negotiate directly with a foreign government. Trippe did it regardless, claiming that PAA was an agent of the U.S. government. The company sometimes referred to itself as the "aerial ambassador of American industry," and Trippe held the firm belief that his airline was bringing a benevolent form of capitalism to less-fortunate nations.[39] By law, Pan Am should have done its bargaining through American embassies, but that would have been too slow for Trippe, who felt an urgency to beat the competition. The French airline Aéropostale (later to become Air France) had already established air routes through much of South America and the Sociedad Colombo-Alemana de Transportes Aéreos (SCADTA) was firmly entrenched in Colombia.

The process would usually start with a series of survey flights and, in the early years, Trippe would often go on these trips and bring his wife, Elizabeth, along. "It was a very exciting event," recalled Sanford B. Kauffman, one of Trippe's many recruits from Yale. "People would come down to see the airplane, and there would be a lot of flag waving. We were often invited in for cocktails at the hotel by high government officials."[40]

Not every nation proved to be so welcoming, however. The government of Colombia refused to grant PAA aerial rights since SCADTA was operating profitably and didn't want competition. Newspapers in Bogotá ran stories about the "hateful Yankee air monopoly menacing all South America."[41] Juan Vicente Gomez, dictator of Venezuela, also tried to bar Trippe's advance. PAA planes were forced to fly via Trinidad until Gomez was deposed and a more pliable president installed. Guatemala was another country that attempted to resist but Trippe appealed to his contacts in the U.S. State Department, pressure was applied, and Guatemala finally granted PAA an air route.

Trippe's agents learned to cajole, bribe, and, in some cases, oust Latin American leaders who dared to oppose the company's advance. They offered partnerships and engineered takeovers of competing airlines as with Compañía Mexicana de Aviación of Mexico, which was acquired in 1929, as was SCADTA, which ultimately succumbed to PAA pressure. "They are afraid that the Octopus of the North is stretching forth its tentacles to devour them," wrote back one of Trippe's agents.[42]

Then there was NYRBA, the New York, Rio, and Buenos Aires Airline, a well-organized North American concern that had already established a ten-thousand-mile route. Trippe made every effort to run NYRBA out of business and was eventually able to buy it outright. Another stumbling block was W. R. Grace and Company, a firm that held monopolistic control over shipping and trading along the west coast of South America. Instead of trying to beat Grace, Trippe eventually merged with it to create Pan American–Grace Airways, popularly known as "Panagra."

Once an agreement with the host nation had been reached, an air route could be chosen. PAA surveyors would mark the ideal landing place by dropping sacks of flour to identify the spot. Construction crews would then hack their way through jungle and begin clearing ground. (In one instance, local villagers stole the bag of flour to bake bread.) In other places, hostile Indians attacked the survey teams but were appeased with dime-store trinkets. Sanford Kauffman's first assignment was to act as station manager at Tela, an isolated refueling stop on the north coast of Honduras. "Our village was truly in a back-of-the-beyond location," wrote Kauffman. "There were no roads except right around the village and at the airport. But even if we had had roads, there was no place to go."[43] At one point Kauffman was delirious from malaria but continued to man his post: "I'd be standing out at the airport with a plane coming in, and I'd just shake," he wrote.[44] There were also political problems.

Kaufmann had been at his post only a few weeks when a revolution broke out in Honduras. Rebels were flying old biplanes and dropping bombs onto his airfield. Kauffman telegraphed Miami headquarters and informed his superiors that PAA planes should not attempt to land but should fly directly on to San Salvador. When the local manager for the United Fruit Company inquired why the mail plane hadn't arrived that day, Kauffman told him about the aerial bombardment. The manager replied: "Why didn't you come and let me know? We're controlling this revolution, and I'll simply tell them to stop bombing you."[45] United Fruit had put the president of Honduras into power in the first place, but when the president hiked the tax on bananas, the company thought it best to have him replaced. "There's a general who would love to be president," explained the agent, "so we're supplying him with funds to buy ammunition and equipment, [and] he'll be the next one." Kauffman got the message and reopened the airport the following day.

The rapid growth of PAA marked a new chapter in aviation. Airports were becoming outposts for economic and geopolitical expansion—ushering in a kind of aerial imperialism that would fall swiftly from the sky with a sack of flour and a trade agreement. By the end of 1929, PAA had more than twelve hundred employees and was operating out of seventy-one different airports. Soon it would be conquering even more territory.

Gateways

The need was well established by the late 1920s, but what exactly was an airport supposed to look like? In early aeronautical literature there was almost nothing written on the subject of style, other than to say that buildings should be "attractive" and "dignified," or that terminals should have a look of "permanence" and "solidity"—this in response to the shoddy state of American airfields. Most architects had never flown and didn't know what to make of this new mode of transportation. Beauty seemed to be less

important than safety. Responsible planning was the key to airport aesthetics, not architectural showmanship.

In a special aviation issue of *Scientific American,* William E. Arthur made a plea for safety and comfort: "The psychology of the first-class railroad terminal is one of inspiring confidence," he wrote. "This psychology would be even more desirable at the airport, where every first-time passenger is more or less nervous."[46] It thus followed that airports should resemble railroad stations.

Nerves were bad enough in the air, but having to sit in a cramped little terminal made the experience of flying even worse. One traveler noticed how fellow passengers twitched in their seats and chewed their nails: "Marie Antoinette on her way to the guillotine was a bluebird for happiness in comparison."[47] When the flight was announced, they filed onto the apron, blinking in the sun, like lambs to slaughter. The first waiting rooms tended to be rather gloomy with small windows, and they were furnished like funeral parlors, featuring rattan chairs and potted plants. Nor was the sense of apprehension alleviated by getting weighed on a freight scale like a hunk of meat. If passenger and luggage weighed more than 180 pounds combined, the fare cost extra.

Most early planning manuals focused on technical issues like paving, drainage, and runway alignment. While passenger terminals should have been the most prominent structures, they were often overshadowed by hangars and maintenance sheds. In a few cases, terminals were placed on a kind of ceremonial axis to distinguish their importance and mark the human point of entry. Long symmetrical approaches from the land side helped to anchor the buildings in place and distinguish them from other utilitarian areas.

The passenger terminal at the Ford Airport in Dearborn was

(Opposite) Ideal Airport, 1928. "The psychology of the first-class railroad terminal is one of inspiring confidence. This psychology would be even more desirable at the airport, where every first-time passenger is more or less nervous." Wilbert J. Austin, designer.

placed on a perpendicular axis to the main road, with a formal entrance and a large parking lot. Designed by Albert Kahn (1869–1942), who also designed the Ford hangars, airplane factory, and airport hotel, the building had white brick walls and uniform pilasters that were vaguely suggestive of classical architecture. Two humble chimneys rose up on either side, while inside was a ticket office and a simple waiting room with terracotta floors and plaster walls. This may have been the first real passenger terminal in the United States but, compared to the large airports of Europe, it was inconsequential. The entire building measured fifty-two feet square and could have fit comfortably inside Croydon's booking hall. Despite its diminutive size, however, architect Kahn was able to enhance the terminal's presence by positioning it in line with the runways and entry road. Kahn understood the psychological importance of defining a separate zone for passengers, one that was located near the center of the airport's geography, well away from the noise and fumes of Ford's aviation works.

Most American terminals built after 1927 would follow the Ford example of a symmetrical facade and depot-style interior with a waiting room and a ticketing office. There was an occasional exception such as the terminal at Buffalo, which had a crisscrossing scissors plan with five separate entrances placed diagonally, and a twenty-by-twenty-foot waiting room. Although crude, this layout suggested a new kind of architecture arising from conditions inherent to the airport. The terminal's oddly baroque plan evolved from its placement at the intersection of two runways, an innovation intended to eliminate excessive taxiing and provide a central point of control.

Juan Trippe also understood the symbolic importance of airport architecture. He believed that a terminal, more than being just a waiting room and a ticket counter, should set the stage for the adventure of flight. In 1928, he hired society architects William Adams Delano and Chester Aldrich to design PAA's Miami terminal. Delano and Aldrich were partners in a New York firm that spe-

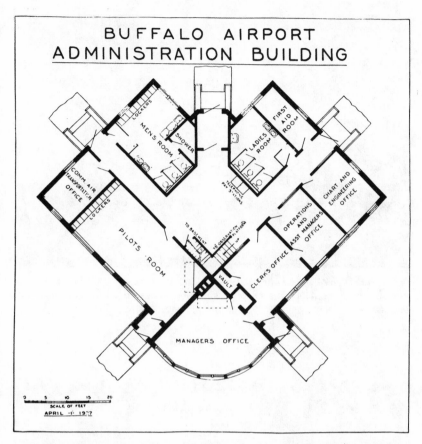

BUFFALO AIRPORT
ADMINISTRATION BUILDING

LOCKERS

MEN'S ROOM

SHOWER

LADIES ROOM

FIRST AID ROOM

COMM AIR TRANSPORTATION OFFICE

LOCKERS

PILOTS ROOM

TELEPHONE PAY STATIONS

TO BASEMENT

TO OBSERVATION PLATFORM

CHART AND ENGINEERING OFFICE

OPERATIONS AND ASST MANAGERS OFFICE

CLERK'S OFFICE

VAULT

MANAGERS OFFICE

0   5   10   15   20
SCALE OF FEET
APRIL -I- 1927

Buffalo Municipal Airport, 1927. A new kind of architecture suggested by conditions inherent to the airport: the terminal was built at the intersection of two runways.

cialized in private clubs and estates on Long Island's gold coast. Like Ford's, the terminal was poised conspicuously in the place of honor at one end of the field, while hangars were well removed. Constructed from concrete, the Miami terminal had an architectural integrity that was uncharacteristic of early airport buildings. The curve of its vaulted roof complemented the shape of the planes. Spectators could stand on a balcony and watch the comings and goings on the field. Porters and pilots were dressed in snappy white uniforms and a brass bell was rung to announce departures. The nautical theme was carried inside the terminal with metal railings,

Rendering of Pan American Airways terminal (36th Street Airport), Miami. Delano and Aldrich, architects, 1928. The concrete structure possessed an integrity that was uncharacteristic of early airport architecture.

Interior of Pan American Airways terminal, Miami, Florida.

canvas dodgers, and wicker furniture. There were large windows at either end that flooded the waiting room with natural light.

By the late 1920s, a concerted effort was being made to define an appropriate style of airport architecture. The *New York Times* predicted that American architects would soon be inventing forms "as characteristic of airports as steeples were of churches."[48] Architect Francis Keally argued that airports must instill confidence and create an atmosphere of "dignity and permanence," but he also believed that such confidence could be established through "beauty" as well as through "orderliness of technical procedure."[49] This was a radical statement at the time—the assertion that beauty, architectural beauty, should have a place in such a utilitarian setting.

First-generation airports in Europe were designed to function as national gateways. Historical themes were alluded to, such as a Palladian manor for Croydon, the Petit Palais for Bourget, and a Renaissance palazzo for Littorio airport in Rome. Similarly, American designers looked to historical precedents. There was virtue in the idea of a gateway and some early terminals were designed to suggest classical gateways or temples, with single, narrow openings onto the field to evoke a ceremonial sense of entry and departure. Architects had applied classical veneers to virtually every other building type, from post offices and banks to railroad stations, so why not to airports? Adapted for aviation, the form of the Athenian propylaeum might bring a humanist element to the realm of the machine. Boston's first terminal had a grand neo-classical entrance called the Memorial Portico. Greek pediments at Oakland's terminal were painted white in imitation of a temple and the underlying steel structure of the United Airlines terminal at Newark was hidden behind a false-front colonnade.

Other designers recognized parallels between the airport and the eighteenth-century formal garden and found them too tempting to resist. In his plans for the Curtiss-Steinberg Airport, the architect Kenneth Franzheim set the terminal on axis with a formal entrance court, while crisscrossing allées echoed the lines of the runways. Such monumental alignments could be appreciated only from the air. Landscape architect Ernest Herminghaus recommended geometric beds of flowers as an aide to aviators. At Fairfax Airport in Kansas City, he extended the axis of the main runway with a 150-foot-long reflecting pool filled with water lilies and fountains. Tulips, petunias, and roses were planted in patterns that were easily visible from the air.[50]

In 1929, a national design competition was held to address the question of airport style. The competition was sponsored by the Lehigh Portland Cement Company of Allentown, Pennsylvania, to "crystallize public attention upon the need for well-designed and properly planned airports . . . [with] practical as well as inspirational value," but the entries showed surprisingly little in the way of originality.[51] A handful attempted to push beyond a conventional beaux arts approach—one architect, H. Altater, proposed an airport shaped like a spoked wheel, which would rest on the roofs of skyscrapers—but most of the 257 entries reflected a mood of cautious conservatism. If passengers' nerves were already on edge, so the thinking went, it was better to design terminals in a familiar and comforting style.

Some entries resembled railroad stations; others looked like college dormitories in the neo-Gothic style that was popular in the 1920s, or mimicked beaux arts opera houses. The third-place entry by Odd Nansen and Latham Squire suggested an eighteenth-century chateau with reflecting pools and walkways that radiated out from a central court. Even though the guidelines called for modestly scaled proposals, most were absurdly overblown and unbuildable—even during the boom years.

Beneath the historical pastiche, there were occasional hints of a scientific approach. The winning entry by A. C. Zimmerman and William H. Harrison was praised for its "logical organization" and an innovative boarding system in which passengers walked through a tunnel to a star-shaped boarding pavilion, a precursor to the modern-day satellite.

Despite prevailing sentiments, there were a few who believed that airport architecture should look to the future and not the past.

The symmetries between the airport and the formal garden were hard to resist.

(top) A long reflecting pool and fountain in front of the terminal at the Fairfax Airport, Kansas City. Beds of brightly colored tulips, petunias, and roses were planted in geometric patterns as an aide to aviators. Ernest Herminghaus, landscape architect, 1929.

(bottom) Aerial view of an airport in which formal allées echo the lines of the runways. Britton Kirton, architect, from an entry to the Lehigh Airport Competition of 1929.

"Airports are new, and the architectural expression of [their] buildings should be *modern*," wrote airport theorist Sterling Wagner, but what exactly did it mean to be modern?[52] In his book *The Modern Airport*, Wagner called for a more functional approach and enhanced the traditionalists. "The machine age . . . does not seem to be satisfactorily expressed by forms of architecture which were developed centuries ago."[53]

Terminals in Washington, D.C., and Chicago were designed in a sleek, pared-down style that appeared to reflect the machine aesthetic of aviation. It was not the stringent functionalism of European modernists, but rather a streamlined surface treatment that industrial designers like Norman Bel Geddes and Raymond Lowey specialized in—a style in which everything from pencil sharpeners to locomotives were given the aerodynamic treatment. This approach, known as deco or moderne, had ironically been inspired by the airplane in the first place. Setbacks and vertical ribbing created a skyscraper kind of monumentality even though the buildings rose only a few stories at their highest points, as was the case with the Swan Island terminal in Portland, Oregon.[54] White stucco walls were delineated with dark coping, as at Washington-Hoover, or embellished with jazzy motifs, like the zigzagging lines of black brick on the municipal terminal at Pittsburgh.

"[The airport] is bound to no architectural traditions," wrote Wyatt Brummitt in 1929. "It is free to express itself in absolutely new terms and forms. . . ."[55] Another critic encouraged American architects to design terminals as "beautiful and as efficient as the shining planes themselves."[56] Architect Robert Smith took heed and proposed a terminal with enormous cantilevered wings that stretched out from its roof. While Smith's plan was never realized, a not dissimilar scheme was actually built in Mexico City. But Wagner warned against this kind of caricature: "The incorporation of aeronautical motifs such as whirling propellers, cylinders and outlines of planes into buildings and general airport design might be possible but architecturally it has no more reason than designing a railroad terminal to look like a locomotive."[57]

Deco modern for the capital's first airport: Washington-Hoover Air Terminal, Washington, D.C. Holden, Stott, and Hutchinson, architects, 1928.

Swan Island Airport, Portland, Oregon. DeYoung and Roald, architects, 1928.

A veneer of streamlined modernity may have helped to sell air travel as a flashy new phenomenon, but it failed to reflect the true dynamism of flight. Terminals still appeared heavy and grounded. Interior spaces were cramped, windows too small, and circulation routes were often cluttered and confusing. Paul Gerhardt's terminal at Chicago, for example, had a narrow vestibule measuring only fourteen feet wide that led to the airfield and created frequent bottlenecks.

America's greatest architect, Frank Lloyd Wright, had little interest in airports, but his oldest son hoped to make a career out of them. Lloyd Wright (1890–1978) fell in love with aviation after witnessing Louis Blériot's flight across the English Channel in 1909. At twenty-eight he got a job designing flying boats for the Standard Aircraft Company in Elizabeth, New Jersey, and later worked for Curtiss Aircraft. Combining his aeronautical experience with a background in architecture and landscape design, Wright junior set out to invent an airport architecture that was unfettered by the past. Like his father, he believed in an "organic architecture," in which forms grew out of the specific conditions of a project, both its site and its needs. Wright drew his inspiration from the attributes of aviation: wingspan, turning radii, lines of sight, angles of ascent. His plans were conceived from an aerial point of view, beginning with the expansive geometry of the airfield itself. There were no ceremonial entrances or quaint architectural gimmicks.

His entry to the Lehigh Airport Competition showed a narrow, lasso-shaped structure that encircled a round field. Hangars, passenger facilities, and runways were integrated into a single unified gesture. The terminal's checkerboard roof sloped at a 1:7 ratio, which Wright knew to be an airplane's rate of ascent: one foot vertically for every seven feet traveled horizontally. This oddly peripheral structure didn't fit any preconceived notion of what an airport was supposed to be. It wasn't trying to look like a classical temple or a Palladian villa. It didn't even look like a building. Wright's proposal was so far ahead of its time that it failed to rate even a

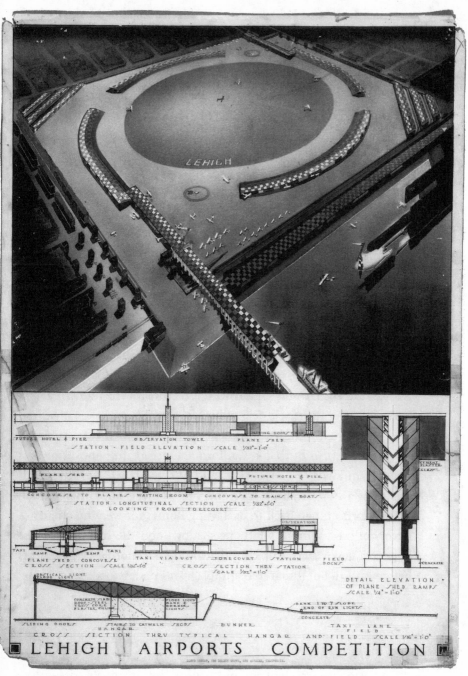

A looping, peripheral airport scheme by Lloyd Wright, son of Frank Lloyd Wright, who hoped to invent a new paradigm. Entry to Lehigh Airport Competition, 1929.

mention from the Lehigh jury, but it foreshadowed the hyper-extended architecture of the future.[58]

During this same period Wright did get an opportunity to design a real airport for the city of Los Angeles. Mines Field was built on a bean field to the south of the city, in Inglewood, on the site of the 1928 National Air Races. The city wanted to develop a municipal facility and had already built a two-thousand-foot runway, a weather station, and several hangars. Wright presented drawings for a passenger terminal that was long and low in the earth-hugging Prairie style of his father. A slender tower rose from the center of the building with a mooring mast for dirigibles.

The plan was enthusiastically approved by L.A.'s Municipal Art Commission, which had veto power over the design of public buildings. The city's airport committee, however, found the design too "futuristic" and favored a more conventional plan. In turn, the art commission refused to accept the compromised version and stood by Wright. The controversy made the front page of the *Los Angeles Evening Herald* under the headline "What Is Art?," with renderings of the opposing plans. "In the eternal problem of what is art," read the *Herald*, "Spanish architecture for the municipal airport wins over futuristic design by Mr. Wright."[59]

Undeterred, Wright proposed yet another plan, this time for Boeing airport in Burbank, California. Once again, innovation was rejected in favor of convention, and Wright failed to achieve his dream of a new airport paradigm. He would eventually abandon these efforts and go back to designing homes for wealthy clients—never fully escaping his father's shadow—but he had opened the door to a new way of thinking. It would take another twenty years before his kind of integrated approach was understood.

Midnight Airports

Aviation was modern and mechanical, but it was also dreamlike and elegiac. The very act of flying was a defiance of the natural order. Early planes had mythological names like Hercules and Goliath. Their engines had names like Jupiter and Pegasus. Cloud poets described the experience as a kind of rebirth and wrote detailed accounts of cumuli and cirrus, comparing their billowing masses to Gothic cathedrals or rocky canyons. "A vast rolling cloud continent," penned one passenger; "a fairy ballroom," wrote another.[60] Even Lindbergh, who was otherwise restrained in his prose, grew lyrical about "weaving in and out of the strange clouds, hidden in my tiny cockpit, submerged, alone, on the magnitude of this weird, inhuman space, I feel as if I'm not alive."[61]

In this twentieth-century version of sublime the point of view is flipped and the clouds are no longer contemplated from ground level but from the pilot's perspective. It came as a revelation to another air traveler that the high wispy clouds he saw while flying over the Netherlands were the same kind that had inspired Dutch landscape painters of the seventeenth century. But now, he thought, modern man could experience them from an angle that Hobbema or Ruysdael never knew.[62]

The opening chapter of *The Last Tycoon*, by F. Scott Fitzgerald, takes place on board a transcontinental flight heading west from New York to Los Angeles. It is June, and Cecilia Brady, the daughter of a Hollywood producer, is returning from her junior year at Bennington College. "The world from an airplane I knew," says Cecilia, who is already jaded with the experience, having made the same trip several times, always aware of what she calls the "sharp rip between coast and coast."[63] Her flight would have been on TAT's cross-country Lindbergh Line that Fitzgerald himself had flown as a contract writer in Hollywood.

As Cecilia's plane flies west, there are intimations of mortality and the foreshadowing of disaster. She feels "solemn and subdued," preoccupied with thoughts of death. The stewardess offers aspirin, Nembutal, chewing gum. She also offers to make up a sleeping berth, but Cecilia is not quite ready for sleep. A storm is brewing along the Mississippi Valley and the flight is ultimately forced to land in Nashville. ". . . the plane was unmistakably going down,

down, down, like Alice in the Rabbit hole . . . Cupping my hand against the window I saw the blur of the city far away on the left." Air travel was a fitting means of transportation for the ambitious characters Fitzgerald depicts in *The Last Tycoon*; it also served as a metaphor for the economic and social gulf that separated the haves from the have-nots. With her plane grounded, Cecilia is struck by the contrast between her glamorous fellow passengers and the common folk milling about the airport grounds: "In the big transcontinental planes we were the coastal rich, who casually alighted from our cloud in mid-America. . . . The young people look at the planes, the older ones look at the passengers with a watchful incredulity. . . ."[64]

The actual airports along the transcontinental caravan appeared like apparitions—each a little stage set suspended in time. Fitzgerald compared them to oases, "like the stops on the great trade routes." The terminal at Kansas City was a gleaming minaret clad in gold and silver tiles. Phoenix had an imposing, "Aztec-style" terminal. Some were modest refueling stops built in isolated places like Clovis, New Mexico, and Winslow, Arizona. But even the smallest shone with an ethereal magic at night. To poet/pilots like Antoine de Saint-Exupéry, the glow of runway lights possessed a preternatural quality: "Out of oblivion the gold has been smelted," he wrote. "There it gleams in the lights of the airport."[65]

Airline companies initially believed that their passengers would be reluctant to fly in the dark and scheduled only daylight flights. Europe took the lead and by 1927, the French airline Compagnie des Messageries Aériennes was flying a regular night route all the way to Constantinople.[66] But American aviation soon caught up. Tall beacon towers, something like landlocked lighthouses, were built at regular intervals along the transcontinental route. "The beacons nearest our ship sweep the horizon with a beam not unlike the prying eye of a searchlight," noted one passenger on an early night flight.[67]

Different rates of flashing and rotation were used to distinguish

Air-Rail Terminus, Columbus, Ohio, circa 1929. F. Scott Fitzgerald compared the cross-country airports to stops on the great trade routes. "In the big transcontinental planes we were the coastal rich, who casually alighted from our cloud in mid-America."

airway beacons from "stray" lights such as streetlamps or trolley cars. According to the Aeronautics Branch of the U.S. Department of Commerce, "The beacon light should have a distinctive characteristic so as to be recognized instantly . . . as a light of aeronautical character . . ."[68] The Commerce Department recommended the use of thousand-watt lamps reflected by parabolic mirrors to create a concentrated beam of light that could be seen from miles away. The government was particularly concerned about brash new forms of advertising that might confuse a pilot—illuminated billboards, blinking arrows, neon slogans—some of which had been specifically designed to attract the attention of well-to-do passengers flying overhead: "The Air Commerce Act authorizes the discontinuance of any false lights or signals at such place or in such manner that it is likely to be mistaken for a true light."[69] Even the prosaic technology of airway lighting invoked a special, separate realm for aviation, calling for a "true light," distinct from the "stray" or "false" lights on ground level.

To receive an "A" rating, an airport had to be equipped with a rotating beacon "with not less than 100,000 candlepower . . . [and] flashes of duration not less than 1/10 second. . . ." The beacon at Cleveland's airport burned with such intensity that an employee was assigned the job of blocking the light with his body so pilots were not blinded when they made their final approach.

Red lights (of not less than fifty watts) were used to mark obstructions, and green range lights were used to indicate the preferred angle of approach. Floodlights were also required. Chicago Municipal Airport used wide-angle Fresnel floodlights mounted on towers. Detroit had fifty large floodlights placed in banks so that no part of the field was ever in shadow. By the end of 1929, more than 275 airports had been equipped for night flying and ten thousand miles of airways were illuminated by 1,352 rotating beacons.

Fitzgerald compared night landings to movie premieres "when the fans look at you with scornful reproach because you're not a star."[70] He understood the odd symmetry between aviation and

Night landing, Pittsburgh Airport, circa 1929.

cinema as well as any writer in America. Movies and aviation had both emerged as by-products of modern technology and given the world new perspectives. The first talkie, *The Jazz Singer,* appeared in 1927, the same year as Lindbergh's flight to Paris. The first in-flight movie was Harold Lloyd's *Speedy,* shown in a Ford Trimotor flying over Los Angeles in May 1928.[71]

Movies and aviation also attracted risk takers like Howard Hughes, who combined a career in both fields by investing millions he inherited from his father's drilling patent. Hollywood lured the future head of TWA into flying in the first place. At the age of twenty Hughes moved from Texas to Hollywood to produce *Hell's Angels,* the WWI flying epic.[72] He used vintage biplanes and hired over 130 pilots to perform the dangerous stunts in which several died. Hughes learned to fly and performed one of the stunts himself. In 1932, he started the Hughes Aircraft Company, took control of TWA in 1939, and bought the RKO studio in 1948. He would put as much energy into designing a half-cup bra for Jane Russell as he did to fine-tuning the Pratt & Whitney engine of his H-1 racing plane.

Architects would look to the movies for inspiration, and it was no coincidence that several who specialized in theater design were hired to design new passenger terminals.[73] In 1929, the architect and set designer H. L. Gogerty "of Hollywood" made the Grand Central Air Terminal in Glendale into a dreamy Spanish confection with hand-finished stucco walls, rustic roof tiles, and arched entry-ways. This was where Fitzgerald landed when he first came to Hol-lywood—and it was where the airplane in *The Last Tycoon* makes its landing after the long flight west: "I could see a line of lights for the Long Beach Naval Station ahead and to the left, and on the right a twinkling blur for Santa Monica. The California moon was out, huge and orange over the Pacific . . . the plane [was] coming down into the Glendale airport, into the warm darkness."[74]

Gogerty's faux Spanish architecture created a fairy-tale sense of suspended disbelief for arriving passengers: "I landed in Los Ange-les with the feeling of new worlds to conquer," wrote Fitzgerald.[75]

A five-story tower rose atop the terminal like a mission belfry, decorated with winged angels holding airplane propellers in place of shields. The interior was adorned with sunburst lintels and serpentine patterns set into the travertine floors.

The airport in Van Nuys had a pseudo-Moorish terminal and was often used in movies that called for an exotic setting. *Laurel and Hardy: Flying Deuces* was filmed there, as was the final scene in *Casablanca*. A four-story tower on the Curtiss-Wright terminal at Mines Field in Los Angeles looked like the belvedere of a Spanish monastery. It was capped by a dome of intricate tile work. Modern hangar doors were ingeniously disguised with arched windows that could be folded back mechanically to allow access for planes.

The idea of the past these airports represented was more like a flashback from *Zorro* or *Robin Hood* than actual history. The most convincing illusion may have been the Boeing Airport in Burbank. The Moorish-style terminal had three levels stacked symmetrically like the Court of Lions at the Alhambra. The only hint of twentieth-century technology was a beacon on the roof. The observation deck made an ideal perch from which to watch Hollywood moguls arriving from the east or spot a client of Paul Mantz, the stunt pilot who operated one of the most essential Hollywood services of the day. Mantz's little airline was known as the *Honeymoon Express* as it flew movie stars to Reno for impromptu weddings and quickie divorces.

There were those who disapproved of California's theme-park approach: "The use of pseudo-Spanish colonial style architecture is not particularly appropriate for a structure serving the most up-to-date form of transportation," grumbled one critic. But the mission style evoked an aura of the "past" in a part of the country that was self-conscious about its lack of history, that is, Anglo history.

Picturesque airports also helped to promote an image of eternal sunshine and unbridled opportunity. Only in southern California would a municipal airport be dedicated to the real estate agent who did the deal, as was the case with Mines Field, named after

Aerial view of Mines Field, future site of LAX, Los Angeles, California, 1929. Terminal and hangars were designed in the popular Spanish mission style.

William M. Mines, a local developer. When the city of Los Angeles officially dedicated the new airport in 1930, a mock aerial attack was staged by the Army Air Corps, but the moment of truth came when a Goodyear blimp maneuvered over the field and dropped a wreath of flowers into the arms of a well-endowed Hollywood starlet named Viola Peters.

There was an equally romantic trend in the South, where airport designers evoked the Confederate past. The press corps raced out to Atlanta's municipal airport to meet Clark Gable and his wife, Carole Lombard, when they flew in to attend the premiere of *Gone With the Wind*. It was an important juncture in modern mythology: the Old South meets the New South as Rhett Butler arrives in a DC-3. The architecture of Atlanta's terminal matched the antebellum theme, its walls gaily decorated with terra-cotta friezes, festoons, and fleurs-de-lis. An ornate balustrade surrounded the semicircular observation deck, and the windows were hung with ruffled curtains. A few years later Atlanta's airport administrators added a plantation-theme restaurant with murals of cotton fields and smiling mammies, while a seventy-three-year-old black employee named Alphon Smith was paid to sit on a bale of cotton and tell Uncle Remus stories.[76] The terminal in Birmingham, Alabama, went even further, with Tara-style columns supporting an overhanging roof and a broad lawn in front for watching airshows and sipping mint juleps.

As planes got faster and airports expanded, the romantic illusions of early air travel vanished. After a few plane rides, the sense of wonder began to wear off and passengers were surprised by how uneventful flying could be. Sinclair Lewis concluded that it was the most "monotonous and tedious form of journeying known to mankind, save possibly riding on a canal boat through flat country. . . ."[77]

Some spoke of a sensation that went beyond mere monotony. "[I feel] utterly separated from the world," wrote one journalist, "set off in a little planet of [my] own and floating on. . . ."[78] Others described a disembodied sense of self, an unsettling disconnection from reality. "We were all lingering—and not quite on purpose," wrote Fitzgerald in *The Last Tycoon*. "Even the stewardess, I think, had to keep reminding herself why she was there."[79] For Fitzgerald's protagonists, the realms of air and earth were predestined for collision. His novel ends with the hero, Monroe Stahr, dying in a plane crash, but it is no hero's death. On its way back to New York,

Stahr's plane disappears into a "white darkness" high in the Rocky Mountains, where the wreckage is covered by a blanket of snow. Fitzgerald based his ending on an actual incident. An airliner had recently crashed in the mountains with a U.S. senator aboard. What intrigued and horrified Fitzgerald about the news report was how the people who discovered the plane had rifled the dead bodies.

In Fitzgerald's version, the wreckage is discovered by children who come across part of the engine and then the corpses, "half concealed by the snow." They proceed to loot the possessions of the wealthy passengers. One finds the jewel box of a beautiful actress. Another finds Stahr's briefcase. "Nobody will know we have been up here," they reassure themselves in a tabloid moment that suggests a new kind of tragedy, one especially suited for the twentieth century, in which the god's fall from the sky is quite literal.

Romantic architecture for United Airport, Burbank, California, circa 1929.

CHAPTER 2

Naked Airport: 1930–1940

Raise the massive Constructions of the future city,
Raise them into the free open sky of the aviator.
—*Paolo Buzzi*

Utopian Perspectives

A passenger on the first scheduled flight from London to Paris in 1919 remarked how the Crystal Palace—that wonder of nineteenth-century engineering—looked like a "child's toy" from two thousand feet in the air.[1] "Everything is new, strange, delightful," wrote another early air tourist, while yet another thought the sprawling suburbs of London resembled a village from above. These were common enough observations during the early period of flight, but they signaled a profound change in perception.[2] "The airplane has unveiled for us the true face of the earth," wrote Antoine de Saint-Exupéry.[3] The pilot's view transformed conventional notions of time and distance and helped create a radically new idea of space. From the air, scale and form were diminished and distorted. Buildings were no longer the proofs of certainty they had been to earlier generations—proofs that had been further eroded by aerial bombardment during World War I when architecture was not merely distorted but destroyed.

Renaissance perspective assumed a certain relationship between viewer and horizon line. This relationship was overturned when the viewer was no longer standing, flat-footed, on ground level. Traditional forms of architecture could be appreciated in a new light. Pilot and author Norman Macmillan noted during a European air tour in 1930 that "churches lose their charm of facade and take on true cruciform." He predicted that "architectural plan form will be more carefully studied."[4] The elevated vantage would transform the way buildings were understood and, in turn, suggest new possibilities. In 1924 Italian architect Virgilio Marchi published drawings of a futurist building as seen from a moving airplane. The edifice appeared animated, almost human. Walls, stairways, and windows opened like gaping mouths as if to reveal a previously unseen dimension.[5]

Instead of being considered a disadvantage the aerial view was seen as a path toward liberation. "The roof is becoming the facade of the house," wrote American architect Francis Keally in 1930. "We can look down upon the world to which gravity has fastened

Futurist building as seen from a passing airplane. Virgilio Marchi, architect, 1924.

us for so many ages."[6] Architects would no longer be slaves of one-point perspective. The front, back, and top of a building were now, in a sense, equal, democratized by the aerial point of view.

Walter Gropius, architect and director of the Bauhaus from 1919 to 1928, understood the obligations this view demanded: "With the development of air transport," he wrote, "the architect will have to pay as much attention to the bird's-eye perspective of his houses as to their elevations."[7] The most frequently published photograph of Gropius's Bauhaus in Dessau, Germany, was one taken from a plane in 1926 that revealed the building's internal logic. The flat-roofed sections of workshop, dormitory, technical school, and painting studio were connected in a pinwheel pattern that could be fully appreciated only from the air. Gropius predicted this shift in perspective would soon generate a promising new kind of city: "Seen from the skies, the leafy house-tops of the . . . future will look like endless chains of hanging gardens."[8]

Le Corbusier was also inspired by the cultural implications of aviation. The Swiss-born architect was obsessed with airplanes— their speed, their functional purity, the simplicity of their form. "The airplane is the symbol of the new age," he exclaimed. "The airplane arouses our energies and our faith." He filled the pages of his journal, *L'Esprit Nouveau,* with aerial views and sensual close-ups of propellers.[9] He devoted a chapter of his book *Vers une Architecture* to aviation, and, in 1935, he published *Aircraft,* an entire volume on the subject.[10] Le Corbusier traced this aeronautical fixation to the spring of 1909 when, at the age of twenty-two, he heard a strange noise in the skies over Paris, chronicling the moment as if it were a divine revelation. The noise was the Comte de Lambert's plane circling the Eiffel Tower at a height of three hundred meters. "It was mad! Our dreams could then turn into reality, however daring they might be . . . men had captured the chimera and driven it above the city." A few months later, Louis Blériot made his famous flight across the English Channel, and Le Corbusier's conversion was complete.

The pilot's view allowed architects and urban planners to imagine a clean slate from which to begin anew. Cameras developed for military reconnaissance were used to make sequential images of the city and gave planners the proof they needed: "Cities, with their misery, must be torn down," wrote Le Corbusier with the moral conviction of a reformer. "They must be largely destroyed and fresh cities built. . . . The airplane is an indictment. It indicts the city. It indicts those who control the city."[11] The past itself was a criminal conspirator: "L'Avion Accuse," wrote Le Corbusier. "The airplane eye reveals a spectacle of collapse."[12] In his own prescriptions for urban renewal, Le Corbusier showed no mercy. His "Voison" plan of 1925 called for entire sections of central Paris to be leveled and rebuilt with towering skyscrapers.

In *Vers une Architecture*, Le Corbusier included a photograph of the concrete hangars at Orly airfield and compared them to the Gothic nave of Notre Dame. The hangars, he explained, were 150 feet high and 250 feet wide, while the cathedral's nave was only

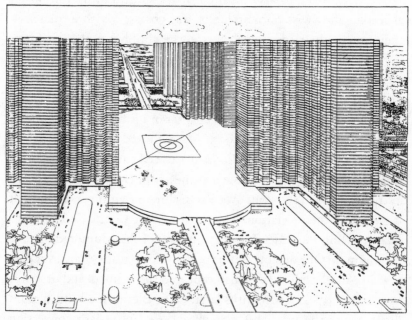

"A city made for speed is made for success." The central air station in Le Corbusier's city for 3 million inhabitants is flanked by four skyscrapers. 1922.

107 feet high and 40 feet wide.[13] The comparison was crude, but it served his purposes: feats of modern engineering were equal and even superior to architectural monuments of the past—the ferro-concrete hangar as cathedral of twentieth-century progress. Thus, "architecture finds itself confronted with new laws," he wrote.

In turn, Le Corbusier envisaged the airport as a new kind of threshold, around which the city—and the nation—would reshape itself. "A city made for speed," said Le Corbusier, "is made for success." He proposed a metropolis of monolithic skyscrapers—*Une Ville Contemporaine pour 3 Millions d'Habitants*—that would have a six-level transportation complex at its core.[14] This Central Station would feature a landing platform on its roof, while the lower levels would service high-speed motor traffic and railroad lines. Small "aero-taxis" would connect travelers to a larger aerodrome outside the city limits. Placing an airport at the city center was a naive and dangerous suggestion, one that would require pilots to maneuver aircraft between high-rise towers and land on a precariously narrow platform. Like most utopian architects of the period, Le Corbusier understood little about aviation: he had never been up in an airplane.

Rival modernist Rob Mallet-Stevens thought of the airport in explicitly symbolic terms and believed that it should provide a bold new entry point to Paris. He condemned nostalgic forms of architecture and called for a revolutionary kind of airport design, one that would hold its own against the outdated monuments of the past: "Tomorrow, travelers and tourists entering the French capital will arrive at the future airport of Paris," wrote Mallet-Stevens. "Their first sight—before the Eiffel Tower, before Notre Dame, before the Louvre, before Paris' many marvels—will be the airport."[15] Another French modernist, André Lurçat, proposed a mile-long runway built atop the Seine. Lurçat's *"bateauporte-avions"* would rest on the Ile des Cygnes and be supported at either end by the Pont d'Iena and Pont de Grenelle. Planes could be launched by catapult while brilliant beams of light would create an aerial corridor for night landings.

"Every generation should build its own city," wrote Italian Antonio Sant'Elia in his *Manifesto of Futurist Architecture*. He called for an architecture that was "agile, mobile and dynamic in every detail . . . like a gigantic machine."[16] At the center of his Città Nuova, Sant'Elia placed a *stazioni aeroplani* with multilevel plazas and ramps—an urban dynamo designed to convert Italy's crumbling antiquity into a machine-age utopia. The station would be linked to train lines and highways by elevators, metal gangways, and swiftly moving pavements. Filippo Marinetti, chief agitator of Italian futurism, was inspired to create a form of "aero-poetry" after taking his first plane ride.[17] Futurist painters distilled the dynamism of flight by using multiple-exposure imagery as Giacomo Balla did in *Swifts: Paths of Movement + Dynamic Sequences* (1913); or to reveal the pilot's perspective in aerial landscapes like Gino Severini's *Flying over Reims* (c. 1915), and Carlo Carra's *Aerial Reconnaissance − Sea-Moon + 2 Machine Guns + North-east Wind* (1914).

When Benito Mussolini came to power in 1922, the airplane became a key icon in his bid to turn Italy into a modern power. A squadron of planes was sent to the Century of Progress Fair in Chicago in 1932 as a show of aeronautical prowess. Upon their return, the planes flew in formation down the *via dell'Impero,* the new highway Mussolini had built atop the ruins of ancient Rome. In keeping with this transformational theme, architect Virgilio Marchi proposed a triumphal new entry to the ancient capital. His *Palazzo dell'aria, veduta aeroplanica* featured a broad roof for landings and oddly medieval ramparts that reached into the Tiber River for seaplanes. In 1935, Marinetti, Angiolo Mazzoni, and Mino Somenzi proposed a linear city with three parallel sections that would stretch across the breadth of the Italian peninsula like extruded pasta. One strand would be for residential use, another for commerce, and the third for industry. The roofs were reserved for airplanes with brightly colored airports placed at fifty-kilometer intervals and illuminated to complement the surrounding landscape: "a blue refueling stop with the reddish orange of the desert,"

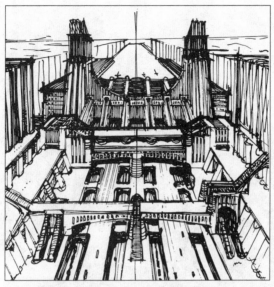

The city transformed. *(top) Stazioni aeroplani,* 1912. Antonio Sant'Elia proposed an airplane station for the center of Milan with multilevel plazas, elevators, and moving sidewalks. *(bottom)* Sant'Elia's design for an airship hangar, 1913.

Palazzo dell'aria, veduta aeroplanica. Virgilio Marchi proposed a new kind of triumphal entry to Rome to be built on the banks of the Tiber River. Planes would be pulled into hangars on metal tracks.

for instance, "or a cylindrical stop with the triangular rocks of the seashore."[18]

Avant-garde architects and artists in the Soviet Union also fell under the spell of the plane cult. Kasimir Malevich adopted the topsy-turvy vantage of the pilot to create a weightless realm of abstract forms in *Suprematist Composition: Airplane Flying* (1915). Malevich's drawing for a "Pilot's House" of 1924 evoked the feeling of an airplane moving through space, while his "Design for an Airfield," also of 1924, had a cruciform shape at its center that suggested both a landing strip and a distorted Christian cross.[19] Constructivist artist El Lissitzky proposed aerial entry to central Moscow with rooftop landing pads on "Cloud Hanger" skyscrapers that were to be built on Strastnoi Boulevard. The firm of G. F. Kuznetsov and E. V. Toropov designed a cantilevered landing apron for the roof of the Soviet Palace of Labor.[20]

London got its share of giddily futuristic proposals, too, including the design by C. W. Glover for an elevated airport in the King's Cross area (1931). It would take the form of a giant wheel supported by the roofs of the tallest buildings.[21] This kind of mid-city scheme was starting to be discredited, however, and Viscount Swinton, British air minister, ridiculed such thinking: "A certain number of rather unintelligent people ask me, 'When are you going to establish an airport in the middle of London.' The answer is when everybody in London has become so air-minded and unaesthetic as to cut down every tree in Hyde Park and turn it into an aerodrome."[22]

Empire Routes

European airlines were not only providing speedy service on the Continent, they were starting to expand their reach around the world. For countries like Great Britain, France, Belgium, and the Netherlands, international service became a way to maintain contact with far-flung colonies. These trunk routes weren't just for

Pilot's house, Leningrad. Kasimir Malevich, 1924.

carrying mail and embassy staffers, however. They were seen as "ligaments of empire" and helped to prolong a colonial system that was already beginning to unravel. "The future of the British Empire depends upon the growth of Imperial air routes," said Sir Alan Cobham, an English aviator who had helped to forge a global link. "Henceforth the nation that controls the air will control the earth."[23] In turn, these empire routes would expose indigenous cultures to modern technology and social conventions from the West. The sight of a European flagship banking over the desert of Jordan or the jungles of Indo-China made an indelible impression on the local population.

Imperial Airways' route across Iraq was initially devised to police the vast, ungovernable expanses of that country.[24] The Royal Air Force (RAF) established the Desert Air Mail route between Cairo and Baghdad in 1920, and Imperial took over the route in

1927, extending it to Basra in southern Iraq. The location of airfields was determined by political as much as practical necessity. Some stops were former RAF fields, such as Heliopolis on the outskirts of Cairo, and Hinaidi, south of Baghdad. In Palestine, Gaza was an intermediate refueling stop. Emergency landing areas were marked at thirty-mile intervals across the expanse of desert between Amman and Baghdad. Furrows were dug into the desert floor as navigational aides pointing the way.

By 1932, Imperial's empire route extended all along the Persian Gulf, with stops in Kuwait, Bahrain, and Sharjah, then crossed to Gwadar in Baluchistan and on to Karachi, India. (The cost of a one-way ticket from London to Karachi was £95.) "Our passengers on the India run were largely civil servants and their wives," recalled Sir Malin Sorsbie, a pilot for Imperial Airways during the 1930s. "I found them a pompous lot."[25] Besides embassy staff, military advisers, and civil servants, however, Imperial also brought engineers to Middle East oil fields, rubber planters to southeast Asia, and salesmen in search of new markets.

W. H. Pilkington, director of an English glass firm, flew from London to Brisbane on business in 1935. He kept a detailed account of his ten-day journey and the thirty-five stops he made along the way. Between Gaza and Baghdad, he was delighted to watch the shadow of his plane trace the oil pipeline across the desert. He was distracted, however, by the fact that fellow passengers had neglected to bring sufficient reading material: "There are five passengers in this plane, and every one of them is reading one of my books," he noted testily. "No one else has come with sufficient literature to get them even as far as Baghdad."[26] When they did reach Baghdad, Pilkington took a tour of the city but found it "smelly." He experienced further offense in Bangkok when his bags were searched by a Siamese official who proceeded to interrogate him about firearms and opium. "Picking up a light novel of mine [he] suggested delightfully that it might be Communist literature."[27]

While most passengers were men traveling for diplomatic or business reasons, a handful of wealthy tourists, including women, flew the India route for pleasure or adventure. Lord Moyne and Lady Broughton flew all the way to Burma to hunt tigers. Lady Maude Hoare, the wife of Britain's current air minister, was the first woman passenger on the India route and she saw it as her duty to show other ladies how to travel lightly on an air journey. Instead of heavy steamer trunks, Lady Hoare used lightweight cloth bags and reduced her wardrobe to a minimum: "a stockinette coat and skirt, with a *crêpe-de-chine* jumper" was one suggestion. She also recommended bringing "gum boots" for wet aerodromes and, for colder climes, a woolen cardigan, and fur coat. Her favorite in-flight garment was a Shetland dressing gown.[28]

Great Britain's tradition of naval supremacy would now, in theory, be transferred to the air, her Commonwealth consolidated, maintained, and further extended with Handley Page flagships thundering off from London to distant points around the world, delivering Foreign Office staff, civil servants, and His Majesty's mail. The new slogan for Croydon Aerodrome became "By Air to Anywhere." By the mid-1930s, Imperial could boast over fifty-nine thousand miles of interconnecting airways that linked more than five hundred stops around the world. The sheer act of maintaining such an aerial network was a significant measure of national will.

High mountain ranges, Bedouin bandits, and extreme weather conditions made Imperial's long-distance trips an adventure for pilots and passengers alike. Planes were fitted with air-cooled engines to avoid overheating in hot climates. The baked earth of the desert flats made suitable landing surfaces, but after rain these often turned to mud. The desert plant camelthorn punctured aircraft tires. Simple "resthouses" were built for passengers, but in some of the more hostile areas forts were constructed from concrete block as at Rutbah Wells in the Syrian Desert and Sharjah on the Persian Gulf. Garrisons of armed guards were stationed at the airfields to protect passengers and property. More substantial facilities with proper hotels and restaurants were erected in Baghdad, Basra, Karachi, and Delhi.

In 1931, Air France inaugurated an airmail service between Paris and Saigon in Indo-China. Belgium's national airline, Sabena, completed a colonial connection from Brussels to the Congo's heart of darkness, and, by 1931, KLM, the Dutch national airline, had established regular passenger service from Amsterdam all the way to Batavia, capital of the Dutch East Indies. KLM flew Fokker F-18s converted for long-range use and equipped with sleeper seats. Stops were made at three-hundred- to four-hundred-mile intervals for refueling. The average one-way flying time was approximately eighty hours, but the trip could take as long as ten days.

By 1934, Imperial had extended its trunk route all the way to Singapore and Brisbane, Australia. The airline also inaugurated a colonial service to Africa, and, by 1932, a chain of airfields stretched the entire length of the continent from Cairo to Cape Town. Planes would follow the Nile south into the Sudan. At Khartoum, a traveler could change planes and go west to Nigeria or continue south to Cape Town across the Sudd swamps and the jungles of tropical Africa. Giant anthills were a common hazard on African airfields, and there was the ever-present threat of yellow fever. (Passengers were sprayed by health officials before leaving their planes.) Malin Sorsbie also piloted Imperial's African route. Unlike the pompous civil servants he flew to India, the Cape Town passengers were carefree and more to his liking. "[They] were totally different," wrote Sorsbie. "They viewed the voyage as a great big lark and we had to put twice as much champagne on board as we had on the flight to India."29

Chronometric Exactitude

When Le Corbusier finally took his first plane trip in 1928, he was surprised to discover that airports had been evolving in their

"The future of the British Empire depends upon the growth of Imperial air routes." Desert airport with rudimentary shelter for passengers, Bahrain, 1934. An Imperial Airways Handley Page HP-42 is being refueled in the background.

own inimitable way. He was going to Moscow to oversee the design of a new government building: "This is how I discovered the air terminals in Bourget, Cologne, and Berlin," wrote Le Corbusier. "I perceived that persons by dint of faith and determination had little by little, higgledy-piggledy, equipped hangars, instruments, buildings, and staff. And that the airports were stations like

railway stations. One set off at a given time and, lo! one arrived with chronometric exactitude."[30]

While safety and comfort were important selling points, it was the clock that became the true arbiter of success in the 1930s. The only way an airline could compete with the railroad and show a profit was to guarantee fast, efficient service. As one journal proclaimed in 1932: "Speed must always be the merchandising factor in aeronautics."[31] Windtunnel studies led to elongated fuselages and aerodynamic lines that helped reduce resistance. Lufthansa offered high-speed service in Junkers Ju-52 airliners that could cruise at 184 mph, as compared to the 100 to 130 mph range of most other passenger planes. The German airline inaugurated a special Blitz service in 1934 using high-performance aircraft like the Focke-Wulf FW.200 Condor that could cruise at 230 mph. The sleek, four-engined Condor made headlines in August 1938 when it was flown nonstop from Berlin to New York in record time.[32]

Speed became the greatest virtue at the airport, too: speed of ticketing, speed of transfer, speed of baggage handling, speed of boarding and departure. Writing in praise of one new terminal, the architect Joseph F. Hudnut noted that the "passage from airplane to automobile is so direct and so effortless that one is scarcely conscious of an architecture: an experience which would appear to be happily consistent with the nature of an organization whose merchandise is time."[33]

The first thing that passengers noticed upon arrival at Fuhlsbüttel airport in Hamburg, Germany, was a large clock that hung auspiciously above the entrance to the modern terminal. Inside, there was a row of smaller clocks that displayed the times in differ-

Chronometric exactitude. Fuhlsbüttel Airport in Hamburg, Germany, was designed to run with the precision of a clock. An entry ramp leads from flying field to customs inspection. Dyrssen and Averhoff, architects, 1929.

ent cities around the world. Indeed, all of Fuhlsbüttel was intended to run like a clock. The sequence of movement from airplane to ground transport was calculated for maximum flow. After disembarking, passengers walked up a long concrete ramp that led from the apron to the arrivals concourse. The architects Friedrich Dyrssen and Peter Averhoff separated airport functions on different levels. The ground floor was reserved exclusively for ticketed passengers, and the basement was for baggage handling; nontraveling spectators were directed up to the restaurant and observation terraces on the upper floors.

A double-carriage roadway and a tramline ran directly in front of the terminal and a traveler could be in downtown Hamburg in a matter of minutes. The concept that Dyrssen and Averhoff pioneered at Fuhlsbüttel would influence the development of other airports and become a standard solution for speeding transit time.

In his 1935 novel *England Made Me,* Graham Greene described a businessman taking a flight from Amsterdam to Stockholm: "He knew the airports of Europe as well as he had once known the stations on the Brighton line," wrote Greene. "Shabby Le Bourget; the great scarlet rectangle of the Tempelhof as one came in from London in the dark, the head lamp lighting up the asphalt way; the white sand blowing up around the shed at Tallin; Riga, where the Berlin to Leningrad plane came down and bright pink mineral waters were sold in a tin-roofed shed; the huge aerodrome at Moscow with machines parked half a dozen deep, the pilots taxiing casually here and there, trying to find room, bouncing back and forth, beckoned by one official with his cap askew. It was a comfortable, dull way of traveling. . . ."34

By the mid-1930s many European airports like "shabby Bourget" were already out of date. Once considered the greatest air hub on the Continent, Bourget had become a national disgrace. Instead of building an entirely new airport, however, the French Air Ministry decided to remodel the old facility and open it in time for the International Exhibition of 1937. A gleaming new terminal by Georges Labro had a 722-foot-long facade of glass. Its hyperextended length and translucency echoed the theme of the exposition—art and technology in modern life—and created a monumentous sense of arrival. A glass control tower projected out toward the airfield and was topped by an octagonally shaped dome. A roof-top terrace could accommodate more than three thousand spectators at a time. Rob Mallet-Stevens had proposed "embarkation footbridges" to extend from the new terminal like the legs of a giant centipede. These were never built, but they foreshadowed the kind of telescoping ramps that would become standard at airports in the 1960s.

In London, air traffic had doubled in 1935. Dense housing was encroaching the periphery of Croydon, and there was no room left for expansion. (Croydon still didn't even have a hard-surfaced runway.)35

A special airport committee of the Royal Institute of British Architects (RIBA) was organized to study the problem. RAF squadron leader Nigel Norman and architect Graham Dawbarn made a tour of airports around the world and published a report suggesting ways to modernize British airports. (As part of their mission, they organized an influential exhibition, called Airports and Airways, in 1937.)[36]

Rejecting the stuffy tradition of the old Croydon terminal, British architects began to adopt the sleek modernity of the Bauhaus. Graham Dawbarn designed a series of stripped-down passenger terminals, including ones at Heston, Birmingham/Jersey, Elmdon Airport in Birmingham, and Perth, Scotland. For the Ramsgate airport, David Pleydell-Bouverie designed an elongated, one-story terminal with a cockpit-style control tower that rose from its center while the terminal's flat roof extended out on either end to further accentuate the airplane metaphor. The most innovative new British airport, however, was being built at Gatwick, twenty-eight miles south of London.

A developer named Morris Jackaman purchased a small airfield in Sussex adjacent to the Southern Railways line, which ran between London and Brighton. If he could offer a faster turnaround

Rendering of Ramsgate Municipal Airport, Ramsgate, England. David Pleydell-Bouverie, architect, 1937.

time, Jackaman thought he could compete with Croydon's service to Paris. He was working late one night, so the story goes, trying to decide what kind of terminal to build, when his father walked into the room and urged him to go to bed. "You're just thinking in circles," he said to his son. Then, like a scene out of a Hollywood movie, Jackaman scratched his head and decided on a circular terminal. He drew up preliminary plans and submitted them to Britain's Patent Office under the title *Improvement Relating to Buildings Particularly for Airports.*

The circular concept had been proposed before, but Gatwick was the first to put it to the test.[37] The terminal would be "an island on an aerodrome," as Jackaman described it, placed in the middle of the airfield and surrounded by a concrete apron. It would be connected to the nearby railway station by an underground passage, and the boarding gates would have canvas-covered gangways that moved back and forth on motorized rails. Passengers could walk from concourse to plane without ever being exposed to inclement English weather and as many as six planes could be loaded at once.

Overseas service from Gatwick to Paris began on May 17, 1936. A passenger could check in at Victoria Station, London, catch the 12:28 P.M. train, arrive forty-two minutes later at Gatwick, walk through the underground passage, and board a British Airway's DH-86. Weather permitting, the flight would arrive in Paris ninety-five minutes later. The entire journey from central London to Bourget took only two and a half hours, a considerable savings in time over Imperial's service from Croydon.

Transparency

During the 1930s, Le Corbusier had the chance to fly with famous aviators like Antoine de Saint-Exupéry and Jean Mermoz. By this point, Le Corbusier had changed his views about aviation and realized that an airport should be built not in the city but, rather, out in the hinterlands. "The beauty of an airport," he wrote, "is in the splendor of wide open spaces!"[38] In the rough sketches he drew for a new kind of airport, the terminal is a mere whisker on the horizon, hardly noticeable, while the plane, exaggerated in scale, sits like a bird god on the tarmac, overshadowing everything around it. Customs, reception, and waiting areas are hidden below ground level so that the open vista of the airfield remains inviolate. Nothing could compete with the machine itself, and thus the only appropriate architecture was one that was practically invisible: just "sky, grass, and concrete runways," he wrote. Later, at the French Congress of Aviation, Le Corbusier made a sweepingly enigmatic statement: "[Airports must be] two-dimensional architecture!" he proclaimed, staring out through spectacles that were as round and thick as an aviator's goggles. "An airport," said Le Corbusier, "should be naked."

In a similar vein, American architecture critic Lewis Mumford suggested half in jest that an airport should be designed from the ground down. Passengers would descend to the planes, which would then be lifted to the runway on a giant elevator like the one at Radio City Music Hall. "The invisible airport," wrote Mumford, "would be the last crown of a disappearing civilization."[39]

"The beauty of an airport is in the splendor of wide open spaces!" Le Corbusier's sketch for a naked airport, 1946.

Indeed, by the mid-1930s, airport buildings started to look less like temples and more like what they really were: outgrowths of modern technology and urbanism. Where the first generation had narrow corridors and overly partitioned interiors, the next generation had a minimum of partitioning and decoration. A free-standing restaurant building at Leipzig's airport was designed by Swiss architect Hans Wittwer, who taught at the Bauhaus. The glass-and-concrete building was stripped to its structural bones. People inside the restaurant watched planes come and go as they ate. There was nothing to block their view, not even a railing. Continuous walls of glass wrapped around all four sides, and, at night, with the lights on, people inside the restaurant appeared to hover in a kind of aerial suspension.

This kind of vanishing act had been going on since the early part of the century in the work of utopian architects like Bruno Taut, who envisioned a world of "crystal architecture," but it found new meaning at the airport, where high visibility was a virtue and an important means of conversion. "Visitors who remain in comfortable restaurants while observing the airplanes as they alight and depart are certain to become patrons of the air transportation lines," wrote one observer. "Nothing could impart greater confidence than for a person to see airplanes arriving and departing frequently without confusion or accident."[40]

A translucent tower of glass rose from the terminal designed by Mario Emmer at the San Niccolò Del Lido Airport in Venice. Gianluigi Girodani designed a glass-enclosed cube that projected toward the Linate airfield in Milan (1937). Double-glazing was used to muffle the noise of airplane engines.[41] The interior of a new terminal by K. J. Mossner at Munich's Oberwiesenfeld was a model of open planning. The few partitions that did exist were made of lightweight materials designed to be nonbearing. Ticket booths and baggage counters were freestanding elements that could be moved for changing needs.

For a new terminal at Bromma/Stockholm, Gunnar Asplund proposed an all-glass bridge that projected seventy meters out

All-glass control tower at the San Niccolò Del Lido Airport in Venice, Italy. Mario Emmer, architect, 1932.

The "traffic hall" at Kastrup Airport, Copenhagen, was designed for the drama of modern air travel. Vilhelm Lauritzen, architect, 1936.

from an embankment, as if the building were in flight. Sweden's airport authority chose instead to build a steel-framed terminal designed by Paul Hedquist in the naked-airport style. It did not call attention to itself but rather to the view outside—the spectacle of the airfield and the surrounding landscape. When travelers entered the building, they were greeted by an eighty-five-foot-long wall of floor-to-ceiling glass.[42]

In 1936, Denmark's Ministry of Works organized a competition for a new terminal at Kastrup Airport on the island of Amager. After reviewing sixty-three entries, the jury chose a submission from Vilhelm Lauritzen, a Danish modernist known for his design of the National Radio Building in Copenhagen. Lauritzen understood what he called "a certain festive optimism that is linked with things in the process of development"[43] and saw Kastrup as an opportunity to explore the relationship between form and flight. Lauritzen made a thorough study of other airports and learned how quickly today's solution becomes tomorrow's failure.

Kastrup's terminal was supported by a system of concrete columns set back from the facade so that exterior and interior walls could be placed for flexibility. The building could be extended at either end, and office partitions were movable. The main "traffic hall" was suffused with Nordic light streaming through long bands of windows and factory-style skylights. The ceiling undulated with waves of acoustic tiles, similar to Alvar Aalto's Viipuri Library, which helped to dampen noise as well as create a rhythmic sense of movement. Wall coverings were made from birch parquet. Rubber tiles were used on the floors and Greenland marble on the walls. An all-glass restaurant protruded onto the apron and brought people as close to the airplanes as safety permitted.

Coming at the end of a decade that saw relentless change in aviation, Kastrup was a high point of airport design. During its first year of operation, more than seventy-two thousand travelers were serviced with great efficiency. But it was more than just a machine for processing passengers. Lauritzen had managed to design a place that celebrated the transitory nature of modern life.

CHAPTER 3

New Deal: 1933–1941

"Here is the magnificent spectacle of a luminous world,
apparently suspended in space . . ."
> —*Official guidebook,*
> New York World's Fair, *1939*

The Flying Candidate

The 1932 Democratic Convention was held in Chicago in July. New York governor Franklin Delano Roosevelt and his advisers waited patiently for the results in the governor's mansion in Albany, where they were able to keep in touch with events by phone. It wasn't until the fourth ballot that FDR received the two-thirds majority needed to win the nomination. When assured of victory, Roosevelt cabled Chicago and announced that he would be arriving by airplane the next day. He would accept the nomination in person—a break in tradition. In the past, presidential nominees had waited until after the convention for a formal ceremony.

American Airways stood by ready to fly the candidate from Albany to Chicago in its most reliable plane, a Ford Trimotor. The pilot was Ray Wonsey. Roosevelt was carried up to the plane on a specially prepared ramp and was seated near the door. His wife, Eleanor, sat in the seat behind him, and their sons Eliot and John came along, too.

The plane left Albany at eight A.M. and started its journey west, south of Utica and north of Syracuse. There were thunderstorms along the Mohawk Valley and the Ford Trimotor was buffeted by headwinds. Roosevelt's son John was airsick most of the way, but the governor chewed gum and felt fine. As assistant secretary of the navy, he had flown quite often and was used to such turbulence.

A number of reporters had been on hand when the plane left Albany that morning, but the "flying candidate" story was building into a major press event as the plane made its way westward. It stopped to refuel in Buffalo, and Roosevelt was greeted by a group of Democratic leaders. Lunch was brought aboard, and the Roosevelts ate roast chicken, cream-cheese-and-olive sandwiches, and chocolate cake. The plane landed again in Cleveland and was cheered by a crowd of five thousand spectators.

The NBC radio network was able to hook up with the plane's cockpit and deliver ongoing reports, which helped to build momentum. At one point, Eleanor was interviewed midair and Roosevelt radioed a message ahead to Mayor Anton J. Cermak of Chicago apologizing for the delay: "Sorry strong head wind makes us a little late." It was all very modern—the plane, the radio hookup—and marked the beginning of a new kind of political event: the airport campaign. Newspapers made the fact of Roosevelt's flying almost as big a story as his nomination. Both items were announced in banner headlines with the same boldface type:

ROOSEVELT NOMINATED ON FOURTH BALLOT;
GOVERNOR WILL FLY TO CONVENTION TODAY[1]

Journalists pointed out the historic nature of the trip: "Jefferson, the father of the Democratic party, rode to his inaugural on horseback," wrote the New York Times, "but the nominee of 1932 flew to the scene of his triumph by airplane from Albany and covered the nine fold greater distance in less time."[2] This was a first. No president or presidential candidate had ever taken to the air before. Here was a leader who embraced the modern age. "Launching his campaign for the Presidency with the first utilization of the airplane in national politics, Governor Roosevelt sped here today through squalls and bumpy air. . . ."[3]

FDR finished composing his acceptance speech somewhere over Ohio. There was a small desk set up in the plane, and a secretary typed up a fair copy while Roosevelt took a few moments to gaze down at the passing landscape. He could see orchards, silos, and country roads winding between the grassy hills—no evidence of the shantytowns and soup lines that had been the blight on Hoover's administration. But he knew the reality on the ground: There were as many as 15 million workers unemployed—25 percent of the nation's workforce. Wages had dropped 60 percent since 1929, and the country's banking system was on the verge of collapse.

A crowd of fifteen thousand waited to greet Roosevelt at Chicago's municipal airport. The headwinds had delayed his arrival by two hours, and the people were restless. After seven hours of flying, the candidate's corrugated metal plane touched down and taxied up to the terminal. People climbed over the fence and swarmed onto the apron. As soon as Roosevelt stepped out of the plane he was engulfed by the mob and his spectacles were knocked off. People wanted to see him and touch him. The press compared the hectic airport scene to Lindbergh's landing at Bourget and for many in the crowd FDR's arrival was no less momentous. Here was a leader who understood the urgency of the moment and the airport made the ideal starting point for his campaign of renewal. By the time FDR's motorcade arrived at the convention hall, party delegates had been worked into a lather: "The convention rose enthusiastically to the voyager of the skies," reported the *New York Times*. "[They] accepted his method of travel and the fact that he endured its rigors so well as a proof of his venturesome spirit and fine physical equipment for the office of President of the United States."[4]

Dinner Key

The nation's economic collapse had ruined commercial aviation. Hardly anyone could afford to fly, and the development of an airway system that had begun so auspiciously in 1927 ground to a halt. Private investment in airports dropped from $35 million in 1930 to a paltry $1 million by 1933. Construction instigated by Lindbergh was left unfinished. There wasn't enough money in municipal coffers to repair existing runways much less build those aerial palaces that had been proposed before the crash. The kind of corporate investment that had fueled the boom of the 1920s vanished, and many of the most promising ventures failed.

Curtiss-Wright's plan for a nationwide syndicate of privately owned airports dissolved. Western Air Express's luxury airway between San Francisco and Los Angeles went bust. Transcontinental Air Transport was also verging on bankruptcy. (The company had just introduced two-way radio service on its transcontinental flights, and several prominent passengers learned of their Wall Street losses in midair.) The airline suffered a $2.7 million loss in the first year of operations alone, and while TAT's president, Clement Keys, managed to keep the company flying into 1930, he was forced to merge with Western Air Express to become Transcontinental and Western Air (TWA). Even Henry Ford, who had invested with such cautious calculation, found that airlines and airports weren't nearly as profitable as cars. His air transport company went out of business in 1932.[5] Experts like Harry F. Guggenheim pleaded with the Hoover administration to create a master plan for a national system with strict regulations, but the government continued to cite the Air Commerce Act of 1926, which restricted federal involvement. Prospects were bleak, and it appeared as if aviation in the U.S. would once again slip behind Europe.

While the crash crippled most airlines, one company was not only surviving but thriving. Juan Trippe and his Pan American Airway system actually grew during the worst years of the Depression. At the end of 1929, PAA hired more than twelve hundred new employees and was operating out of seventy-one airports. Flush from international mail contracts, PAA held a virtual monopoly on overseas air travel out of the United States. Between 1930 and 1934, its gross business expanded by 150 percent.

In 1931, Trippe commissioned the Sikorsky Aircraft company to produce the S-40 as an instrument for connecting PAA's far-flung network. It was, announced Trippe, "the first example of the great air liner of tomorrow that will speed trade and good will among the nations."[6] The S-40 was versatile and could land almost anywhere; its fuselage was shaped like a hull, and its twin pontoons gave it stability on rough seas.[7] The S-40 would open new economic frontiers throughout Latin America as it spread American influence and Trippe's promise of goodwill. It could carry more than four tons of payload and forty passengers, and it had a flying range of 950 miles. The flight from Miami to Barranquilla, Colombia, would require only a single refueling stop in Jamaica.[8] Trippe called his new fleet of S-40s the American Clippers, evoking the romantic era of seafaring.

In 1934, Trippe opened Dinner Key, a million-dollar seaplane station in Coconut Grove, Miami, that would serve as the official gateway to PAA's expanding empire. During its construction Trippe claimed the right of eminent domain with authority to condemn lands. James Yonge, the airline's attorney, convinced the Florida state legislature that such a privilege was necessary so that the new airport would not be boxed in by future real estate speculation. As historic precedent, Yonge cited the rights-of-way granted in the nineteenth century for railways and canals. The new airport, he argued, would also bring more jobs into the state. The legislature was easily persuaded and PAA was granted carte blanche to claim whatever land it needed.

Work crews cleared mangrove swamps and built a peninsula that jutted into Biscayne Bay in alignment with the prevailing northwesterly winds. An approach channel was dredged and a ramp was built so that the S-40s could be hauled ashore for maintenance. When completed, Dinner Key was hailed as Trippe's pièce de résistance and considered the most advanced American airport of the day. It was certainly the most elegant. Tall, swaying palm trees lined the processional drive that led to the main terminal. The three-story building was designed by Delano and Aldrich, the same society firm that designed PAA's first Miami terminal. The color scheme was meant to suggest the "brilliance of sky, sand, and sea."9 Walls were cream-colored stucco. Trim was dark blue. A terra-cotta frieze incorporated PAA's logo of a winged globe combined with a sun-burst motif.

Once inside, passengers were greeted by porters dressed in navy-style uniforms and led into a sumptuously decorated concourse with pale gray walls and terra-cotta floors. The coffered ceilings were decorated with zodiac signs and touches of iridescent paint to give them a celestial sparkle. But all the ornament was only icing on the cake. The real architecture was the far-reaching network of airways that Trippe had managed to forge with such tenacity. A large globe of planet Earth sat prominently at the center of the Dinner Key concourse. Its surface was highlighted with a cat's cradle of dotted lines that stretched from Miami south across the West Indies and down through South America. To some, these lines were marks of accomplishment: Trippe was only in his thirties and already controlled an empire that spanned twenty-five thousand miles and touched thirty-two countries. To others, the lines represented a pernicious form of American imperialism: "Pan American Airways are stretching their tentacles all over the world!" wrote one critic.10 But from either perspective, the magnitude of the enterprise was impressive.

One passenger who took particular interest in the workings of Dinner Key was the writer Alice Dalgliesh who had booked a ticket to fly PAA's entire Latin American circuit. She was planning to spend two months collecting material for a book about her experiences, *Wings Around South America*.11 Dalgliesh was accompanied by Katherine Milhous, an illustrator who would sketch scenes along the way.

As Dalgliesh recounts, a brass bell was rung in the airport and a voice called through a megaphone: "Plane for Barranquilla!" Dalgliesh, Milhous, and the other passengers filed out of the waiting area and down through a boarding ramp covered with a canvas awning. "We go through a doorway which looks like the entrance

Aerial view of the International Air terminal, Dinner Key Airport. Delano and Aldrich, architects, 1934.

to a train platform, and down to the dock where the seaplane Colombia is riding on the water. She is silver, with red stripes on her wings."[12] The spacious cabin of the plane is divided into eight compartments. Walls are paneled with walnut. Windows are draped with silk curtains.

The Clipper plane was towed away from the dock, and the plane taxied out to the open waters of Biscayne Bay. Dalgliesh had never flown before and was pleasantly surprised by the smoothness of the flight. "On we go with scarcely any sensation of motion," she wrote, reassured by the fact that PAA had never lost a passenger in a flying-boat accident. Soon it was time for lunch—soup, a meat course, and dessert—and the smartly dressed steward set a table with a green cloth and unbreakable dishes. After lunch Dalgliesh begins to take notes but stops short when ink from her fountain pen leaks onto her blouse. "When the plane reaches a certain height the outside pressure on the pen diminishes, but the inside pressure remains the same," notes Dalgliesh with scientific detachment, resolving to write with a pencil for the rest of the trip. PAA's South American network will provide the adventuresome tourist with many new perspectives from the air and startling contrasts on the ground. Most importantly, it will immerse Dalgliesh into South American culture in the shortest amount of time. What in the past would have taken months now takes days.

On the flight to Quito, Ecuador, the plane climbs to fourteen thousand feet and crosses the Andes: "Fold after fold of crumpled yellow-green velvet, with patches of darker green dotted with white flowering trees and small Indian villages," notes Dalgliesh. "Here and there a curl of smoke rises from a solitary hut." At no point in her narrative does the author suggest that the Pan American system might be a "tentacle" of Yankee imperialism. Apparently unaware of the political subterfuge it took to establish such a route, she is delighted to find the comforts and efficiency of "modern American civilization" in the "midst of a people living on a primitive scale." Even at remote refueling stops, Trippe's airline has provided the most up-to-date facilities. "Here [in Chile], with nothing but desert and bare mountains around it, is a modern airport building with huge plate-glass windows and furniture of chromium and red leather." At the airport in Quito, Dalgliesh sees her first Indians—"very light gold-colored people who look quite oriental"—and Milhous does a hasty sketch.

But after the first few days of their whirlwind odyssey, Dalgliesh is bothered by a nagging sense of urgency. The airplane begins to set the pace of the trip. There is no time for lingering or the kind of thoughtful reflection that was possible during steamship days. "Airplane reservations cannot be changed," laments Dalgliesh, "so we must leave the quaint streets and terra-cotta roofs of Quito." The means become the end as the scope of narrative narrows to immediate airport impressions. At one stop, she describes only the terminal "set against a background of blue-green mountains . . . Its roof is the brightest green, and it is fringed with scarlet poinsettias. We stay here long enough to refuel, to have a drink of lemonade, then we are off again." Another terminal is "a doll's house, white, covered with climbing geraniums and set here like a tiny oasis in a desert."

Their plane lands in Asunción, Paraguay, during a tropical downpour and Dalgliesh doesn't even leave the plane. She looks out from the relative comfort of the cabin and sees "native huts, coconut trees, red-clay roads, and a dripping greenness." At the Santos-Dumont Airport in Rio, there is a cageful of blue-and-green parrots, and a crowd of "demonstrative" Brazilians waiting at the gate. But Dalgliesh is most impressed by the new airport buildings that were designed under the influence of Le Corbusier and his naked airport theories. (Le Corbusier came to Rio in 1936 as an adviser on the Ministry of Education building.) A hangar by Marcelo and Milton Roberto has a daringly cantilevered roof that appears, in section, like the wings of a condor. A sleek new seaplane terminal by Attilio Corrêa Lima is clad in yellow travertine. Slender columns skewer the structure from floor to roof, while spiral staircases, both inside and outside, create a sense of movement. "Not only are the buildings handsome," writes Dalgliesh, "but there are pergolas leading to the seaplane docks; arbors, palms, and flowering trees. Even the sidewalks outside the buildings make a lovely pattern, their concrete squares criss-crossed by ribbons of grass."

A few days later, the writer and illustrator are on their way back to Miami: "The sun is setting, and there, in the golden light, is the International Airport," writes Dalgliesh. "We step onto the soil of our own country with pride and a sense of achievement." But it was a sense of achievement clouded by uncertainty. How was one expected to digest such fleeting impressions from so many different cultures? As one Latino had scolded her: "You North Americans hurry so!" Impressions of the landscape and the indigenous cultures were reduced to snapshots. Instead of a deepening understanding, Dalgliesh was left with a sense of imminent departure.

WPA Airports

President Roosevelt understood the importance of aviation as being a practical as well as symbolic necessity in the nation's recovery. Improved commercial airlines would speed the movement of people and goods, thereby stimulating the economy. Within months of his inauguration in 1933, FDR established the Civil Works Administration (CWA), and among its expenditures were $11.5 million for airport construction. The CWA was essentially a back-to-work program that covered wages and helped employ more than seventy thousand jobless men. At Candler Field in Atlanta, for instance, six hundred workers were hired to rebuild the runway and dig draining ditches. The government paid daily wages but gave nothing for equipment or material, so most of the work was done with shovels and pickaxes.[13] Federal support increased further in 1935 when the Work Projects Administration (WPA) came into being and a Division of Airways and Airports was established under the WPA's chief engineer. Teams of surveyors, engineers, and architects collaborated on a massive renewal of the country's aerial network. New airports were built, and older ones were brought up-to-date. WPA officials conducted field studies in thirty-eight states to determine which communities needed assistance and which needed to build entirely new facilities. Aerial photographs were taken of existing conditions. As planes got heavier, the old turf fields were no longer adequate so new kinds of hard-surfaced runways were developed like that in Cleveland, where an all-weather "landing mat" was laid with asphaltic-bound macadam.

Buffalo airport received $1 million in WPA funds for airfield expansion and a new terminal. The city of Philadelphia opened a municipal airport on Island Road (1940). The Los Angeles Airport received funds to build a 4,650-foot runway and a modern terminal. WPA funds helped to build the new Portland-Columbia Airport in Oregon (1935), after the Bureau of Air Commerce declared the Swan Island facility unsafe for DC-3s. Fill was dredged from the Columbia River to create six hard-surfaced runways. An administration building and hangars were also built. Besides such structural changes, the WPA also sponsored aesthetic improvements.

The Federal Art Project financed a four-part *History of Aviation,* painted by Eugene Chodorow and August Henkel for the main lobby of the terminal at Floyd Bennett Field in Brooklyn, New York. Each wall depicted a different theme: the *Mythology of Flight* on the east wall, *Aviation in War* on the north. The artists took three years to complete the job, but as soon as the mural was installed, there was trouble. The anti-Communist paranoia infecting federal agencies prompted rumors that the Floyd Bennett murals were rife with Marxist content. According to one official, the Wright brothers were dressed in outfits that looked suspiciously Russian. There was a red star on a navy plane where there should have been a white star. There were also several characters who appeared to be "strangely un-American in expression and garb," reported the *New York Times.*[14] One of the aviators sported a thick mustache that made him look like Joseph Stalin. WPA administrator Colonel Brehon B. Somervell ordered an immediate investigation, and the murals were destroyed.[15]

A similar fate lay in store for the 1,530-square-foot mural that Arshile Gorky painted in the lobby of Newark Airport's new terminal. The Armenian-born painter called his work *Evolution of Forms Under Aerodynamic Limitations* and divided it into ten panels. Each panel represented a different aspect of aviation: *Early Aviation, Activities on the Field, Mechanics of Flying,* and so on. Fragments of airport iconography such as propellers, searchlights, and gas pumps were combined with biomorhpic shapes and slabs of color—"such local colors as are to be seen on the aviation field,"

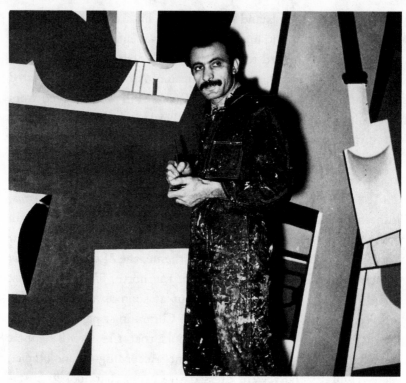

Arshile Gorky working on mural for Newark Airport, 1936.

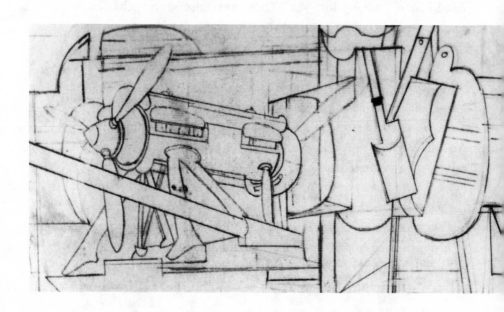

wrote Gorky. In 1935, a maquette of the mural was exhibited at the Federal Art Gallery, and the press attacked it for being "unreal and absurd," a disgrace considering the fact that public funds had paid for it. In his defense, Gorky wrote, somewhat cryptically: "I have used [these symbols] in paralyzing disproportions in order to impress upon the spectator the miraculous new vision of our time." But it would take the intervention of New York's Museum of Modern Art to calm the storm—reassuring critics that this was indeed a true work of art, worthy of public funding. Gorky was allowed to continue working on the project and finally mounted the mural in 1937, but it was painted over a few years later.[16]

If there was such a thing as a WPA style of architecture it was an eclectic mix, ranging from nondescript modern to faux Tudor and neoclassical. Frederick A. Gutheim, a critic, condemned the federal building program in general and felt that it had failed to produce a single building of distinction.[17] WPA-sponsored airports tended to imitate regional sources rather than break fresh ground. A terminal for El Paso, Texas, was designed in an Alamo-meets-Buck-Rogers style of faux ruined stucco and stonework. In

Study for aviation mural, Newark Airport. Arshile Gorky, 1935–36.

1937, San Francisco built a Spanish-style terminal with terra-cotta tiles and coffered ceilings. Albuquerque's new terminal, opened in 1939, was modeled after Pueblo Indian architecture with adobe walls and rustic timbers. The waiting room had murals of Indians hunting bison. When WPA airports went modern, they were usually in the deco streamlined look of so much Depression architecture. Air terminals at Cleveland, Houston, and Detroit had the same squat profiles, with central towers and symmetrical wings. They might have been mistaken for high schools or post offices. Windows were relatively small. Walls were thick and load-bearing. It was a style that some referred to as "WPA Modern," but these terminals lacked the lightness and functional clarity of modernist airports in Europe.

The WPA terminal at Newark Airport had a pared-down look with horizontal bands of windows and narrow swept-back wings— not unlike the Fuhlsbüttel terminal in Hamburg by Dyrssen and Averhoff—but there was no separation of incoming from outgoing passengers, and no thought given to future expansion. The interior had the cramped feeling of a bus terminal. Ceilings were low, and there wasn't enough natural light. Instead of a single open area, there were six separate waiting rooms. "The station plan is so cut up," wrote one critic, "it will hinder rather than help the expediting of passenger traffic."[18] Despite its architectural drawbacks, however, Newark proved to be a success in other ways.

American planning studies of the 1930s stressed the need for a "direct and expeditious" connection between the city center and the airport. Newark was the model for such a connection. The Pulaski Skyway was an elevated highway that stretched above the Jersey meadowlands from the Holland Tunnel all the way to the airport.[19] This six-mile-long superstructure—"a marvel of concrete and steel"—made Newark the fastest track between Midtown Manhattan and the skyways. The *New York Times* reported enthusiastically that "the air traveler alighting at Newark can reach the New York side of the Holland Tunnel, under normal conditions, in nine and one-half minutes."[20] This was the reason that the U.S. Post Office

337—El Paso Municipal Airport, El Paso, Texas

Municipal Airport, Houston, Texas

Municipal Airport, Little Rock, Arkansas

Postcard views of WPA-period airports: El Paso, Houston, Little Rock.

chose Newark over Floyd Bennett Field as its New York air terminus. Over two hundred thousand passengers passed through the airport in 1935, making it the busiest in the world. As one journalist wrote, Newark was the "symbol of a new age, *the age of high speed.*"[21] This kind of infrastructural linkage represented a new awareness. The airport was now seen as part of a greater urban matrix. Instead of redefining the city center, as visionaries like Le Corbusier had predicted, the city itself would reach out toward the airport and reshape itself in a horizontal expanse.

Meanwhile, theories of airport design were being challenged. The airport, like the airplane itself, was a problem to be solved by rational planning. Speed was the primary goal: speed of transfer, baggage handling, boarding, and departure. Joseph Hudnut, dean of architecture at Harvard, felt that too much time was wasted on symbolism. Efficient circulation between ground and air was more important. "I find it difficult to believe that [the] glorification of travel is a necessary condition of traffic control," he wrote.[22] In the face of modern technology, archaic architectural statements were meaningless. Richard Neutra, the Austrian-born architect, argued that the airport's true nature was one of transition, not style: "Speed and fluidity in the transition from air to ground is what is needed more than a *grand court d'honneur* in front of an airport."[23] Architect John Walter Wood agreed. Wood spent much of the 1930s inspecting airports and compiling data.[24] A successful airport, he concluded, should be operated like a "smoothly functioning organism, providing a steady and fluent movement of aircraft, passengers, merchandise, mail and surface vehicles." He compared the well-planned terminal to a "gangplank" between air and surface vehicles.[25]

"Speed is the cry of our era, and greater speed one of the goals of tomorrow," exclaimed Norman Bel Geddes, one of America's star industrial designers, who would turn his attention from vacuum cleaners to airports during the 1930s.[26] With considerable foresight he envisioned a system that would automate the movement of planes and passengers with clockwork precision. His diagrams looked more like machinery than conventional architecture. "To-day," wrote Geddes, "the confusion is such that passengers from an arriving plane find themselves mingling and jostling with bag-gagemen, postal employees, mechanics, guards and pilots."[27] In his new paradigm, there would be no mingling and jostling. Passen-gers would glide through underground tubes on moving sidewalks and ascend by elevator to a loading slip. They would then board their plane via a cantilevered gangway that could be adjusted to fit any size of aircraft. Using his patented system, Geddes predicted that an airplane could depart every minute "in a most orderly fash-ion with ample time for servicing."

As concepts of passenger movement advanced, so too did the science of air traffic control. By the mid-1930s, Newark Airport

Air terminal #1, 1932. Automated airport system by Norman Bel Geddes.

led the rest of the country in this new science. Pilots would radio in their course and airspeed to dispatchers along the route; they would then relay the information by phone to the control center. The progress of each flight was tracked on a horizontal map using small brass weights known as "shrimp boats." This process became a model for other airports and, in 1936, when the government created a national air command, Newark was chosen as one of its primary control centers.

While the myth of the individualistic pilot was still operative, the ultimate authority was beginning to move from the cockpit to the control tower, from pilot to air traffic controller. "This is a new profession," wrote aviation writer John Tunis. "It is something

Rotary airport moored off the southern tip of Manhattan. Norman Bel Geddes, designer, 1930.

which air travel has developed. [Traffic controllers] speak a queer, staccato language . . . Like traffic cops they must have eyes on all sides of their head."[28] Hollywood celebrated this new kind of hero in *Ceiling Zero*, a 1935 airport romance, directed by Howard Hawks, in which James Cagney plays an errant, barnstorming pilot who is pitted against Pat O'Brien as the sensible, safety-conscious manager of Newark Airport. As outright propaganda for commercial aviation, the movie demonstrates how the airport is now run scientifically: how electronic maps are used to track aircraft and radio beams guide planes through fog. Cagney's character still believes in flying by the seat of his pants. He is romantic and reckless while O'Brien is sober and sensible.

Airport of the New World

Fiorello La Guardia had been dreaming about airports since World War I when he served as a pilot-bombardier on the Austro-Italian front.[29] He was elected mayor of New York City in 1933 and set out to re-create the city with a zeal that bordered on the messianic. He centralized government agencies, consolidated the city's bureaucracy, and cut the kind of waste and graft that had tarnished the office of his predecessor, James J. Walker. He also vowed to bring New York's crumbling infrastructure up-to-date—to build new highways, bridges, and parks. And for this he had a loyal friend in the White House. "Our Mayor is the most appealing man I know," said President Roosevelt. "He comes to Washington and tells me a sad story. The tears run down my cheeks and the tears run down his cheeks and the first thing I know he's wangled another $50 million."[30]

One of La Guardia's greatest challenges was to bring New York into the air age: "Aviation is established," he said. "Nothing can stop it."[31] The city needed an airport that was worthy of its importance. New York was the biggest port in America, with 50 percent of all foreign trade passing through its harbor. It was also the biggest manufacturing center and had the tallest buildings in the world. "So much more is expected of us than other cities," said the mayor, but he felt burdened by Floyd Bennett Field, a third-rate airport he had inherited from Walker's administration. Floyd Bennett was located on an isolated stretch of marshland on Jamaica Bay and was connected to Manhattan via Flatbush Avenue. Traffic crawled all the way through Brooklyn with stoplights and local traffic jams.

La Guardia tried to make the best out of the situation and convinced American Airlines to run a New York–to-Boston flight out of Floyd Bennett, but it was a bust. The other airlines took heed and continued to fly out of Newark. He urged postal officials in Washington to make Floyd Bennett the official air terminus for New York. He promised to make improvements—repave the runways, install better lighting and radio equipment, none of which solved the basic problem: It still took too long to drive mail from the central post office in Manhattan out to Brooklyn. The postal service wouldn't budge. Then, returning from a trip to Chicago, La Guardia pulled one of his infamous publicity stunts. When his plane landed at Newark instead of Floyd Bennett, the mayor complained to the airline attendant that his ticket read "Destination: New York" not "New Jersey." He refused to get off the plane unless it flew him to Brooklyn, which it did with the mayor as its only passenger. "Remember," he said to the crew as he disembarked, "Newark is not New York." The incident made an amusing item in the tabloids, but it did little to change the situation.

La Guardia realized that he would simply have to build a new airport in a better location. But where? City planners favored converting the old Holmes Airport, a privately owned facility in Queens. Others suggested putting an airport on Governors Island since it lay enticingly close to New York's financial district. At one point, there was serious discussion about building a seaplane base on the East River Drive between Twenty-second and Twenty-fourth streets. Then there was the usual spate of science fiction, including an airport on the roof of Pennsylvania Station and Norman Bel Geddes's motorized island off Battery

Park.[32] The mayor was open to almost any kind of idea—anything that might help push New York into the air age. At one point, he envisioned an entire network around the city's periphery: "New York will have a ring of airports within a few minutes distance of the business and commercial center," he declared.[33] But he would finally settle for a single facility built in North Beach, Queens, on the former site of a Curtiss-Wright airport.[34] While the property called for major expansion, it was ideally located—a twenty-minute ride from Midtown Manhattan by way of the new Grand Central Parkway and the soon-to-be-completed Triboro Bridge.

La Guardia was able to convince the federal government to give $27 million toward the building of his new airport. More than half the total cost would be paid by the WPA. North Beach became the first airport in the United States to receive public funding on such a scale.[35] Dubbed "La Guardia's Folly," the project soon came under attack by opponents who felt it was too grandiose and well beyond the needs of a community that had a perfectly serviceable airport at Floyd Bennett. Even Robert Moses, the city's own commissioner of parks, was against the idea. One editorial cartoon depicted La Guardia dressed as an aviator standing over North Beach clutching a sack of public money.[36]

But none of this distracted the mayor, who, with characteristic bombast, declared that the new airport would open in time for the New York World's Fair of 1939. Considering the amount of work needed at the site, this sounded like an empty boast. In September 1937, a New York City Police launch brought him across Flushing Bay to North Beach for a ground-breaking ceremony and photo op. He climbed behind the controls of a giant steam shovel and ceremoniously moved a pile of dirt—the first of many such piles used to fill the 357 acres of marshland. A temporary trestle was built across Bowery Bay from Rikers Island to transport 14 million tons of refuse from the city's garbage dump and subway excavations. As the landfill mounted, a six-sided peninsula began to take shape. A thousand carloads of cement and 3 million gallons of asphalt were

Editorial cartoon, 1938. The expensive new airport being built at North Beach in Queens had many opponents and was dubbed "La Guardia's Folly."

used to make runways and aprons sturdy enough to support the weight of heavy new aircraft like the DC-2. Runway #1, the longest in the world at six thousand feet, was positioned in accordance with prevailing, northwesterly winds. Runway #2, at five thousand feet, ran from south to the north in line with a radio landing beam.

The official architects of record were Delano and Aldrich, Juan Trippe's favorite firm, but the real architect, the master architect, was La Guardia himself. He oversaw every phase of development from the paving of runways to the choice of lighting fixtures in the restaurant. He visited the construction site every week to encourage workers and supervise last-minute changes. "La Guardia just nurtured that [airport] like a plant," recalled one acquaintance. "I think he spent every Saturday and Sunday out there watching every bit of sand that was put in."[37] Construction schedules were compressed, and five thousand men worked in rotation, three shifts, six days a week for close to two years until the airport was completed. The mayor's Christmas card for 1939 carried a romantic rendering of the new terminal by Hugh Ferriss.

October 15, 1939, was the perfect day for christening the new airport. There wasn't a cloud in the sky and a gentle, northwesterly breeze blew across Flushing Bay. A crowd of 325,000 were there at North Beach to celebrate La Guardia's triumph. Police sirens wailed as limousines arrived with the dignitaries: the mayor himself; Postmaster James Farley; officials from the WPA, including John M. Carmody, Col. F. C. Harrington, and Corrington Gill. Navy planes swooped over the field in a V-formation. Flags of all nations snapped from the roof of the terminal. A fleet of DC-3s waited on the apron, their wings gleaming in the autumn light. Brehon B. Somervell officially presented the airport to the city of New York. In his brief address, the WPA supervisor explained how it had been built in a record amount of time, in adverse weather conditions, and despite considerable opposition. "I hope you are pleased with it," he said. "It is a credit to the WPA."

When the mayor got up to speak, he made a special point of thanking the people who had actually done the work, including many who had been previously unemployed: "Here is one of the greatest monuments to the industry and skill of American labor . . . the living answer of the industry of these men who found themselves unemployed through no fault of their own."[38] But just as he began to speak, a young woman darted out of the crowd and raised a placard that read: NEWARK IS STILL THE WORLD'S GREATEST AIRPORT. She paraded briefly in front of the stand before being whisked away by two policemen. Then, without missing a beat,

Mayor La Guardia continued his speech and dedicated the new airport to world peace: "To bring tidings of happiness to commerce," he said, "and friendly relations with all the countries whose planes will land at this airport."

There had been disagreement over what to name the new airport. On opening day it was still being referred to as "New York City Municipal Airport," but near the end of the ceremonies, three skywriting planes circled overhead and spelled out five words in giant looping letters of white smoke: NAME IT LA GUARDIA AIRPORT. Everyone cheered, and eighteen days later the city council made the gesture official. It would now be called New York Municipal Airport, LaGuardia Field, and soon shortened to just "LaGuardia." Everyone got caught up in LaGuardia fever. C. R. Smith, president of American Airlines, signed a long-term contract, calling the airfield the "world's greatest development in civil aviation since Lindbergh flew the Atlantic."[39] And while that may have been an exaggeration, LaGuardia was certainly a leap forward in airport planning. Seen from the air, the 558-acre complex made a single, sweeping gesture, linking up disparate parts—appearing to grow as much from the curves of the Grand Central Parkway as out of the bend of the shoreline—a natural offspring of the city and its infrastructure. The curving line of the boarding pier; the oval boat basin; the bulkheads; the diagonals of the runways and the looping overpasses of the highway interchange formed a new kind of urban landscape—one that was surely as impressive as anything found at the world's fair.

While most members of the press praised the new airport, Lewis Mumford, architecture critic for *The New Yorker*, blasted it in his Skyline column. In Mumford's view the main terminal was "a series of bungles, missed opportunities and hideous misapplications of ornament [that came] very close to equaling the all-time architectural low."[40] At least, he concluded, you could get into a plane and fly away. An early rendering by Delano and Aldrich shows a fairly utilitarian facade broken up by horizontal bands of windows and darker brick, but the final version was much more

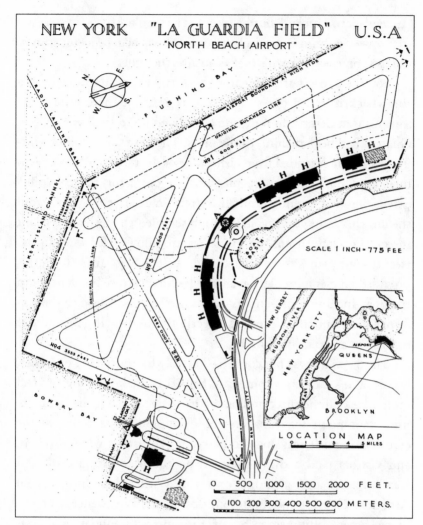

Master plan for LaGuardia Airport, New York. The 558-acre complex was a break-through in airport planning. It opened in time for the New York World's Fair of 1939.

ponderous. Strident vertical ribs and decorative grillwork gave it a vaguely totalitarian look, an impression that was reinforced by the stainless steel eagle perched ominously on the roof. Exterior walls were buff-colored brick, and the coping was black masonry. Mumford accused the architects of designing a "faked entrance" that had nothing to do with the modern spirit of aviation. Interiors were fussy, thought Mumford, designed in what he described as a "funeral-parlor motif," but he reserved particular scorn for the control tower, a "miniature lighthouse," which had been seemingly plopped on the terminal's roof as an afterthought.

For the most part, Mumford was right: the terminal was a throwback to the depot style of the 1920s, but there were other features that deserved praise and even lived up to the hype that La Guardia had been dishing to the press. The Skywalk, a long boarding dock that extended from either side of the terminal, was a revolutionary move in airport planning, a precursor to the "pier" extensions that would sprout from terminals after the war. From the air, this long curving structure resembled the feeler of a giant insect. The length and radius of its arc allowed for as many as twenty-four planes to be loaded at once. The Skywalk's two levels provided efficient circulation and helped to decrease bottlenecks in the flow. Incoming passengers didn't need to pass through the terminal at all but could proceed directly through their gate and out to the taxi stand or parking lot.

The Skywalk was not conceived merely for functional purposes, however. It's curving promenade helped to make the airport feel more like a public place and not an exclusive club for the rich—an important point for a mayor who championed the rights of the common man. It was open to everyone. Turnstiles were installed, and visitors paid a dime to stand on the observation deck and watch planes arrive. "High over the Whitestone Bridge is an American Flagship inbound from Boston and Providence. The airplane comes gliding smoothly over the airport boundary and your eye follows its every movement. . . ."[41]

From the start, the airport had been sold to the public as a gateway to the 1939 New York World's Fair: "Airport is Urged as Fair Adjunct," ran a headline in the *New York Times* on July 19, 1936. The fairgrounds were built atop the ash heaps of Flushing Meadow, Queens, just a few miles from La Guardia's new airport. The Trylon and Perisphere theme center symbolized a new American optimism. The country was beginning to recover from its economic crisis, and there were reasons to celebrate. The exhibition pavilions

The Skywalk boarding pier at LaGuardia Field, 1939. This revolutionary structure allowed twenty-four planes to load at the same time.

were white and bilious, as if filled with helium and ready to float away. In keeping with the World of Tomorrow theme, there was a particular emphasis on aviation. The Department of Commerce installed a full-scale control tower to demonstrate the exciting new world of traffic control.[42] In the Transportation Zone, just across the Bridge of Wings, sat the Aviation Pavilion, in which architect William Lescaze evoked the feeling of flight with interlocking vaults that rose in succession to create a soaring exhibition space with actual airplanes suspended from the ceiling. Across the esplanade was the Chrysler Pavilion and Raymond Loewy's Rocketport display, with its half-scale model of a rocket-powered airliner that would, one day, fly passengers from New York to London in three hours.

The most popular exhibition, however, was GM's Futurama, designed by Norman Bel Geddes. Ten million people, an average of twenty-eight thousand daily, took the "magic, Aladdin-like" ride that simulated an air trip across the United States in the year 1960. Visitors sat in specially designed sound chairs that glided around the perimeter of a thirty-five-thousand-square-foot model. "You somehow get an almost perfect illusion of flying," wrote one journalist. The miniature landscape of the future featured seven-lane highways, suspension bridges, and modern farms, where fruit trees grew under glass domes.[43] At various points across the countryside, Geddes placed dirigible stations and small, regional airports that were connected to cross-country train lines. In the middle of the continent was a circular airport with three giant elevators that carried airplanes down to subterranean hangars. The Futurama ride ended at a city of glass towers and a giant airport three miles in diameter. "Its entire area is paved," said the narrator's voice, "making it possible for planes to land or take off in any direction and in large numbers."

La Guardia's new airport was promoted as yet another exhibition, "a $50,000,000 floor show," as one magazine raved. Another dubbed it "Fiorello's Futurama," and pointed out how this was not a science-fiction display or miniature diorama, however, but the real thing. "The extravaganza is 'on the boards' twenty-four hours a day and has a cast of thousands . . . a great parade across the largest skyport of them all."[44] When the duke of Windsor visited the world's fair in 1939, he was delighted by the imaginative exhibitions, but was most impressed by what he saw of LaGuardia; he thought its control tower the most "marvelous and enlightening sight" of his trip.[45]

Mayor La Guardia had kept his promise. He boasted to FDR that his new airport was "the greatest, the best, the most up-to-date and the most perfect airport in the U.S. It is 'the' airport of the New World," he said, beaming with one of his legendary smiles. The turnstile to the Skywalk observation deck raised $150,000 in the first year of operation. And, best of all, the U.S. Postal Service made LaGuardia its primary terminus for the New York area. By 1940, it was the busiest airport in the world, with a daily average of 250 landings and three thousand passengers. The success surpassed even the mayor's expectations. La Guardia's folly had become La Guardia's legacy—the standard against which other airports would now be judged.

The People's Airport

On a sultry summer night in 1938, Franklin D. Roosevelt had a nightmare. He dreamed of a terrible plane crash at Washington-Hoover, the capital's airport. It was something that had been plaguing his conscience since he took office. While cities like New York were benefiting from federal airport assistance, the nation's own capital was stuck with an embarrassing relic from the 1920s. Pilots despised Washington-Hoover and rated it the most dangerous airport in the United States. There were high radio towers obstructing the western approach. Highway 1 and a smokestack made the eastern side equally precarious. The main runway was bisected by a road, and guards had to be posted to flag down traffic whenever a plane took off. Miraculously, there hadn't been any major accidents yet, but a catastrophe was waiting to happen. The fact that so many important politicians and foreign dignitaries used the airport made the situation even more critical.

"It is a disgrace to the United States," said Harry F. Guggenheim, patron of air safety. "The airport for the capital should bear comparison with the magnificent fields of Europe."[46] The Department of Commerce threatened closure if safety standards weren't

Editorial cartoon, 1938, depicting FDR and his cabinet running from a crashing airplane. While the New Deal encouraged the building of new airports, the nation's capital was serviced by the outdated and dangerously inadequate Washington-Hoover Airport. One veteran pilot claimed there were better landing fields in Siberia.

met. Famed aviator Wiley Post joked that there were better landing grounds in the wilds of Siberia, and a satirical cartoon in the *Washington Herald* depicted FDR and his cabinet running in panic from a crashing airplane.[47]

As soon as the president awoke from his nightmare, he vowed

to take action. Invoking executive powers, FDR ordered the Civil Aeronautics Authority (CAA) to begin planning for a new airport on an emergency basis. Preliminary plans were ready by the fall of 1938, and the president approved the $13.5 million needed for construction. A 750-acre site was chosen at Gravelly Point, on the western banks of the Potomac River, just a mile from the old airport. The Army Corps of Engineers built a dike and pumped tons of gravel and sand from the bottom of the Potomac to raise the marshy site as much as twenty feet.

Howard Lovewell Cheney was the architect of record, but as with La Guardia, the real architect, the man with the vision, was FDR himself.[48] During his first term in office, he had an interest in public architecture and even made design suggestions on several projects including the Jefferson Memorial and Bethesda Naval Hospital. Vague outlines of a "national" airport had been forming themselves in his imagination since 1938, and he already had a good idea of what he wanted. The firm of Fellheimer and Wagner proposed a futuristic, Buck Rogers–looking terminal, but the president wanted something in keeping with the neoclassical style of the Capitol. He was even said to have drawn a rough sketch for the architects, who then carried out his wishes. The front would have a colonnade of eight slender columns, just like the portico at George Washington's home, a few miles downriver. The Mount Vernon motif was repeated on the airfield side with another set of columns rising in front of a curving wall of glass. To push the analogy further, the belvedere on Mount Vernon's roof was reconstituted as an all-glass control booth atop the new terminal.

Despite historic allusions, the terminal's mock Colonial shell concealed a modern interior and the latest in airport technology. A soaring wall of glass, "a great prism . . . high enough to admit the sky," rose within the main lobby and looked onto the airfield. One of the first "automated" baggage systems allowed suitcases to be weighed on a scale set into the check-in counter. The bags were tagged, pushed through a trapdoor, and slid down a spiraling chute

Washington National at night. Rendering by Hugh Ferriss.

The People's Airport, Washington National. Both the front and back facades were designed to evoke the classical colonnade of George Washington's home at Mount Vernon. Howard Lovewell Cheney, architect, 1940.

to an underground distribution area. The control tower featured an electronic "progress board" that was adapted from a device used on Wall Street. (The CAA wanted to make National its model airport—a working laboratory for new ideas.) The runways were designed to support the new generation of heavier, faster planes. The longest was almost seven thousand feet, longer than runway #1 at LaGuardia. Rotating turntables were set into the loading apron for speedy positioning of planes, and servicing facilities were placed in subterranean pits.

National's sponsors were quick to remind everyone of the airport's true symbolism. Here was the new threshold to the nation, built entirely with public funds, and officially called the "people's airport." In case anyone missed the point, the CAA published a romantic rendering that showed the terminal hovering majestically between the Congress building and Mount Vernon. "Visitors and Washingtonians will flock to the field as to one of their favorite parks."[49] Buses brought sightseers out from the city. Those who owned their own car could park on a terraced embankment and watch the "theater of the air" as if at a drive-in movie.

"From a distance," reported the *New York Times*, "the terminal looks like a glistening palace of silver and glass."[50] But others weren't as complimentary. Joseph Hudnut wrote, "The portico of Mount Vernon, translated into concrete, struggles in vain to impose its serene spirit on the long ranges of utilitarian forms at either side," and he compared the roof—with searchlights, weather vanes, and a glass control tower—to a "battleship on top of a temple."[51] Despite such contradictions, the federally funded airports of the New Deal set the stage for future developments. They were ambitious in scale and defined a new kind of peripheral zone, toward which the urban fabric would gradually extend itself with highways, bridges, and transit lines. Washington National and LaGuardia would serve as models for the airport cities of the postwar period and help to define a new kind of urban space, one that was horizontal and sprawling rather than vertical and dense.

CHAPTER 4

Air Power: 1939–1957

*"Mass travel by air may prove to be more significant
to world destiny than the atom bomb."*
                                                —*Juan Trippe*

Über Airport

In the opening sequence of Leni Riefenstahl's documentary film
Triumph of the Will, Adolf Hitler makes a Wagnerian descent from
the sky in a Junkers D-2202 to the Nuremberg rally of 1934. The
subjective eye of the camera peers out the window of the plane as it
breaks through a bank of clouds and skims over the rooftops of the
old medieval city. When the plane lands, Hitler steps onto the airfield and is greeted by the crowd as if he were a machine-age god.
Hitler, like Roosevelt, understood the propaganda value of aviation. It was both modern and mythic, and he knew how to use it to
dramatic effect. Nowhere would aviation assume such a symbolic
role as it did in Germany. Under Hitler's command, the airports of
the Third Reich became gestures of national unity. Hitler also
understood the military advantages of airpower. If Britain ruled the
waves, Germany would rule the skies and soon surpass all other
countries in aircraft production.

While LaGuardia and Washington National were still under
construction, reports began to drift back from Europe about a
"colossal airport" arising on a scale that was "hard for even Americans to imagine," wrote Albion Ross in the *New York Times*. The

reporter described the awe-inspiring sight of Berlin's Tempelhof airfield and its new semicircular terminal.[1] Daniel W. Tomlinson, a TWA executive, toured Tempelhof a year later and declared it a marvel of German genius. "[It] is the greatest thing I've ever seen," he said. "The ground space is twenty times greater than that of the Grand Central Station in New York."[2] Three-quarters of a mile long, Tempelhof's new terminal was indeed an awesome achievement. Newspapers ran photographs of its seemingly endless facade and wrote about the new facility as if it were already in operation. In fact, the terminal wouldn't be finished for several more years, but the point was made.

For several years, Charles Lindbergh had been goading Americans about German air superiority. He visited the country six times between 1936 and 1938 and was shown the newest aviation works and airfields. The Treaty of Versailles had forbidden the building of military planes or airports, so commercial aviation played a stealth role. While the Nazi facilities were officially built for civilian use, there was little doubt about their true purpose. At Tempelhof, Lindbergh was invited to pilot an experimental passenger plane. He was even allowed to inspect a top-secret testing station in Pomerania where the Messerschmitt (ME) 109 fighter plane was being developed. "I have never been more impressed than I was with the aviation organizations I saw in Germany," wrote Lindbergh.[3]

But one didn't need to go all the way to Europe to witness German airpower. The first transatlantic flights by Deutsche Lufthansa began landing at Port Washington, Long Island, as early as 1936.[4] When a Focke-Wolff Condor landed in Rio de Janeiro on June 29, 1939, it was treated as a major news event. The plane, with a black swastika emblazoned on its tail, had flown from Berlin in a record time of thirty-seven hours, four minutes. (The actual crossing of the Atlantic took less than ten hours.)

Tempelhof played an early role in the Nazi power grab. In 1933, the Reich's minister of propaganda, Joseph Goebbels, announced that May 1 would be celebrated as a "Day of National Labor," and

Hitler's über-airport: Romanticized rendering of Tempelhof Field, Berlin. Ernst Sagebiel, architect, circa 1936.

labor leaders from all over Germany were invited to attend an air show at Tempelhof. Close to a million showed up to hear speeches and watch aerial displays by famous WWI aces like Ernst Udet. "Decorations" were planned by Hitler's favorite young architect, Albert Speer, who framed the speaker's platform with swastika banners and created a "cathedral of lights" with 150 searchlights shining into the sky.[5] Hitler welcomed the assembled workers and assured them of their role in the new Germany. The next morning, union headquarters across the country were seized, and labor leaders who had come to the air show were arrested. The spectacle of the airport had been used to lure the unionists into a giant trap.[6]

Architecture helped to take Hitler's mind off more troubling issues. He appreciated the language of classical form and monumental scale. "If I continually put architectural problems into the foreground," he once wrote, "that is because they lie nearest my heart." Working with Albert Speer, Hitler formulated a plan to transform Berlin into a modern world capital. A long ceremonial avenue would lance the heart of the city, beginning in the south with a central rail terminal and continuing north along a monumental plaza toward Tempelhof, which would anchor one end of the plan and become the Reich's aerial gateway.[7] The führer wanted Berlin to have the grandeur of ancient Rome, but it had to be a modern Rome, with an airport at one end, a railroad station at the other, and a high-speed autobahn encircling the entire city.

By the mid-1930s there were more than 220,000 passengers using Tempelhof annually but the old airfield was in desperate need of expansion. Air Marshal Hermann Göring announced that Tempelhof would be transformed into the greatest airport in the world.[8] When the scale model was unveiled in 1936, it filled a room in the Air Ministry building. Its architect, Ernst Sagebiel, knew how much Göring loved models—in the attic of the air marshal's house was a model train set with miniature mountains and Bavarian cottages—so every detail was precise. Little Nazi flags flew from the roof, and tiny Junkers planes lined up in formation on the field.

There were even miniature lights rigged around the perimeter of the oval landing area.

Sagebiel had been a construction supervisor for Erich Mendelsohn and was familiar with that architects' early airport drawings. With the rise of the Third Reich, Mendelsohn, along with so many fellow modernists who were Jewish, fled for his life. Sagebiel stayed in Germany and joined the party. He soon gained favor with Göring and was put in charge of the Air Ministry's building division along with the rebuilding of all German airports.[9]

At Tempelhof, Le Corbusier's "naked airport" would meet the Germanic cult of power. The idea was to create a symbolic gesture, a phoenix rising from the ashes of the Versailles treaty. The new terminal embraced the perimeter of the airfield with a narrow, five-story structure. An entry court led from the Platz der Luftbrücke to a seven-story reception hall. The limestone walls and concrete piers were oppressively thick compared to those ephemeral glass pavilions that Hitler had condemned as "architectural Bolshevism." He believed architecture to be the most persuasive form of national philosophy. "These buildings," he said, "are bearers and guardians of a higher culture [and as such should] represent the highest justification for the political strength of the German nation, the moral justification for the raw realm of power."[10]

The official Reich style was rigid, austere, and monumental in scale, inspired by the buildings of the nineteenth-century Prussian architect Karl Friedrich Schinkel, but with little of Schinkel's finesse. When the Nazis took control in 1933, Germany's progressive design movement went into retreat. Hitler railed against the "degenerate" art of Weimar and promised an end to the "artistic pollution" of the German people. He denounced the buildings of Mendelsohn, Gropius, and Ludwig Mies van der Rohe as so many "cubist monstrosities" and decreed that all new buildings should convey the dignity of the classical past.[11]

In his memoirs, Speer referred to the Reich architecture with a degree of irony as "our Imperial Style."[12] All public buildings, especially airports, were required to express a "German strength

and German greatness." Sometimes referred to as "stripped classicism," it was a ham-fisted style that was, ironically, adopted by
both the right and the left to represent their respective ideologies.
(The Soviet terminal at Vnukovo Airport in Moscow had the same
strident piers as Tempelhof repeated along its dreary facade.)

The first section of the new Tempelhof went up in record time
and was officially dedicated by Göring in December 1937. It was
the largest airport structure ever built. As one of Hitler's confi-
dantes reported, Tempelhof "[grew] out of the spirit of the Luftwaffe, tough, soldierly, disciplined."[13] One block was connected to
the next by a curving wall of limestone, punctured by hundreds of
identical windows. All airport functions were consolidated into a
"a single body animated by a single spirit."[14] To emphasize the
sense of regimented space, there were carved friezes depicting military exploits from Germany's past.

Hitler was pleased. Sagebiel's design appealed to his sense of
continuity. Architecture was meant to do just that: serve an ideal,
reaffirm an ideology. There was enough room on the observation
deck for sixty thousand spectators and this made it a perfect setting
for Nazi pageantry. Access to the observation deck was through
fourteen towers that stood as monolithic sentries around the land-
side of the building.

More than six hundred planes would be able to land and take off
in a single day, while thousands of passengers could pass through
the terminal without confusion. The circulation plan was based on
the same scientific principles used at Fuhlsbüttel Airport, Hamburg. Separate levels were designated for each function: freight,
baggage, passengers. Underground ramps led to a central loading
area, where baggage would be sorted and then loaded onto the planes.
Planes could maneuver up to the boarding points under cover of a
forty-foot-wide canopy that protected passengers in bad weather.

Tempelhof signaled the beginning of a new phase in airport
history. "The dethroning of the individual is the most essential
principle of our now victoriously conquering movement," said propaganda minister Goebbels, and the Reich's airport was an archi-

tectonic reflection of this mob philosophy.[15] The message was assimilation and control.

Just prior to World War II, Graham Greene recorded his impressions of a night landing at Tempelhof. The lights of the cabin were dimmed, and Greene could see the airport below, brilliantly illuminated in scarlet and yellow boundary lights. When the plane banked over the heart of Berlin, he could make out the trams and automobiles moving down the Kurfürstendamm. The sight was inspiring—just as he remembered it from an earlier trip—but then the plane made its final descent: "One could see the headlamps sweeping the asphalt drive," wrote Greene, "the sparks streaming out behind the grey Lufthansa wing, as the wheels touched and rebounded and took the ground and held. That was happiness, the quick impression; but on the ground, among the swastikas, one saw pain at every yard."[16]

Camouflage

"You're getting on that plane with Victor where you belong," says Humphrey Bogart to Ingrid Bergman on a misty runway in Warner Brothers' 1942 production *Casablanca*. The cinematic moment marks a shift in the popular perception of departure. Travel took on a new sense of urgency in a world where international tensions mounted, treaties were broken, and disputed territories were annexed by force. The lyrical mood of aviation's early period gave way to strict controls and displays of architectural bombast. The airport became a backdrop for international intrigue—the final escape route for refugees, spies, and star-crossed lovers like the characters played by Bogart and Bergman.

The former gateways to utopia became targets for aerial bombardment. The modernist terminal at Schiphol Airport in Amsterdam was flattened by the Luftwaffe on a spring morning in 1940. So was the V-shaped terminal designed by Chomel and Verrier at Bron Airport outside of Lyon. When Paris fell in June

"You're getting on that plane with Victor where you belong." Claude Rains, Paul Henreid, Humphrey Bogart, and Ingrid Bergman on the tarmac in the final scene of *Casablanca*, Warner Brothers, 1942. The airport becomes a backdrop for international intrigue.

1940, Labro's glass terminal at Bourget was converted for military use. After the Germans occupied Denmark, Lauritzen's terminal at Kastrup—a building designed to celebrate the mobility of modern life—became a Luftwaffe base for bombing raids against Norway.

American airports were also preparing for the worst. After the surprise attack on Pearl Harbor in December 1941, a Japanese invasion seemed imminent. Emergency measures were taken to prevent sabotage, and all civilian airports were taken over by the federal government. Soldiers were brought in to patrol airfields and antiaircraft guns were mounted on terminal roofs. On the night of February 26, 1942, defense batteries at Los Angeles Airport opened fire on nonexistent Japanese raiders—a case of nerves in what came to be euphemistically called the "Battle of Los Angeles." A similar incident created havoc at LaGuardia Airport when an anticipated air raid turned out to be a hoax.

While designers had once attempted to make airports as visible as possible—Lloyd Wright's checkerboard runways and the bright flower beds of Ernest Herminghaus—every effort was now made to conceal them. Camouflage artists transformed hangars and runways so as to blend in with surrounding landscape. Los Angeles Airport was concealed with a patchwork netting that made it look

Airport defense, 1943. Soldiers stand guard on the roof of LaGuardia's terminal, New York.

like a dairy farm from the air. Animators from the Disney studio helped to camouflage Burbank's airport with a canopy of chicken wire soaked with glue and feathers. Whenever it rained, the airport smelled like a barnyard. In Santa Monica, the Douglas bomber plant was ingeniously disguised as a suburban subdivision, with streets and lawns painted onto the roof. Mock suburban homes were made from canvas and plywood.

No new civilian airports were built during the hostilities, but visionary designers did their part in the war effort. Raymond Loewy, the famous industrial designer, proposed an elevated airport for Midtown Manhattan that could also serve as a defensive shield against aerial bombardment. Norman Bel Geddes developed several projects for the military, including a "television-controlled aerial torpedo," a portable hangar system, and a mid-ocean air base camouflaged to look like a floating iceberg.[17]

FDR's "Arsenal of Democracy" manufactured 50,000 warplanes a year and companies like Boeing and Douglas refitted their plants for wartime production. Douglas converted its DC-3, the most successful prewar passenger plane, into the C-47, and it became the workhorse of military transport. The air force assumed command of civilian aviation, and while service was seriously curtailed, some scheduled flights continued to fly. The airline companies were allowed to retain their corporate identities and make profits, but they were required to help with the airlift of servicemen and supplies throughout the duration. Most of the commercial airline fleet was commandeered by the Air Transport Command (ATC), to ferry personnel and supplies.

Terminals built at ATC bases were usually rudimentary, prefabricated structures, but a few exceptions were custom-built. Charles M. Goodman, project architect of National, designed a terminal for the ATC airport in Washington, D.C. Since it was serving so many VIPs, the terminal had a few extra comforts, including a landscaped courtyard and a lounge with modern bentwood chairs. There was also a stylishly furnished room where passengers were briefed on mid-ocean downings. A three-dimensional display explained first

Mock suburban landscape on the roof of the Douglas Aircraft plant in Santa Monica, California, circa 1943.

aid, navigation, and the finer points of surviving in a raft.[18]

Even before the war started, the Pentagon had begun to plan a defensive air network through Latin America. The secret program was called the Airport Development Plan (ADP), and Pan American Airways was paid $12 million dollars to build twenty-five land and nine seaplane bases in fourteen different countries. The new airports would form a defensive shield—something like an aerial Maginot Line—against German intervention, stretching more than five thousand miles from Miami in the north to Natal, Brazil, in the south.[19] The ADP airports were spaced at intervals of approximately 450 miles. The Treasury Department footed the bill, but Pan Am would own the bases outright after the war. The airports were built in isolated places like Amapá, Brazil, located on a tributary of the Amazon River. Supplies had to be brought in by canoe. In San José, Guatemala, the malaria rate among airport workers was 100 percent. If local landowners proved uncooperative, their property was simply expropriated through pressure from the U.S. State Department. When a Japanese landowner in Mexico refused to sell his land, the Mexican militia removed him by force.

Most host countries cooperated because they were getting free airports out of the deal. President Rafael Trujillo of the Dominican Republic insisted that the ADP airfield be built in the rocky hills of Miraflores instead of the flat area of San Pedro de Macorís. Anastasio Somoza, the dictator of Nicaragua, wanted the airfield built right behind his presidential palace in Managua so, it was rumored, he could make a hasty escape in the event of a coup d'état.[20]

While never used for defensive purposes, the ADP airfields did serve as links in the supply route to Allied forces abroad. Pan Am was also commissioned to build airfields across the belly of Africa so that supplies could be flown to British forces in Egypt. Natal, on the Brazilian coast, was the western jumping-off point, linking to Monrovia, Accra, El Fasher in the Sahara Desert, Khartoum, and finally Cairo.

While Pan Am remained the leader in international service, the war opened the door for free-market competition. Both Eastern and American Airlines, which had previously been restricted to domestic service, came under contract with the army to fly to Latin America, once Trippe's exclusive domain. The army also commissioned TWA to deliver armaments to British forces fighting General Rommel in the Libyan Desert. TWA's four-engine Stratoliner was converted for the cause. Its deluxe furnishings were stripped out and extra gas tanks were added to give it transatlantic range. TWA would fly as many as ten thousand crossings to Europe, assuring the company a commanding position after the war.

In 1944, the Civil Aviation Assembly, a gathering of Allied officials, met in Chicago to discuss the role that commercial aviation would play in the postwar world. New bylaws for international air travel were hammered out. Some participants felt that the United States had an unfair advantage and would have the market cornered as soon as peace was restored. British and Dutch representatives were particularly concerned and tried to establish rules that would protect their interests. Foreshadowing cold war divisions, the Soviets refused to participate in the conference. They preferred to establish a self-contained internal network and write their own civil air code.

The urgent necessities of war compelled engineers and designers to experiment. "Unusual material, designs, and methods of fabrication not used in normal times are entirely justified under prevailing conditions," wrote Herbert Whittemore of the National Bureau of Standards.[21] Prefabricated hangar parts were made out of laminated plywood sheets, to save priority materials like steel. Engineer Herbert H. Stevens invented a pneumatic airport hangar with a thirteen-acre domed roof made from rubberized canvas. The air-supported structure would need only a tenth of the steel normally used for such a building.[22]

Concrete in particular found a new identity during the war. It was cheap, easy to use, and fast to work with. Sweeping arches could be made to support thin concrete shells. Clear spans of over three hundred feet could be achieved without ties or bracing. WAR SPEEDS CONCRETE PROGRESS, read an advertisement for the Lone Star Cement Corporation in 1943: "War-time demands have accelerated the trend toward concrete as a medium of design. Combining freedom of expression and structural economy, architects and engineers are now using concrete to enclose space with shell domes, curved walls, plane surfaces—whichever is most effective functionally. . . ."[23]

Nowhere did the demands of war provoke such improvisation

as in Italy, however, where a new kind of airport monumentality was realized in the concrete hangars of engineer Pier Luigi Nervi. A dozen of these giant hangars were built for the Italian air force between 1938 and 1942, including ones at Orvieto, Orbetello, and Torre del Lago. Nervi's hangars were bold expressions of their function. Their concrete forms were cast with a minimum of reinforcing and could stand on their own as architectural entities. Nervi's

"War-time demands have accelerated the trend toward concrete as a medium of design." Advertisement for the Lone Star Cement Corporation, 1943.

soaring hangars were destroyed during the war, but photographs of the structures survived. These would be published frequently and serve as inspiration for a later generation of designers.

Developments made during the war set the stage for peace. New materials and building technologies helped to modernize airport construction. New kinds of aircraft and international air routes reshaped the world while radar and other wartime developments would make commercial flying safer and more efficient.

Friendship

The thermometer at Washington National was already pushing ninety degrees when the president's limousine crossed the Arlington Memorial Bridge and turned onto the Mount Vernon Parkway. Harry Truman sat in the back scanning the morning papers. The *Washington Post* had a story about David Greenglass, the former army sergeant charged with espionage for his part in the Fuchs spy ring. The *New York Times* had a story about the Hollywood Ten refusing to cooperate with the House Un-American Activities Committee. Communist regimes were springing up around the globe, while at home anti-Communist paranoia was reaching fever pitch. "Better Dead than Red" was the slogan of the day. It was June 1950, and the American way of life seemed in jeopardy.

While the president's plane taxied to the runway, all other flights in and out of National were put on hold. The DC-6, painted red, white, and blue and decorated with eagle feathers on its tail, was officially called the *Independence* after Truman's hometown in Missouri. Among the press corps, the plane was known as the "Flying White House," the prototype for Air Force One. Like FDR, Truman was accustomed to flying. As a senator, he had flown back and forth to Washington from Kansas City.

(overleaf) A new sense of monumentality: the skeletal framework of an air-force hangar in Orbetello, Italy, 1939. Pier Luigi Nervi, engineer.

The DC-6 turned at the far end of National's longest runway, revved its engines, and set off on its short flight to Baltimore, where Truman was scheduled to dedicate a new airport. A battalion of dark clouds was building on the western horizon. The president had been briefed about a system of violent thunderstorms wreaking havoc across the country. There had been a bad air accident somewhere near Milwaukee that morning. The details weren't available yet, but he worried that there would be many more such accidents. The skies were too crowded. New controls and federal standards were long overdue.

The *Independence* landed at Baltimore's Friendship Airport at eleven A.M. The U.S. Marine Corps Band played "Hail to the Chief" as the plane taxied toward the reviewing stand. Crowds moved listlessly in and out of the new terminal, which was draped with red, white, and blue bunting. "Good Night Irene," one of the most popular songs of the period, played over the loudspeaker system.

The dedication ceremony was the high point of an entire week of special events: concerts, exhibitions, and special flights for handicapped children. Aviation movies played continuously in the terminal hall. Pretty models glided across the tarmac wearing "Fashions for Flight," and Mayor D'Alesandro presented a collection of TV sets to a children's hospital. In his welcoming speech, the mayor explained how the new airport was a miracle of engineering, planning, and cooperation between federal, state, and municipal governments. The white cuboid terminal was designed by James R. Edmunds at a cost of $3,724,000 and had over an acre of interior floor space. The architecture was austere and possessed all the charm of a nuclear test site, fitting its role as the first airport of the cold war. The interior was a showcase of American enterprise and featured a four-star restaurant, a cocktail lounge, conference rooms, and game rooms with pinball machines and slot machines. There was also a children's nursery, a barber and beauty shop, a bank, and a bookstore.

The archbishop of Baltimore gave a blessing and prayed for peace. The president kept his own speech to eight minutes and the message was similar: No one wanted to go to war with Russia.

Americans were sick of war. "We would not build so elaborate a facility for our air commerce," said Truman, "if we did not have faith in a peaceful future." The cover of the dedication brochure was illustrated with a white dove. Even the name of the new airport, "Friendship," had been chosen in the spirit of peace.

As soon as he finished, the president continued on to Missouri. The pilot was able to skirt the worst of the storms and make a safe landing at Kansas City. Later in the day Truman would learn the full extent of the accident that had happened that morning. All fifty-eight passengers and crew were killed when a Northwest Airlines plane crashed into Lake Michigan.[24] It was the worst air disaster in American history, and Truman went to bed haunted by the image of charred bodies washing ashore. He was just starting to fall asleep when the phone rang again. There was more bad news. This time it was his secretary of state, Dean Acheson, who informed the president that the North Korean army had just crossed the thirty-eighth parallel and invaded South Korea.

A Nation on Wings

After years of sacrifice, Americans were ready to enjoy the freedom and prosperity of the postwar era. Expectations were high. People had disposable income saved in war bonds and federally insured savings accounts. Hundreds of thousands of GIs returned stateside expecting good jobs. They wanted to get married and have families. They wanted to own their homes and fill them with the latest appliances. Most of all, they wanted mobility. Population patterns and demographics shifted dramatically. Along with all the physical movement came social movement.

After a war that had uprooted so many, people thought little of moving from one coast to the other for a new job or a change in lifestyle. American cars were faster and more affordable than ever before. The Federal-Aid Highway Act authorized the building of an interstate highway system that transformed the American landscape and sped the exodus from concentrated cities out to the greener pastures of Levittown and similar enclaves. America was on the go, as journalists of the day put it. Commercial aviation would play a significant role in this transformation and help to create a more fluid society at a time when, as W. G. Sebald wrote, "restlessness became a cardinal virtue."[25]

Wartime travel restrictions were lifted a month after V-J Day, and commercial aviation was allowed to resume regular service. "After a world war won chiefly by aviation, people everywhere are anxious to use the plane for peace," reported one magazine.[26] In 1945, 6.7 million passengers flew on U.S. domestic carriers. The following year, 12.5 million took to the skies. The airline companies responded with bigger planes, cheaper flights, and clever marketing gimmicks. Upstart companies sprang up overnight, and warplanes were hastily converted to meet the growing demand. One of the first civilian airliners to go into service after the war was the giant B-377 Stratocruiser that Boeing converted from the B-29 Superfortress, the same plane that dropped the bomb on Hiroshima.

For the first time airlines began to offer lower, affordable "air coach" fares and all-expenses-paid package tours. Smaller charter companies undercut the big airlines—a lowly salesman could afford to fly to a conference in Atlanta, a grandmother could fly to Seattle to visit her grandson. The era of mass air transit was under way. In 1954 scheduled airliners carried over 30 million passengers within the United States. By 1955, more Americans were flying than riding on railroads, and, by 1956, there were more than 40 million flying on American carriers.

Nowhere was this frenzy of movement more apparent than at the overcrowded airports. To make the point, *Life* magazine dispatched a team of photographers to document a twenty-four-hour period of air travel across the country.[27] A total of 1,095 planes took off that day (June 3, 1956) and carried 136,823 passengers. According to *Life,* air travel had "engulfed the U.S. and changed its habits." It was modern, "convenient, fast, [and] undramatic to the point of being commonplace. . . . Throughout the day men of affairs moved into and out of busy air terminals as they tried to keep to hectic schedules that require the swift travel of flight." *Life* also pointed out that every level of society was represented in the new "democracy of the air." Along with businessmen there were Hollywood stars, politicians, newlyweds, senior citizens, children, and even animal trainers.

The black-and-white photographs that accompanied the article depicted a sequence of figures in motion. In some cases they were blurred at the edges to evoke the frenetic energy of the airport environment. There was the movie star Victor Mature running to catch a flight at Midway; a young senator from Massachusetts named John F. Kennedy eating a snack at National; another politician, Leonard Hall, grabbing his luggage; silver-haired Rosalie Kirby kissing her poodle farewell before boarding a flight to Chicago; nine-year-old Christopher Venn waving good-bye to his sister at Logan. What *Life* did not document that day was the decrepit state of American airports.

"Democracy of the air." John F. Kennedy on campaign trail at Portland Airport, Oregon, 1959. Photograph by Jacques Lowe.

At the end of the war, architect Marc Thompson was sent on a cross-country mission to inspect civilian airports and report back to the Civil Aeronautics Administration. Thompson had designed air bases for the navy and was well qualified for the assignment, but nothing could have prepared him for the conditions he encountered. Runways were too short and landing systems dangerously obsolete. The passenger terminals were filthy, overcrowded, and outmoded—some dating back to the Lindbergh era. Originally designed to process a few hundred passengers a day, those same terminals were now coping with thousands. Chicago's municipal airport, for instance, handled 1.3 million passengers in 1946, twenty times more than it had in 1941, while LaGuardia struggled to process 2.1 million passengers in 1946.

The old DC-3s had carried only twenty-one passengers. The new Lockheed Constellations carried eighty; the Douglas DC-6 carried eighty-six; the Boeing Stratocruisers, the bruiser of the bunch, could carry more than a hundred. When two or more of these planes arrived at the same time, there was inevitable chaos on the ground. Trying to book reservations was also a nightmare. Phone lines were usually jammed, and many found themselves being bumped from flights at the last moment. Savvy travelers found it easier to go to the airport and simply wait for the next available flight. Most airports still used archaic methods of baggage handling. After arriving, passengers would have to find their suitcases amid a mountain of others. As one traveler complained, "It takes longer to get your baggage at Washington National than it does to fly from Chicago."[28]

Some facilities became so inadequate that passenger services were moved into temporary structures likes tents and Quonset huts. Atlanta's picturesque terminal from the 1930s could no longer handle the mobs of postwar travelers, so the city converted a military hangar to civilian use. At the Willow Run Airport in Ypsilanti, Michigan, a cavernous aircraft factory was turned into a terminal. Such makeshift arrangements may have been fine for soldiers during the war, but paying passengers expected better treatment.

Anxious confusion extended to the overtaxed control towers as well. By 1952, a plane was taking off or landing every eight seconds, and traffic controllers were haunted by the specter of midair collision. Busy airports like LaGuardia reached peaks of over fifty planes an hour, and a new system called "stacking" was introduced to keep aircraft holding at different altitudes. One plane was reported to have circled Washington National for five hours before being allowed to land.

While *Life* always tried to report air travel in a positive light, other magazines published nightmare accounts of filthy terminals, canceled flights, and dysfunctional public address systems, what one journalist referred to as "Ordeal-by-Loudspeaker." The golden age of airport bashing had begun. *Fortune* ran a twelve-page indictment called "What's Wrong with the Airlines." The *Saturday Evening Post* ran "Why Air Passengers Get Mad," and *Harper's* followed with "Our Airsick Airlines."[29] Accompanying the articles were photographs of anxious people crowding around ticket counters, searching for lost suitcases, waiting in long lines, or slumped in broken chairs.

By all accounts, Midway was the worst. "Chicago's airport is a slum," reported *Fortune*. "Chewing gum, orange peels, paper and cigar butts strew the floor around the stacks of luggage. Porters can't keep the floors clean if people are standing on them day and night."[30] By 1946, Midway was handling over a million passengers annually, making it one of the busiest airports in the world. The small deco terminal, which had seemed the height of elegance in the 1930s, was now a liability.

Bad weather made matters even worse. Air traffic reached an all-time crunch on "Black Wednesday," September 15, 1954, when more than forty-five thousand passengers were delayed at New York airports because of heavy fog. Hundreds of airliners were stacked in holding patterns above LaGuardia and Idlewild, awaiting instructions from the ground. More than just a local problem, the backup created a ripple effect across the country and forced thousands of cancellations.

Another crisis was caused by the proximity of residential development. A number of planes had crashed into a neighborhood near Seattle's airport and as one glide-path resident put it: "If you are going to live at the end of a cannon like that airport, you've got to expect it to go off sometime."[31] In February 1952, an airliner also crashed into a densely populated section of Elizabeth, New Jersey, three miles south of Newark Airport.[32] The plane was said to have plunged "like a lightning bolt" into the city streets, spilling aviation fuel, which then ignited into an inferno. Eleven people on the ground and twenty-eight passengers were killed. It was the third such crash in an eight-week period, and the citizens of Newark demanded action. Officials responded by closing the airport until further notice, but people wanted it closed for good.

In response, President Truman appointed Lieutenant General James H. Doolittle to head a national airport safety commission. After several months of inquiry, the commission concluded that the dangers posed by airports must be tolerated as a consequence of modern urban life, pointing out that more people were killed riding bicycles than from falling aircraft. (Doolittle declared Newark safe and called for its immediate reopening.) This did little to assuage the fears of local residents, but the commission did persuade the president to establish "no-build" hazard zones extending half a mile from the ends of airport runways and enact zoning laws that would prohibit construction of housing within these approach areas.[33] Truman also increased appropriations for airport safety. Pilot examinations were tightened. Air traffic control systems were upgraded and navigational aids improved. Nineteen fifty-four proved to be a turning point with not a single airline fatality reported.

But there continued to be a debate over how airports could safely be integrated into the social landscape. At the end of the war, Lewis Mumford predicted that the airplane would soon be "as much a part of our daily lives as the motor car."[34] In the National Airport Plan for postwar America, the CAA proposed the construction of 3,050 new airfields and the improvement of hundreds of preexisting fields at a cost of $1.25 billion. One federal official compared it to the highway program: "By investing $25 billion in roads during the last twenty-five years, we have made it possible for the United States to become a nation on wheels," he wrote. "For a much smaller investment, we can start the United States on its way toward becoming a nation on wings."[35]

In spite of obvious dangers, the Urban Planning Section of the CAA published diagrams that showed how residential communities could be neatly "tucked in between runway approaches and separated by parkways."[36] While dubious at best, this approach was indicative of the postwar mind-set: Air age versions of Ebeneezer Howard's Garden City would sprout around the periphery of airports, engendering a new kind of economic development. As some pointed out, precedents for this kind of airport community had proved to be successful during the war years. "Far from avoiding the vicinity of airports, first-class residential developments have gravitated to ports in many cities," noted the editors of *Architectural Record*.[37] Westchester, for instance, was built around the edges of Los Angeles Airport and housed ten thousand defense workers.[38]

There was a belief held by some postwar planners that new airport systems could reinvigorate the failing economies of older industrial cities. Such thinking had its roots in the utopian twenties and came with a desire to sweep away the old urban imprint with massive slum clearance and highway-building programs. This kind of tabula rasa approach was to be expected in Europe where cities had been destroyed by aerial bombardment, yet it proved equally alluring in mainland America where no bombs had fallen.

Toledo, Ohio, had a population of 350,000 and was the third largest water port of the Great Lakes. While once a bustling hub of commerce, it was slipping into decline. White, middle-class families were fleeing to the suburbs and businesses were abandoning the downtown area. During the summer of 1945, civic leaders sponsored the "Toledo Tomorrow" exhibition in the hopes that it would inspire support for urban renewal. Crowds stood in line to view the center-piece of the exhibition, a sixty-foot model showing what the city

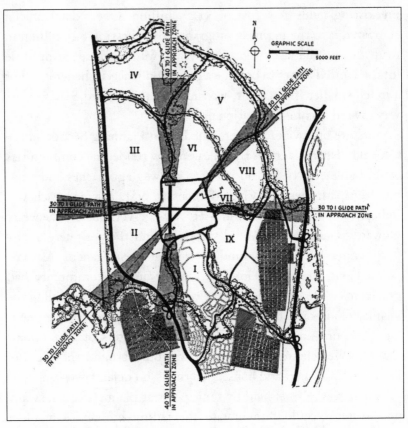

"First-class residential communities can be tucked in between runway approaches and separated by parkways." A postwar plan for suburban development near an airport published by the Urban Planning Section of the Civil Aeronautics Administration (CAA), 1945.

might look like in the future years of peaceful prosperity. (The *Toledo Blade*, a local newspaper, paid the $250,000 cost of construction.)[39]

Blighted downtown areas would be razed to make way for highways, parks, and a new transportation hub. Freight yards, coal docks, and grain elevators would be relocated to a new industrial zone while polluted areas along the river would be reclaimed for recreation. But the key to Toledo's renewal would be a matrix of airports designed to bring the city into the modern era. (This was the work, once again, of Norman Bel Geddes, who had proposed a similar scheme in his Futurama model at the New York World's Fair of 1939.) Air, rail, and bus traffic would converge within a multilevel complex called the Tri-Terminal, located on a tract of reclaimed marsh near the business district. Express highways would lace their way through the heart of the city, enabling out-of-towners to reach the central airport without delays. Three small "feeder" airports would be built on the banks of Lake Erie to provide round-the-clock service for air freight. "Freight planes of the future," explained one of Toledo's planners, "will look like pigs— great balloons with small wings."

Toledo Tomorrow was a wishful glimpse into a future that was never meant to be. Not only was it beyond the means of municipal funding, but the basic premise—that centralized renewal could revive a dying city—was completely out of step with the times. In fact, the U.S. population was becoming more dispersed, and commercial aviation was one of the underlying causes. "[The airplane] will decentralize our daily activities to a degree proportional to its speed," wrote Charles Froesch and Walther Prokosch in their influential study, *Airport Planning*, of 1946.[40] The authors predicted that new kinds of urban clusters— what they called "air cities"—would supplement the old city centers, sprouting in previously unpopulated areas just as new communities had once arisen at junction points along the transcontinental railway. "It may not be fanciful to suggest that some future suburbs will be 100 or more miles from the center of a metropolis," they wrote.[41]

America's most famous architect, Frank Lloyd Wright, held a similarly decentralized point of view and believed that airports should be spread out across the countryside, well removed from urban density. "As flight develops," wrote Wright in 1957, "air-rotor or helicopter depots will be connected with the cross-country rights-of-way on which once were laid the hard rails."[42] In plans for his unbuilt Broadacre City, Wright placed an airport outside of town, near the golf course. For shorter, daily commutes, he envisioned citizens of Broadacre and piloting their own personal "aerotors," which could hover above the ground like flying saucers.

In the decade following World War II, major new airports

would indeed be built in the hinterlands, well outside city centers. Midway in Chicago was already hemmed in by residential development. The city's Regional Planning Association considered several options, including building an airport on stilts above a railroad yard; filling in the Lake Calumet wetlands; and creating a man-made island in Lake Michigan. Instead, Chicago's planners chose to build the future O'Hare at Orchard Place, fifteen miles to the northwest.[43] This would be a nationwide trend.

Friendship Airport was built ten miles south of Baltimore and thirty miles north of Washington, D.C. Pittsburgh's new airport was located twelve miles west of the city center, and New York's new facility at Idlewild was built fifteen miles from Times Square. All would be connected to their respective downtowns by hard-paved umbilical cords: O'Hare by Interstate 90; Friendship by the Baltimore-Washington Expressway; and Idlewild by the Van Wyck Expressway.

During the first summer of peace, a group of mayors found themselves trudging across a windswept plain in Queens, hoping to learn something about airport planning. They were following their indefatigable host, Fiorello La Guardia, on a tour of his airfield-to-be at Idlewild. "Let me tell you something about the magnitude of this airport. It embraces 4,495 acres," he boasted. "It will be a great monument, and the world's finest airport." This was hard to imagine, however, since all the mayors could see was a lunar landscape of low scrub grass and the fading imprint of an abandoned golf course. There were also remnants of a dilapidated hotel and a row of squatter shacks built along the banks of a salt-water inlet.

La Guardia had learned important lessons from the airport that bore his name. Only two years after its opening, LaGuardia Field had reached a state of crisis. The airport's man-made peninsula was sinking into Flushing Bay. Concrete aprons sank at an average of six inches a year and in some places there were collapses as deep as six feet. Worst of all, there was no room for expansion.

It was clear that the city needed to build another airport, and this time La Guardia wanted to make sure there would be room for growth into the twenty-first century. The Army Corps of Engineers began preliminary fieldwork at the new site in 1942, pumping 43 million cubic yards of sand out of Jamaica Bay to raise the field above the high-water mark. Nine million dollars from the sale of Floyd Bennett Field to the U.S. Navy helped to pay for initial costs, but wartime priorities put a cap on spending and progress was slow.

Preliminary plans for Idlewild show a surprisingly formal layout, with a long ceremonial axis leading to a semicircular plaza. Hangars and freight depots were to be placed around the edge of the field, "much as stables are spotted around a racetrack," explained the architects Delano and Aldrich.[44] Their $10 million passenger terminal was designed to accommodate thirty thousand passengers a day. Its layout was, for all intents and purposes, a modern version of the Roman Colosseum surrounded by a neoclassical colonnade. "The building [has] great dignity and beauty," wrote La Guardia, "yet not an inch of space is wasted."[45] However inappropriate, there was an ironic sense of symmetry to an air terminus being based on an arena for gladiatorial battle. In place of ramps leading to the lions, there were eight "loading decks" leading to the airplanes.

The scheme was published in the *New York Times Magazine* with a self-congratulatory essay by the mayor: "We are building the finest airport in the world, at a cost of $71,000,000, not in the hope that some day there will be need for it, but because commercial aviation *will* need it as soon as it is completed," wrote La Guardia.[46] In odd contrast to the mayor's optimism, however, were the Sturm und Drang renderings by Hugh Ferriss that accompanied the article. Drawn with deep charcoal shadowing, Delano and Aldrich's terminal looks more like a stage set for *Faust* than a municipal airport. Day is turned into night. Airplanes swoop out from their loading positions like so many birds of prey. Automobiles stream under the terminal's gaping colonnade, while masses of people huddle along the side of the building as if lining up for

Judgment Day. The architects wanted to evoke the ancient past, but Ferriss somehow captured the noir uncertainty of the post-Hiroshima future.

In the end, the scheme was never realized. After completing his third term, La Guardia retired. William O'Dwyer became mayor in 1945 and inherited the unfinished project, but he was not the enthusiast that his predecessor had been. O'Dwyer saw the airport as a financial burden. Seventy-one million dollars had already been spent but most of it had gone toward filling the marshy slough on Jamaica Bay, and an estimated $100 million was needed to finish the job. Alternate proposals for the site were suggested, such as turning it into an industrial park or low-income housing, but O'Dwyer was eventually convinced, however reluctantly, that New York had to build a second airport.

The old design was scrapped, and a new planning team headed by Wallace Harrison took over. Harrison brought an urbanistic vision that was ideally suited to the scale of such an undertaking. Court architect to the Rockefeller empire, Harrison had collaborated on Rockefeller Center and designed the Rockefeller apartment building as well as several other projects for the family.[47]

By the time Harrison started working on Idlewild in 1946, estimates for air traffic into New York had increased dramatically. The revised terminal would need to accommodate close to a hundred boarding positions. This called for a more radical approach, certainly not the outdated formalism of Delano and Aldrich: "Thus only may we preclude early and untimely obsolescence," wrote Harrison.[48]

At the center of his scheme was a glass-faced monolith that soared above six lanes of traffic streaming in from the Van Wyck Expressway. Passengers would alight onto concrete islands and ascend by escalator to a central lobby as if to heaven. (Harrison had used similar escalators for the Trylon and Perisphere theme center at the 1939 New York World's Fair.)

In 1947, *Fortune* magazine reported that retail concessions were now accounting for more than a third of airport revenue: "Travel,

The central terminal at Idlewild Municipal Airport, New York. Passengers would ascend to the lobby by escalator and walk through a shopping arcade before boarding their planes. Wallace Harrison, architect, 1947. Rendering by Hugh Ferriss.

A terraced restaurant looks out over the airfield and the Peripheral Building in a proposed scheme for Idlewild Municipal Airport, New York. Wallace Harrison, architect, 1947. Rendering by Hugh Ferriss.

especially on vacation or expense account, puts people, including greeters and handkerchief wavers, in a spending mood. And when people have time on their hands—as they often do at an airport—they will spend out of boredom."[49]

Harrison was one of the first to fully comprehend the potential of retail marketing at the airport. In his plan for Idlewild, the passenger became a kind of consumer guinea pig, guided along a route that was calculated to "produce a maximum of concession revenue." After checking in, passengers had no choice but to walk through a shopping arcade: "Along this route are the well-advertised, high revenue-producing stands, shops, food and liquor-vending establishments, and direct access to the newsreel theatre."[50] At the end of the arcade was a terraced restaurant with panoramic views of the airfield.

When it came time to depart, passengers would proceed to the Peripheral Building, a narrow two-mile-long structure that girdled the terminal area. With its undulating, uterine forms—almost baroque in plan—it was odd-looking, but revolutionary in the way it integrated intra-airport transport and boarding access into a unified whole. Passengers could ride custom-designed buses (precursors of today's people movers) along the elevated roadway to reach one of eighty-six boarding pods that had been placed at five-hundred-foot intervals around the perimeter. Each pod contained its own waiting room, newsstand, and snack bar.

Harrison envisioned Idlewild as a monumental machine for processing air travel—so vast in scale that it staggered the imagination and foreshadowed the kind of infrastructural systems that the modern airport demanded. In many ways it was too far ahead of its time, and by the time Harrison presented the scheme to O'Dwyer, the new mayor had already changed his mind and decided that airports were too expensive for a city to own and operate. Shortly thereafter he signed a fifty-year lease with the Port of New York Authority to operate Idlewild on a self-sustaining basis. After several months of analysis, Thomas Sullivan, the Port Authority's chief of aviation planning, decided on yet another

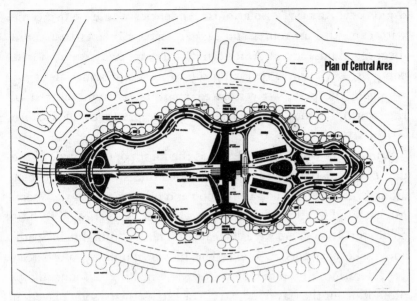

Plan of Central Area

The oddly baroque master plan for Idlewild. The two-mile-long Peripheral Building could accommodate eighty-six planes at once. Wallace Harrison, architect, 1946. (Each circle denotes a boarding position.)

design strategy, and Harrison's innovative concept was soon modified beyond recognition.[51]

Around the World in Eighty Hours

After the war, America found itself playing a new role in global politics. The balance of power had shifted. Old empires crumbled, while former colonies struggled toward independence. The British withdrew from India and Burma in 1946. The Dutch granted independence to Indonesia in 1949. At the same time, an American empire was stretching around the globe "wherever airliners could deliver businessmen," bringing with it a consumer-friendly form of imperialism.[52] "The modern airplane creates a new geographical dimension," wrote Wendell Willkie. "There are no distant places any longer: the world is small and the world is one."[53] Gunboat diplomacy gave way to a kind of airport diplomacy. America's isolationist tendencies would be overcome with expanded air routes and bigger, faster airplanes that could disgorge thousands of American tourists to every point of the compass. "Aviation is removing the barriers of distance and time which in the past partly isolated many lands from the rest of the world," wrote Eddie Rickenbacker, president of Eastern Airlines.[54]

Around the World in 80 Days was the most popular movie of the day, based on Jules Verne's story about Phileas Fogg and his race around the world by hot-air balloon and other means of transport. Michael Todd's all-star production was shot as a series of Technicolor vignettes. There were châteaux in France, bullfights in Spain, and snake charmers in India. The movie's publicity blurb read "252 locations! 13 different countries!," making it sound like a promotion for the travel industry. The catchy theme song played in elevators, shopping centers, and airport lounges. Popular magazines carried tales of modern-day Phileas Foggs attempting to travel around the world in eighty hours. "I Flew 14,000 Miles for Dinner," ran a story in the *Saturday Evening Post*. "I left London on Tuesday, February 14, 1956, at 1:22 PM," wrote globe-trotting journalist Noel Barber. "I flew four days and five nights [and] I couldn't have been fresher when I stepped off the plane at London Airport at 8:45 on the Saturday morning, February 18, 1956."[55]

Time/Life publisher Henry Luce promoted air travel as fervently as he did anticommunism. He understood that every tourist, armed with a Kodak camera and a Samsonite suitcase, was a soldier against international communism. His wife, Congresswoman Clare Boothe Luce, expressed the prevailing mood when she declared: "American postwar aviation policy is simple: we want to fly *everywhere*," and with newly extended networks, U.S. citizens *could* fly almost anywhere.[56] To emphasize the point, Luce's *Life* sent artist Edward Reep on an air trip to capture the exotic allure of airports around the world. Reep returned with watercolor scenes of Buddhist monks strolling through Don Muang Airport in Bangkok, Punjabi women under the veil in Karachi, and fishermen working the waters near the airport in Tokyo. Airports, claimed *Life,* "were the new gateways to the wide world . . . bits of cosmopolitan swank set in tropical jungles, buttoned-up hutments of warmth on an arctic tundra, palaces of glass in central Europe."[57]

In a speech commemorating the first flight of the Wright brothers, President Truman made a solemn pledge: "We Americans stand ready to do our part, to make the world's airways paths of peace—to use our planes for travel, for pleasure, for commerce and for all the peaceful pursuits that make up our daily lives."[58] A copy of Truman's message was carried from the White House all the way around the world by a retired air force pilot who flew on regularly scheduled American air carriers—proof positive that the world's airways were free and open. It was, however, the great air apostle himself, Juan Trippe, who put the postwar attitude most succinctly: "Mass travel by air may prove to be more significant to world destiny than the atom bomb."[59] In place of confrontation, overseas air travel would act as a kind of nonnuclear deterrent.

In 1956, about the time that Soviet troops were marching into Hungary, Rickenbacker composed a passionate plea to the American public: "Let us go forward boldly," he wrote, "making sure of our rightful place in the air, for freedom and for good."[60] It was a patriotic call to duty: Travel by air. *Life* published a special issue devoted to the wonders of the air age and America's preeminent place in it. A genuine "revolution" was under way, explained the editors, one that was as earthshaking as the Russian or French revolutions.[61] Every overseas airport would serve as an outpost for American foreign policy, creating a context for free-market capitalism. Along with the airports came hotels, shops, restaurants, and other injections of American culture. After all, businessmen and tourists needed clean, comfortable, climate-controlled places to stay when they traveled abroad. In 1946 Juan Trippe established the Intercontinental Hotel Corporation (IHC) and began to build hotels in partnership with the Waldorf-Astoria. The idea proved to be a lucrative sideline to the airline business and, by 1954, Trippe's subsidiary was operating nine different hotels overseas.

Trippe and the airline executives understood the restless urge to see the world. A whole generation of Americans had experienced international travel as guests of Uncle Sam. More than a million GIs flew overseas during the war in ATC transport planes. They were not afraid of flying. They had been to Paris and Guam when the bombs were exploding. Many of them wanted to go back and visit the places they had seen as soldiers, bringing their families with them this time. The idea of vacation took on a whole new dimension. A middle-class holiday no longer meant a trip to Yellowstone Park or the Jersey shore. Brightly colored posters lured travelers south in winter with seductive images of palm trees and bikini-clad women, or north to the Alps. In 1946, the first full year of peace, only 538,000 people from the United States had flown abroad. By 1950, more than a million had.

Planeloads of Americans were streaming across the Atlantic, but European airports were unprepared to greet them. Many of the gleaming terminals of the prewar era had been destroyed. Others were still in a state of ruin, their runways pocked with craters. Civil airports in the Netherlands, Belgium, and France had been bombed into oblivion. The once-great air center of Paris was still operating out of the old 1930s terminal at Bourget. (A new airport—built at Orly—wouldn't be finished until 1961.)

The Dutch government made the rebuilding of Schiphol a priority. KLM's resourceful director Albert Plesman purchased a fleet of surplus warplanes and put his airline back in business as soon as hostilities ceased. The "new" Schiphol opened in July 1945 with a repaved runway and only a few temporary buildings—air traffic control was operated from the back of a van—but more importantly, it was a symbol of national recovery. As Prince Bernhard of the Netherlands put it "Our great Schiphol airport has risen phoenix-like from the ashes and ruins of war."

Germany was forbidden to operate its own airlines after the war (Lufthansa didn't resume service until 1955), but airports in Berlin played a major role in the first showdown of the cold war. When the city was partitioned into four occupation zones, Tempelhof airfield fell within the American sector. It had been heavily shelled by the Red Army in 1945 but repairs were made, and by May 1946, the first commercial flights were leaving for North America. In June 1948, Stalin blockaded all land, rail, and canal access into Berlin. Instead of capitulating, the United States and Britain began to fly round-the-clock sorties of food and other supplies into the beleaguered city of 2.5 million. As soon as one plane touched down, it would be unloaded and sent back into the air. "The sound of the engines was like music to our ears," recalled one young Berliner.[62] A plane was taking off or landing every three minutes.

During the blockade, more than 2 million tons of cargo were flown into Berlin's three airports—Tempelhof in the American sector, Gatow in the British, and Tegel in the French. (There were 277,264 flights in and out of Tempelhof alone.) The airlift was so succesful that Stalin relented and ended the blockade in May 1949. Apart from keeping Berlin out of Soviet control, the airlift was also a propaganda coup in the opening round of cold war brinksmanship. Tempelhof, former symbol of Nazi oppression, had become the "airport of democracy" and other Reich airports would be similarly transformed, such as the Rhein-Main Airport in Frankfurt, which became the main U.S. air base in West Germany and gateway for international arrivals. The Nazi Imperial Eagle that had once decorated the front of Frankfurt's terminal was replaced with a dove of peace. The terminal at Munich's Oberwiesenfeld was rebuilt and turned into a studio for Radio Liberty to broadcast anti-Communist propaganda into East Germany.

But the war had taken its toll and it would take millions of dollars in economic aid before European airports were restored to their former glory. In 1955, fourteen American cities, including Atlanta and Kansas City, had more air traffic than the busiest airport in Europe. Paris had less traffic than Louisville, Kentucky.[63] Not surprisingly, Switzerland, free of wartime deprivations, was the first to build a major new facility. Kloten airport in Zurich

American bombshell Jayne Mansfield arrives in postwar Germany. Frankfurt Airport, 1957.

opened in 1953 and was considered the most deluxe in Europe: "Operated not as a runway for transients," wrote one journalist, "but as a first-class hotel."[64] The terminal by Alfred and Heinrich Oeschger featured lounges with showers, playrooms for children, and one of the best restaurants in Zurich. Such were the rewards of neutrality.

The busiest European airport was Heathrow, located fifteen miles west of London. Heathrow had played an important role as an RAF base during the air defense of London. New concrete runways were laid in 1946, and transatlantic planes began to make use of them immediately. Waiting rooms and customs offices, however, had to be housed in tents and trailers. The first permanent building wasn't finished until 1955, just in time to greet the hordes of American tourists that swarmed Europe that summer. There were more than eighty-two thousand arrivals and departures that year. What came to be known as Terminal 2 was an undistinguished brick building with long boarding fingers. It was the first of several buildings designed by Frederick Gibberd and Partners.

By 1954, almost 2 million were flying off to Europe and other points around the globe. Competition for the overseas market had intensified. Pan Am no longer held a monopoly but had to share the pie with TWA and other companies like American, Braniff, and Northwest. TWA inaugurated its "sky-tourist" fare to Europe in 1952. Willis Lipscomb, a marketing genius at Pan Am, countered with the famous "fly now, pay later" scheme in 1954. Working with the Household Finance Corporation, Lipscomb devised a credit plan so that passengers could pay off their fares in monthly installments. *Life* magazine proclaimed the summer of 1955 to be the "greatest vacation exodus ever."[65]

During this first wave of postwar travel, transatlantic planes still needed to make refueling stops. Assuming its role as the "doorstep to Europe," the government of Ireland developed Shannon Airport in County Clare, on the westernmost coast of Ireland. The Canadian government expanded runways at Goose Bay, Labrador, and at Gander, Newfoundland, to handle the growing stream of international flights. English novelist Christopher Isherwood passed through Gander on his way back to London in the early 1950s and recalled a "tiny sparkle of lights in the wilderness. . . . The big bare white waiting-hall, with its table of simple refreshments, seemed very much a frontier-post; here were the last cup of coffee and the last bun in the Western Hemisphere."[66]

But the airlines were soon able to avoid the refueling stops altogether. "No Goose, No Gander," announced one airline, promoting its nonstop service. Pan Am started direct service to Europe on June 1, 1956, in the new Douglas DC-7C ("Seven Seas") with a range of 4,606 miles. TWA introduced its nonstop New York–to-London route in the Lockheed 1649A Starliner, which was able to fly six thousand miles without refueling.[67] The old transatlantic stops became ghost ports. By the end of 1956, more Americans were crossing the ocean by plane than by ship. As if to signal the ultimate demise of the ocean liner, the *Andrea Doria* sank that same year after colliding with the *Stockholm* off Nantucket.

A Curious Preoccupation

"Airports are safer now, but they all look too much alike," wrote pilot/novelist Ernest K. Gann in 1953. "They have sacrificed character for vastness."[68] In response to the precipitous rise of postwar air traffic, airports were indeed bigger than ever, anticipating future needs, and pushing the limits of architectural convention. American architects responded to the dilemma of postwar aviation with predictably overwrought solutions. "Terminal buildings, serving an exclusively contemporary mode of transportation, show a curious preoccupation with the monumental," wrote one critic, as many postwar terminals continued to perpetuate the classicism of the prewar era, only on a bigger scale.[69] A design similar to Delano and Aldrich's stillborn plan for Idlewild was built at Chicago Midway.[70] The central rotunda of Paul Gerhardt's terminal was shaped like a fluted column, overscaled and truncated, not unlike the faux ruins of Le Désert de Retz, the folly garden that François de Monville built in eighteenth-century France.

The roof of the Chicago terminal telescoped up in concentric tiers with a Cloud Room restaurant on one level and a control tower perched on top like the decoration on a wedding cake. Midway's was the first big air terminal to open after the war, and its style of overblown classicism, however anachronistic, set the tone for other airports. Even terminals with a modernist veneer—like those in Seattle, San Francisco, and Miami—perpetuated the idea of the gateway as architectural proof of arrival and departure, with large central blocks and symmetrical wings.

Allusions to ancient ruins at a cold war airport. *(top)* The terminal at Chicago Municipal Airport was designed as a truncated classical column. Paul Gerhardt Jr., architect, 1946. *(bottom)* Broken column folly at the Désert de Retz garden in eighteenth-century France.

Vue Perspective de la Colonne.

Greater Pittsburgh's new "super airport" opened in 1952, the year that the first U.S. hydrogen bomb was detonated in the Pacific. It was built at a cost of $29.8 million on sixteen hundred acres of land in Moon Township. Designed by Joseph Hoover in a tough battleship style, it was the largest and most expensive terminal to date, and the first to challenge Tempelhof in scale. The press called it the Taj Mahal of air terminals. It rose seven stories with walls of shiny black granite. Stretching out from its center was a boarding wing called the "finger-dock," which could handle more than sixteen airliners at a time. On the entry side of the terminal passengers were greeted by a formal forecourt and semicircular colonnade.

Meanwhile, behind so many imperial facades, something else was happening. The true morphology of the airport was making itself felt. Bigger planes and bigger crowds were forcing terminals to stretch out in odd new directions, laterally, with long narrow boarding piers like Pittsburgh's finger-dock. Decentralization was the true mark of postwar airports, not the monumental gesture. The kitsch classicism of Midway was an anachronism, a case of mistaken architectural identity. As Albert F. Heino put it: "We are passing the day when all persons going to an airport must go through the front door."[71] Heino, one of the leading airport theorists of the period (and chief architect for United Airlines), believed that an air terminal should be treated as a functional machine, not a civic monument. "It is to be hoped that we shall have no [more] baroque, renaissance or classic air terminals," he wrote. "An air terminal is a machine."[72]

The paradigm had changed. Old models for comparison were inadequate. No longer could an airport be seen as a single entity. Heino compared the airport to a machine with many interconnected parts. Others looked to urban planning for models of comparison: "Every airport, from the smallest to the most complex . . . is very much akin to a town plan or neighborhood development," wrote the airport specialist Walther Prokosch. "A complex of structures has to be organized in relation to each other as well as

An ungainly new look in postwar American airports: long appendages sprouted to handle more planes. *(top)* Greater Pittsburgh was called the "Taj Mahal" of American terminals when it opened in 1952. Its "finger-dock" could handle more than sixteen planes at a time. Joseph Hoover, architect. *(bottom)* Friendship Airport in Baltimore (1949) had a boarding pier that was longer than the main terminal. James R. Edmunds, architect.

Terminal Building
Friendship International Airport
Baltimore, Md.

with relationship to the runway pattern."[73] Ansel E. Talbert, aviation editor of the *New York Herald-Tribune*, may have been the first to use the term "airport city" as a way to suggest a more complex kind of urban phenomenon. This soon became a commonly cited analogy "The largest of America's modern commercial flying fields might well be called 'airport cities,' " wrote Talbert in 1953. "They include theaters, banks, restaurants, barber and beauty shops, book shops, clothing stores, jewelry shops . . . instantly available to air passengers arriving or waiting to depart."[74] Airports were becoming self-sufficient entities, displacing traditional patterns of urban growth and setting the stage for the sprawl to come.

Greater Pittsburgh Airport boasted that its new terminal was a "city within a city," with a nightclub, a roof deck for twenty-seven hundred spectators, restaurants, and an outdoor dining terrace. Passengers who had time between flights could watch a movie in the full-sized theater or go shopping at one of a dozen retail stores. On-site hotels were seen as a good source of additional revenue, and Pittsburgh had a sixty-two-room hotel within its terminal. The Hyatt chain opened its first airport hotel in 1954 at Los Angeles International—it was a ranch-type motel with a palm-fringed patio and swimming pool—and New York hotelier Louis Ritter opened a hotel at LaGuardia that featured air-conditioning, soundproofing, and rooms that were shock-mounted on a foundation designed to eliminate vibrations from the nearby airplanes.[75]

During its first year of operation, Pittsburgh's beefy terminal was swamped: over a million passengers passed through its black granite arcades.[76] Planners in Baltimore had been equally optimistic, but initial statistics were alarmingly low. The giant terminal was as cold and austere as a nuclear test site. While it had been designed in anticipation of the travel boom, the mobs never came. Fewer than seventy thousand passengers used the airport in the first full year of operations. (Only four planes arrived from overseas all year.) Most regular fliers—businessmen, government officials, foreign diplomats—preferred to fly out of Washington National because of its convenient location. Traffic increased somewhat after the Baltimore-

Washington Expressway opened in 1952, but by then Friendship already had the reputation of being a white elephant. *Life* magazine did nothing to dispel this notion when it published an article called "Baltimore's Lonely Big Airport" illustrated with photographs of empty runways and cavernous interiors: "Deserted lobby sparkles bleakly at 7:15 in the evening," read one caption. "The observation deck looms emptily above the ramp," read another.77 Friendship, however, proved to be one of the rare cases of *over*estimating.

Airports would continue to grow in fits and starts, reinventing themselves as aviation advanced to its next phase of evolution. If no other lesson had been learned in twenty-five years of trial and error, it was that airports were never finished. They were in a constant state of flux, flirting with obsolescence, reshaping themselves, and adapting to new technologies. As veteran pilot Hal Blackburn put it: "To the best of my knowledge I never landed on a completed airport."78

But how did one go about designing a structure that was never complete? *Business Week* heralded a change of temperament in 1954 with an article titled: "Airports Turn to the Engineers," giving the impression that traditionally trained architects were ill equipped to cope with the complexity of airport design.79 Engineers and efficiency experts would come to the rescue with slide rules and flowcharts. The airport became a laboratory where specialists would calculate space and time in precise increments. A formula was devised for every part of the process. Journals published time-motion diagrams with black lines drawn to represent the movement of passengers through hypothetical terminals. Dotted lines indicated baggage routes, and ghostly white outlines represented zones of future expansion. One firm sent a team to New York to conduct a study of rush-hour crowds passing through Grand Central Station. The airport planners clocked the commuters as they walked from train to street. They measured the busiest routes and analyzed areas of backup and bottleneck. For Cleveland's new terminal of 1956, the firm Outcalf, Guenther and Associates copied the layout of a school for the blind because of the simplified logic of its circulation system.

The holy grail for airport planners, however, was how to move large numbers of people between terminal and plane. Airport manuals of the postwar period recommended all manner of systems— some lunatic, some brilliant—for accomplishing this task. In the forward docking concept, planes were guided onto steel tracks set into the apron and mechanically nosed toward the boarding gate.[80] A patented device called Loadair was unveiled by the Whiting Corporation in which an airplane would taxi onto a dolly and be pulled toward the terminal sideways by means of electric-powered cables. An experimental version was installed at Idlewild, but it proved unwieldy and dangerous.[81] Rather than winching the planes closer to the building, the building would begin to reach out toward the planes with loading bridges and adjustable platforms. "Since we cannot bring all airplanes to the terminal, it seems we must take the terminal to the airplane," wrote Albert Heino, one of the first to develop a credible boarding system.[82] The equation was simple: the faster the planes taxied into position, picked up their passengers, and got back into the air, the greater was the profit. "Airplanes are non-productive when resting on terra firma," wrote Heino, who unveiled his unit terminal theory at a conference of airport managers in Fort Wayne, Indiana.[83] Each unit would contain its own services, he explained: check-in, baggage conveyor, waiting room, etc., and drastically reduce the distances that passengers and baggage needed to travel between ground and air. "Decentralization of the airline terminals make possible a direct access to each plane by ground transportation," wrote Heino. "The bus, limousine or private car may be driven to the door of the airline, where the passenger alights a few feet from his airplane."[84]

There was understandable resistance to Heino's philosophy of unit design. To airport authorities and architects, it seemed repetitive and boring. But as Heino and the efficiency experts explained, these narrow utilitarian structures, strung out like army barracks, weren't buildings at all. They were "units" and weren't supposed to be pretty or symbolic. They were products of pure necessity.

The roots of the unit terminal theory can be traced back to the

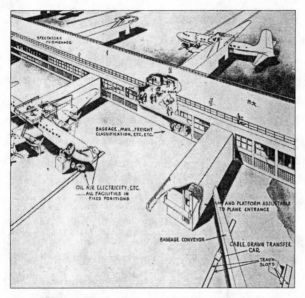

The Loadair docking device was introduced by the Whiting Corporation in 1950. Planes were pulled up to the terminal on dollies that ran on steel tracks.

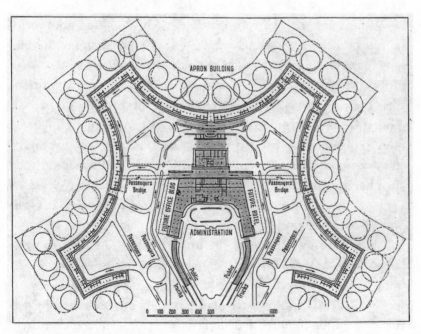

"We must take the terminal to the airplane." The apron building at Logan International Airport stretched out from the original terminal and was designed to handle fifty planes at a time, 1951.

prewar period, to LaGuardia's Skywalk and pioneers like Joseph Hudnut who had envisioned the ideal airport as being a "series of gates placed at intervals in a long and uniform barrier . . . [Such a] design would be based necessarily upon a unit system," wrote Hudnut. "That is to say, upon the repetition of several elements having the same function and an equal importance."[85] In his airport survey of 1946, Marc Thompson had prescribed long, shedlike structures referred to as "concourses." Wallace Harrison concocted the two-mile-long Peripheral Building for Idlewild, and Norman Bel Geddes proposed his own gate unit system in 1947 with a long slender terminal that could process several thousand passengers at a time.[86] Logan Airport in Boston built an eccentrically shaped structure called the "apron building" as part of its postwar expansion program. It was seven thousand feet long, forty feet wide, and provided access for fifty planes. A new terminal built for Newark Airport in 1952 had two long "loading arcades" that stretched 575 feet onto the apron.[87]

While they may have had different names—"unit terminal," "apron building," "loading arcade"—they were designed for the same purpose: to speed the transfer of human bodies and maximize profit. If architecture reflects something of the human condition, then these narrow sheep runs embodied the prosaic linearity of modern life: the treadmill of corporate employment, the narrow margin of profit, the anxiety of a salesman running for his flight. They were not designed to memorialize heroic deeds, but rather as antimonuments to the likes of Willie Loman and Sammy Glick.

It would take the refined eye of an architecture critic like G. E. Kidder-Smith to find beauty in the ungainly new airport vernacular. After touring Europe in the mid-1950s, Kidder-Smith published *The New Architecture of Europe*, in which he analyzed 225 buildings in sixteen different countries. He singled out a new air terminal at Gatwick for particular praise. Its most noteworthy feature was a nine-hundred-foot-long boarding pier made from steel and glass. It possessed a functional purity and quality of what Kidder-Smith called "airport-ness." In other words, it had

Studies in *airportness*. "As soon as one arrives one feels that this is an airport and no other transportation service." (top) Glass-and-steel boarding pier at Gatwick Airport. Yorke, Rosenberg, and Mardall, architects, 1957. (*bottom*) Renfrew Airport, Paisley, Scotland. Rowan Anderson, Kininmonth, and Paul, architects, 1956.

integrity and wasn't trying to imitate other types of architecture. "As soon as one arrives one feels that this is an airport and no other transportation service," he wrote. "One is architecturally, indeed physically, projected onto the field and made a part of its excitement, for no solid wall ever rises between the passenger and his aerial transportation."[88] This marked a significant shift in perception, one that would be exploited fully in the coming jet age. Airports owed nothing to the past, but possessed their own distinctive character, their own *airportness*.

CHAPTER 5

Jet-Land: 1957–1970

"And a 'soaring' airport is getting to be the most In of all."
—Time, *March 29, 1963*

Soaring

Throughout most of the 1950s, there was a commonly held assumption that jet engines burned too much fuel and therefore weren't suitable for long-range passenger service. Most airline companies continued to buy dependable prop planes like the Constellation and the DC-7. The British developed the Comet jetliner, but it had serious flaws and progress was set back by a series of fatal crashes. When Boeing produced the 707 jet prototype, all of that changed. As in earlier phases of aviation, military necessities led to civilian advances and the first successful passenger jet was a by-product of cold war deterrence. The sleek body and swept-back wings of the 707 evolved from the B-52 bomber to become one of the most elegantly proportioned planes ever built.

As usual, Pan Am's Juan Trippe led the way and was the first to order a fleet of 707 airliners. On October 16, 1958, First Lady Mamie Eisenhower stood with Trippe on a wooden platform at Washington National and dribbled a bottle of water collected "from the seven seas" over the silver nose of *Jet Clipper America*. The 707 then set off on the first nonstop commercial jet flight to Europe. The trip took more than seven hours. "In one fell swoop we have shrunken the earth," announced Trippe.[1] *Time* magazine went a step further and calculated that the jet had shrunk the earth by exactly 40 percent. The 707s had a range of over three thousand miles and could fly at six hundred mph, leaping over time zones and international date lines. Time itself seemed more elastic. Night rushed into morning and then back to night again. Passengers became "cocooned in time," as poet John Betjeman put it: "We never seem to catch the running day / But travel on in everlasting night. . . ."[2]

Jets also spawned a new surge in travel. In 1959 more than 51 million passengers flew out of U.S. airports. In the first two years of jet travel passenger figures almost doubled. During the summer of 1961, it was estimated that more than eight hundred thousand Americans visited Europe. Transatlantic traffic increased by 20 percent every year thereafter.

It was a "Jet-Winged World," announced *Newsweek* magazine. While DC-3s had inspired the streamlined style of the 1930s, the first generation of jets decreed the 1960s aesthetic, and changed the look of everything from furniture to fountain pens. The jets themselves—the DC-8s, Boeing 707s, Caravelles—became touchstones for modern designers. Other forms of transportation—including automobiles, buses, and trains—began to imitate the slender look of the jets.

The prefix "jet" was used to sell products evoking speed and modernity and was attached to everything from laundry soap to vacuum cleaners. The Jetsons were the TV family of the future, while the New York Jets were the newest team in the National Football League. Coinages like "jetway," "jetwash," and "jetport" entered the vocabulary, along with a new physiological condition known as "jet lag." (Sleeping pills and/or amphetamines were the prescribed remedies.) Affluent socialites jetted to fashionable watering holes and became known as the international "jet set."

Jet travel also inspired a new look in fashion—for both the stewardesses, who dressed like runway models, and the passengers. *Vogue* advised simple lines and muted colors for the independent

A "jet-winged world" demanded new forms. United Airlines hexagonal boarding satellite at San Francisco International Airport, 1960.

jet-setting woman: "The pale grey suit, its fresh white collar and cuffs, the white straw hat it's worn with, all such were impossible, or at least impractical, before the jets with their clean, unhectic swiftness."³ *The New Yorker* reported the case of a woman who flew from New York to Paris just to have her hair done at a stylish salon and then came all the way back for a ball at the Plaza Hotel that same evening.

The increased sense of mobility would contribute something to the cultural upheavals of the 1960s. The Beatles were a global phenomenon made possible by a combination of jet speed and television. They conducted their first world tour by jet plane and planted the seeds of a musical revolution at every airport along the way.

Trains and ocean liners went into decline as airline tickets became less expensive. Cunard's *Queen Mary* took her last voyage in 1967, as did New York Central's famous pullman train, the *Twentieth Century Limited*. Standby and charter fares brought a new freedom to the younger generation, who could now afford to travel abroad. During the summer of 1960, more than 120,000 American students stayed in European youth hostels. The "junior year abroad" became part of every undergraduate's coming of age. Previously out-of-the-way destinations were now within reach. New kinds of resorts, like Club Méditerranée, specialized in short-term, theme-driven vacations. By the end of the 1960s, Club Med had more than thirty exotic "villages" scattered around the world.

On May 25, 1961, President Kennedy committed the country to a new frontier: ". . . landing a man on the moon and returning him safely to Earth." Indeed, nine months later, astronaut John Glenn orbited the earth three times in the *Friendship* 7 space capsule, traveling eighty-one thousand miles in less than five hours. Passengers on a transatlantic jet flight seemed only one step away from Glenn's outer orbits as Pan Am, half seriously, accepted reservations for the first commercial trip to the moon.

One of the paradoxes of jet travel was its lack of sensation. Speed, jet speed, was something you hardly felt. "My passage through space was unnoticeable and effortless," wrote historian Daniel J. Boorstin, after a jet flight to Amsterdam in 1960. "I had flown not through space but through time."[4] Even though hurtling forward at six hundred mph, the supersonic traveler experienced no sense of momentum. "The jet-man," wrote French philosopher Roland Barthes, "is defined by a coanaesthesis of motionlessness . . . an excess of speed turns into repose."[5]

While the early days of flight created a new awareness of landscape and architecture, the view from the jets made everything look the same. Distinctions were blurred at an altitude of twenty-three thousand feet. "The airplane robbed me of the landscape," complained Boorstin.[6] The only real sense of transition would come in the transfer from one sealed conveyance to the other: from automobile to plane—checking in, hurrying to the boarding gates. But once inside the plane, nothing much happened.

The lack of sensation would be compensated for by the in-flight screening of movies and other forms of distraction. As French critic Paul Virilio noted, the onboard projector would "reinvent the passing parade of a landscape that disappears and freezes in the distancing brought on by altitude."[7] And if movies weren't sufficient then the jet terminals themselves would become environments of pure sensation and supply the missing narrative: a sense of movement, transition, and excitement that flight itself no longer provided.

"What I want," said TWA's president, Ralph Damon, "is a building that starts your flight with your first glimpse of it and increases your anticipation after you arrive. The spirit of flight, inside and out, and nothing less will do."[8] Adjectives such as "winglike," "birdlike," "soaring," "swooping" were used to describe the new airport architecture that often mimicked the look of the jets themselves with air-foil roofs and cantilevered "wings." United Airlines announced that its crescent-shaped terminal in New York was as "streamlined and spacious as the new DC-8 jets it will service."[9]

The new terminal at Lambert Field, St. Louis, was hailed as a "Jet-Age Grand Central Station." Its thin-shell structure was a miracle of modern engineering. Minoru Yamasaki, a forty-year-old Japanese-American architect, wanted the roofs of his terminal to soar rather than anchor themselves to the earth. Three cross-vaulted spaces were connected in a rhythmic sequence to form a 412-foot-long concourse. Panels of heat-resistant glass, 120 feet wide and 32 feet high, filled the elliptical voids between the vaults like grinning mouths. As one critic wrote, the terminal prompted "a feeling of being suspended." Another praised the way its roof vaults seemed to float "like bulbous clouds."[10] It was the first of a new breed, and other architects soon introduced undulating rooflines and hovering forms to create the illusion of constant

(overleaf) Opening day at Lambert Field, St. Louis, 1956. Minoru Yamasaki, architect.

motion. In some cases the terminal interiors were completely revealed through a gaping expanse of safety glass. This added further to a sense that traditional notions of time and space had been usurped. Walls were splayed at extreme angles, twisted and curved. Roofs were engineered to float on pinpoint supports. Interiors were equipped with moving sidewalks, escalators, automated doorways, and revolving baggage carousels. In some cases, kinetic forms of art were commissioned to further emphasize a sense of perpetual motion.

But with all the talk of soaring birds and waveforms, something else was going on with the curves and cleavages of the new jetports. Struggling to find a suitable metaphor for the billowing roofs at Lambert Field, critic Buford L. Pickens compared them to "strange tripartite bras."[11] The cascading veils of glass suggested a kind of architectural striptease—a dimension to the "naked airport" that Le Corbusier had never anticipated.

Sex had always been used to sell commercial air travel—early airline companies lured male passengers with chorus girls dancing on wings—but during the 1960s, the comparisons between jet travel and sexual adventure were explicit. At the heart of every 1960s terminal was the cocktail lounge, a place to strut, flirt, and anesthetize any feelings of preflight dread. Playboys and party girls wandered through departure lounges catching their reflections in floor-to-ceiling mirrors, exploiting the anonymity of international time zones. Sexy dancers entertained jet-lagged businessmen at the Tiger A-Go-Go lounge at San Francisco's airport where, reported *Newsweek*, "two voluptuous tiger kittens, clad in a minimum of tiger skin, waist-length hair switches, and tiger-gold pumps wriggled epileptically at both ends of the bar while some 250 patrons whooped, whistled, banged their glasses, and cheerfully talked of catching later planes."[12] Stories appeared in men's magazines about anonymous encounters on transatlantic flights, while the greatest achievement for jet-setting Don Juans was membership in the so-called Mile High Club: full penetration at twenty-three thousand feet. Advertisements showed leggy stewardesses standing in front of the phallic new jets, inviting male passengers to "come fly with me," while best-sellers like *Coffee, Tea or Me?* chronicled the "aerial and amorous adventures of swinging young 'stews.'"[13]

The center aisles of the new jets became "catwalks in the air." Couture fashion designers like André Courrèges, Pierre Balmain, and Oleg Cassini were commissioned to design seductive uniforms. American Airlines stewardesses wore miniskirts and white mesh stockings. National had kinky tiger prints. United Airlines introduced short, A-line dresses in bright colors with runway stripes down the front.

"Come Fly with Me." United Airlines stewardesses, LAX, circa 1963.

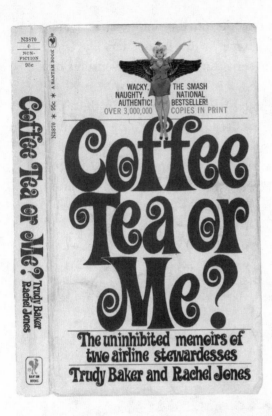

The stews on Southwest wore hot pants and white vinyl boots. But the most overt display of high-flying fashion was on Braniff. "When a tired businessman gets on an airplane, we think he ought to be allowed to look at a pretty girl," said Mary Wells, the advertising agent responsible for Braniff's marketing strategy. Italian designer Emilio Pucci dressed the "Braniff Babes," as they were called, in wildly patterned leggings and bubble space helmets made from Plexiglas. "It was wonderful to watch Braniff hostesses feel so beautiful and begin to walk like models, one foot in front of the other, tra la la, on the planes," wrote Wells, who introduced a promotional gimmick in 1965 called the "Air Strip," in which stewardesses removed successive layers of clothing during the progress of a flight.[14]

Braniff's makeover went beyond uniforms, however, and included everything from planes to swizzle sticks. Each plane in the company's fleet of 707s was painted a different shade of bright blue, green, yellow, red, or brilliant turquoise. The seats inside were covered in matching Herman Miller fabrics. There were seven different color schemes in all: "You can fly with our airline 7 times and never fly the same color airplane twice."[15] The company's new advertising slogan was: "The end of the plain plane. We don't get you there faster. It just seems that way." Top interior designers were also brought in to redesign Braniff's check-in counters and waiting areas in equally daring motifs. For Braniff's home base at Love Field in Dallas, Alexander Girard created a mod entry with op-art murals and ceilings faceted with tiny dangling mirrors. The departure lounge had Marimekko-style decorations, and the baggage carousels in the arrivals hall were painted with undulating bands of color.

A modern form of airport romance had been evolving for some time, but the game came to fruition in the jet age with its own cast of stock characters and plots. Airline thrillers like Ernest K. Gann's *The High and the Mighty* and Hank Searls's *The Crowded Sky* established the basic formula in which pilots were brave and handsome, passengers were skittish and demanding, and stewardesses were beautiful and willing. The hardware of aviation was juxtaposed with the soft contours of stewardesses' bodies. "[The pilot's] eyes

Braniff stewardess in uniform designed by Emilio Pucci.

passed down the line of her immaculate white blouse," wrote Gann, "pausing only a moment to sense again the full breasts beneath it."[16]

Her Majesty's secret agent, James Bond 007, always found a moment between flights to flirt with beautiful women: "At London Airport, Bond unconcernedly went through the baggage and ticket routine, bought himself an *Evening Standard,* allowing his arm, as he put down his pennies, to brush against an attractive blonde in a tan traveling suit who was idly turning the pages of a magazine," wrote Ian Fleming in *Diamonds Are Forever.*[17] In *Crash*, English novelist J. G. Ballard made Heathrow a fetishistic backdrop for characters who cruised London's airport periphery in a "state of intense excitement, thinking of the strange tactile and geometric landscape of the airport buildings, the ribbons of dulled aluminum and areas of imitation wood laminates."[18]

Terminal City

Airports of the 1960s offered urban planners a new template for the modern city—one that would resolve the problem of the old city center by ignoring it altogether. Gigantic new complexes were built expressly to accommodate jet travel. They were no longer like cities, but were real, self-contained urban nodes, servicing millions of passengers a year and hiring thousands of employees. By the mid-1960s, Idlewild/Kennedy was providing employment for over nineteen thousand people earning collectively over $150 million a year. Jet-age airports would have their own police and fire departments, power plants, fuel dumps, dentists, doctors, hotels, conference centers, and, in some cases, theaters, nightclubs, and churches.

As *Newsweek* reported: "The drab and drafty barracks-like airports of a decade ago have mushroomed into sprawling, self-contained urban complexes where travelers can sleep, shop, imbibe Scotch and status at a VIP lounge, fill a tooth, or dance the frug."[19] Companies built their plants as close to airports as possible, which

The
Crowded
Sky

by

Hank Searls

author of

THE BIG X

speeded the evisceration of old downtown areas. "The airport area is like the city for businessmen now," said the manager of an airport hotel in the early 1960s. "They fly in during the morning, meet here all day, have a few drinks and dinner, and fly out that night."[20] This was a peripheral kind of urbanism that foreshadowed the "edge cities" of today.[21] Attempting to explain the trend, *Time* magazine ran a five-page feature called "Airport Cities, Gateways to the Jet Age" in 1960. The mother of all airport cities, explained *Time,* was Idlewild.

To follow the development of Idlewild from its inception in the 1940s to 1963, when it was renamed John F. Kennedy International, is to witness the evolution of the modern airport in all its excesses and failures.[22] Over such a span of time, it is impossible to point to a single person, an auteur, who can be wholly credited with its creation. It would take several mayors and legions of administrators, planners, architects, engineers, landscape architects, and other specialists to accomplish the task.

On June 1, 1947, Austin J. Tobin, executive director of the Port of New York Authority (PNYA), signed a fifty-year lease with the city of New York for the Idlewild territory. Along with its control of bridges, tunnels, bus terminals, and docks, the authority was now guardian of the city's airports. (Besides getting a token rent, the city would receive 75 percent of net revenues.) The airport's name was officially changed from New York Municipal to New York International Airport (NYIA), but Idlewild, the name of the old golf course, was the one that stuck.

Tobin, the grandson of an Irish immigrant dockworker, had begun his career at the PNYA in 1927 as a law clerk. He worked his way up to executive director in 1942 and ruled over the waterways and skyways of New York for the next thirty years. Tobin, like Robert Moses, wielded enormous power but kept a low profile—the *Wall Street Journal* called him a "brilliant bulldog." His mandate was to integrate the metropolitan airports into a system that could keep pace with escalating air traffic.

Tobin hired Thomas Sullivan as the authority's deputy director of aviation and by 1953, Sullivan's team had completed a tentative scheme called "master plan E," which called for a single centralized terminal with enough space for fifty-five boarding gates. By this time, however, traffic estimates were escalating. In 1949, only 250,000 passengers passed through the drafty halls of Idlewild's temporary terminal, but it was estimated that by 1957 there would be over 5 million. Airline executives pleaded with Tobin. They wanted more space and anticipated the need for 150 gates or more. Eddie Rickenbacker of Eastern and other executives threatened to take their business to Newark Airport so Tobin and Sullivan reconsidered the options.

It was apparent that a single centralized terminal would need to be over two miles long to handle the flood of expected travelers. Such a building would strain the envelope of architectural feasibility, not to mention the well-being of passengers who would have to trudge down long corridors to reach their planes. At some point in the discussion, in some dim chamber of the Port Authority's headquarters at 111 Eighth Avenue, someone put forth a novel concept. Forget the idea of a single terminal. Break things up. Decentralize. ("Dispersal" was the official term used.) Rather than a single megastructure, the airport would have a cluster of separate structures connected by a looping access road, all fitting within a 655-acre area called Terminal City.

It was a concept derived from the early "unit terminal" experiments of Albert Heino: the distance between car and plane would be reduced, and the airline companies would be given control over their own environments. Drawings from the period show ten terminals poised like remnants of Harrison's Peripheral Building but broken up into shorter sections, like sausage links that had been cut from the original loop. In the earlier drawings, all units were identical, cookie-cutter modernist, the "long and uniform barriers" that Joseph Hudnut once prescribed. But now each terminal would be different and the airline companies would hire their own architects to outdo one another in architectural bravado.

Critics of the concept complained it would create a hodgepodge of contrasting styles, a cheap circus atmosphere. But that was exactly what was wanted, something flamboyant, a tourist attraction to advertise the airlines. "A showplace atmosphere is being built into New York's International Airport at Idlewild," reported the *New York Times* in 1957, "and over the next few years the airport will gain a reputation not only as the world's best and most modern air terminal but as a major sight-seeing attraction in the metropolitan area, on a par, say, with Rockefeller Center and the United Nations."[23]

Idlewild would be more than just a brash promotion for New York and the wonders of jet flight. It would be an advertisement for the American way of life at a time when democracy itself seemed under imminent threat. The airport's opening years coincided with peak events of the cold war: the U-2 spy plane incident in 1960, the raising of the Berlin Wall in 1961, the Cuban Missile Crisis in 1962. Billed as the modern gateway to the "free world," Idlewild displayed all the virtues of American culture—abundance, diversity, mobility, freedom—within a single sweeping gesture. (There was a reason the central area was called Liberty Plaza.) Pressing the point, Harrison Salisbury of the *New York Times* reported that the terminal area alone was bigger than the total acreage of Moscow's airport.[24] For millions of hopeful immigrants this would be the first impression, before the Statue of Liberty or the Empire State Building: the showy terminals and dancing fountains of a jet-age Ellis Island.

This vision of Idlewild was still in the future, however. Work at the site dragged along and the Port Authority was receiving hostile criticism.[25] The airport, explained Tobin in his own defense, was the most complex kind of undertaking, one that required "the combined talents of Rube Goldberg, Nostradamus and Einstein."[26] Under pressure from Robert Wagner, New York's new mayor, Tobin finally held a press conference in January 1956 and unveiled a scale model of the final version of Terminal City.

In the past, airports had been designed with the pedestrian in mind. Idlewild would "substitute driving for walking," as one planner put it, and create an environment that was designed as much for the automobile as it was for the airplane: "The accomplished marriage of the automobile and the airplane in the travel pattern is thus accommodated."[27] A similar kind of thinking was reshaping the entire American landscape during this period. More than ten miles of roadway were built in and around the airport grounds, with overlapping pretzels, high-speed interchanges, and enough parking for six thousand cars. Terminal City was starting to look more like a suburb than a city—its kidney-shaped loop closer in spirit to the subdivisions of Long Island than the clustered spires of Manhattan. Perhaps the most conspicuous display of car culture was the Gulf gas station placed at the ceremonial entrance to the airport. But this wasn't just any gas station. It was a white, flat-roofed temple to the gods of internal combustion designed by Edward Durrell Stone, the architect who had designed the United States embassy in New Delhi. His Idlewild gas station was a miniaturized clone of the embassy, complete with the same flat, overhanging roof, slender columns, and sculpted *brise-soleil* in front.

No provisions had been made for rapid-transit links, even though two of the city's subway lines came within striking distance, and a stop on the Long Island Rail Road was only a few miles away. Instead of mass transit, millions were spent on a new highway system. Original calculations predicted that ten thousand people would arrive by car at Idlewild every hour during peak periods. That might have been manageable, but the numbers quickly doubled, and as soon as it opened, the Van Wyck Expressway was jammed with traffic.[28]

In spite of its highway-style organization, an effort was made to impose a classical axis on the Idlewild landscape and unify the tangled web of roadways and runways. At the center would be the 220-acre Liberty Plaza expressly designed for the pedestrian, not the car, and intended to "relax the tensions of travel by enchanting the eye." This appears to have been the work of Wallace Harrison, who was rehired as "coordinator of exterior architecture." His mission was to advise on the overall placement of buildings, roads, and landscaping so that Terminal City would be as beautiful from the air as it was from the ground.[29]

Harrison had developed a particular talent for applying thematic glue to complex urban projects as he had at Rockefeller Center, the 1939 New York World's Fair, and the United Nations Headquarters. For Idlewild he wanted to provide an overarching allegory and a sense of historical gravitas that the airport otherwise lacked. Harrison and his team studied the layouts of eighteenth-century formal gardens. From the air, the long allées and reflecting pools of Versailles were surprisingly similar to the runway geometries of Idlewild.

A pedestrian bridge would extend from the main arrivals terminal and connect with a ramp that encircled the 220-foot-diameter Fountain of Liberty. At night, the fountain was illuminated with candy-colored lights that flashed on and off in an "ever-changing spectacle" on a repeating, six-minute cycle.[30] The central plaza stretched northward with three smaller fountains and alternating beds of tulips. Here Harrison appears to have taken his cue directly from an early layout of Versailles, where three similar fountains had been aligned in diminishing diameter to create the illusion of a forced perspective. At its midpoint, the plaza bisected an artificial lagoon to form a giant cruciform that could be seen from high in the air.

Thus, the gardens of Versailles, the antithesis of democratic values, were a model for Liberty Plaza. Both Versailles and Terminal City, however, were designed to suggest a sense of limitless possibility. Just as the distant outposts of Louis XIV's empire had been symbolized by the grand alignments of Versailles, so, too, did the air corridors of Idlewild symbolize the trajectories of American capital reaching around the globe. The glass hall of Idlewild's arrivals building replaced Louis's château in its position of honor. The long transverse axis of the "canal" at Versailles became the "lagoon" at Idlewild. The Basin of Apollo became the Fountain of

Echoes of Versailles at Liberty Plaza, Idlewild/Kennedy International Airport, New York, 1960.

Liberty, and in place of the Petit Trianon there was a little glass temple to technology: the Central Heating and Refrigeration Plant that contained the airport's mechanical heart.

This utility building marked the end point of the long axis that cut through the heart of the airport. Its mechanical workings were displayed in full fetishistic glory through a facade of glass. Valves, pipes, absorption chillers, water boilers, and generators were painted different colors: red for hot-water plumbing, green for chilled water, orange for electric conduits, etc., to create what one visitor called "a pastel forest of color-coded piping."[31]

Thousands of sightseers visited Idlewild when it finally opened, lured by the promise of bright lights, inventive architecture, and in-transit celebrities. They walked through Liberty Plaza and gazed out over the green lagoon. The sound of splashing fountains was drowned out by the roar of jet engines. For a few years the plaza was a popular showcase, "a sort of permanent world's fair," as one magazine reported, but it wouldn't last long. The fountains, tulips, and gravel walkways were torn up a few years later to make room for parking.

Around the circumference of Idlewild's theme park center arose a series of unit terminals, known as the "Seven Wonders." The first to open was the International Arrivals Building (IAB) designed by J. Walter Severinghaus, a "gravely soft and measured" architect who worked for Skidmore, Owings, and Merrill.[32] His experience building airfields for the U.S. government in Morocco made him a logical choice for handling the air-to-ground complexities of the arrivals building.

The IAB was designed to be an architectural fulcrum for the overall airport scheme. It would process millions of passengers arriving from overseas, with special areas for immigration, customs, and health services. Even though it was called the arrivals building, it would also house departure lounges for fourteen different foreign airlines that didn't have their own terminals. The $30 million IAB would be the largest structure built at Idlewild, designed for pure function as an interface between the airplane and the automobile.

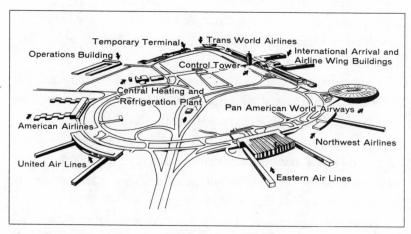

Map of the Idlewild loop and the "Seven Wonders," 1962.

Long thin arms stretched out on either side of the central hall in arcades of aluminum and glass. To draw attention to the central arrivals area, Severinghaus added a parabolic roof that looked as if it might spring into flight at any moment, but was ceremoniously "grounded" by massive concrete anchors. The silver arch made a highly visible landmark from both the ground and the air.

Outgoing passengers used the second floor of the terminal, while arriving passengers deplaned on the ground floor, passed through immigration, and then entered a customs inspection area with supermarket-style counters. These devices, with their rubber conveyor belts, added to an impression that one had arrived in the ultimate consumer state. A glass-enclosed mezzanine known popularly as the "fishbowl" provided the voyeuristic pleasure of watching arriving passengers muddle through customs.

"Now, at last, New York opens its glittering portal to a jet-age world," reported one journalist when the IAB opened its doors.[33] Columnist Harrison Salisbury kindly compared it to a "chromium temple of travel," but the IAB was closer in spirit to a corporate campus. The building stretched out in a kind of modular insanity. It was twenty-three hundred feet long, the equivalent of eleven city blocks. Multicolored diagrams were printed up to help people find their way around, but the terminal was impossible to grasp as a single entity. To fit into the commemoration brochure, a rendering of the terminal's facade had to be printed on three foldout pages.

In contrast to the IAB's uniformity were the independent airline terminals, a grab bag of late modernist trends. As soon as one terminal was finished and hailed as the cutting edge, the next came along to upstage it. Eastern Airlines' terminal opened in October 1959 with ramps suspended from stainless steel cables that were stretched tautly from the ceiling like the strings of a celestial harp. Cars could drive right through the terminal beneath a glass-and-steel porte cochere. United's terminal opened the same year and was praised for its restrained elegance and logical circulation. Its cantilevered canopy suggested the shape of an aileron and echoed the curve of the Idlewild loop. Northwest Airlines built a terminal next

"A chromium temple of travel"—the International Arrivals Building at Idlewild, 1959. Skidmore, Owings, and Merrill, architects.

to Eastern's that featured a two-level entryway protected by a honeycomb of concrete toadstools. Eastern, United, and Northwest were eclipsed by American Airlines, however, whose $14 million terminal was designed to evoke the company's exotic South American destinations. Across the facade was the world's largest stained-glass window—an abstraction of thick, fractured glass—while inside was a mural by Carbyé, a Brazilian painter, depicting lush jungles and tropical birds. All of these architectural wonders, however, would soon be overshadowed by Pan Am's new terminal that seemed the cutting edge of airport design, at least for a few months.

Juan Trippe wanted a terminal that would announce to the world that his company still ruled the skies. To that end he encouraged architect Walther Prokosch to go all out and create the ultimate terminal. Prokosch, who had coauthored an influential book on airport planning, believed that scientific management was the

(opposite) Supermarket-style customs in the IAB at Idlewild, 1960.

answer: "Every device must be pressed into service to effect the maximum usefulness of all parts of the terminal," he wrote and proceeded to experiment with as many new devices as the $12 million budget would permit.[34]

Trippe wanted to avoid the long appendages that encumbered other terminals, so the structure was shaped elliptically. Passengers would never have to walk more than a few hundred feet to their planes. The four-acre roof was engineered to hover like a giant umbrella—its fin-shaped girders supported by a ring of thirty-two concrete piers. Jetliners could nose up beneath a protective overhang like "animals to a trough." A steel "passenger bridge" was then swung out and attached to the door of the plane.

From the land side, the terminal was entered through a hundred-foot-wide opening that was protected from the elements by an invisible curtain of warm air blown through nozzles in the floor. The air curtain was protected by a wind screen decorated with signs of the zodiac sculpted by Milton Hebald. The architecture was enhanced by an ingenious lighting scheme designed by theatrical lighting expert Jean Rosenthal, "to further dramatize the spacious interior and sweeping exterior."[35] Each column was lit from below so the whole building appeared to hover at night. The roof was perforated by a ring of small openings that, from the sky, appeared like a bright necklace. The Panorama Restaurant floated high above the main concourse like something out of the *Jetsons,* complete with space-age decor and clear Lucite furniture.

The terminal opened in June 1960 and was hailed by the press as a "tour de force."[36] How could anyone top this? It made Idlewild's other terminals look primitive. But Pan Am would be upstaged a few months later.

Uplift

The peripatetic architect Eero Saarinen had just flown halfway around the world, but he was out of breath from running the last

The car meets the plane at Northwest Airlines terminal, Idlewild. White and Mariani, architects, 1960.

Pan Am terminal, Idlewild. Walther Prokosch of Tippets-Abbett-McCarthy-Stratton, architect, 1960. Rendering by Hugh Ferriss.

twenty yards. He rushed into the conference room and apologized for being late. "Sorry," he said. "The plane was delayed in Fiji." The startled jurors had already worked their way through 230 entries and made a preliminary cut for the new Sydney opera house. Not seeing anything that caught his eye, Saarinen went through the rejects, so the story goes, and noticed an unusual entry by Danish architect Jørn Utzon. It showed a series of interlocking shell vaults that resembled sails soaring out toward Sydney Harbor. Saarinen pulled it out of the pile and began to convince the others that this was unquestionably the most interesting submission, "capable," he explained, "of becoming one of the great buildings of the world." By the end of the day, the decision was unanimous and Utzon's proposal was the winner.

Just a few weeks before his trip to Australia, Saarinen had signed a contract to design TWA's new terminal at Idlewild. The company's motto was "Up, Up and Away with TWA," and its president, Ralph Damon, was hoping to boost the company's image by every means possible. Saarinen wanted to make a bold statement—something that would stand out from Idlewild's other flamboyant terminals.

During his flight back from Sydney, an idea began to emerge. With Utzon's opera house still fresh in his mind, Saarinen sketched curves and vaults on the back of the airline menu, allowing his pencil to do the thinking. One sketch had a pair of swelling forms resting on two narrow points that looked like the talons of a hawk. Another sketch resembled a turtle with its head retracted. By the time Saarinen's plane landed in Detroit, the fragmentary forms were starting to congeal into something.[37]

A few days later, Saarinen was eating breakfast, pondering the grapefruit rind that sat on his plate. He flipped it over to make a simple dome, then cut a few incisions with his knife and began to play with the V-shaped flaps of rind.[38] When he arrived at his studio, he continued to refine the details and figure out how to turn a grapefruit rind into a terminal. Saarinen had studied sculpture and, in some ways, felt himself a sculptor before anything else. He proceeded to cut shapes out of cardboard. He modeled lumps of clay and made plaster casts. He and his staff built dozens of models to further their understanding of the structure and how it might come to rest on such narrow supports. (At one end of the studio they assembled a model out of cardboard that was so big Saarinen was able to climb inside and make changes.)

While Utzon's opera house may have provided an initial spark of inspiration, Saarinen was influenced by other sources including the expressionist drawings of Erich Mendelsohn, such as *Sketch for a Hall* (1915) with its overlapping waveforms, and Minoru Yamasaki's terminal at Lambert Field, St. Louis. (Saarinen had seen the St. Louis terminal at various stages of its construction and at one point he even asked Yamasaki to see the drawings.)

But Saarinen wanted to take his concept a step further. The soaring roofs at St. Louis rested on a plinthlike foundation that essentially anchored them to the ground. The effect was serene but static. Saarinen wanted the architecture of his terminal to be a "place of movement and of transition," he wrote. "We wanted an uplift."

The two wings of his early sketches evolved into four intersecting vaults that measured 50 feet high and 315 feet long. The larger sections were like the wings of a bird that stretched laterally in daring cantilevers to the north and south. The smaller sections formed a beaklike canopy over the front entrance, while the concrete "tail" covered a sunken waiting area. "The shapes of the vaults were deliberately chosen in order to emphasize an upward-soaring quality of line, rather than the downward gravitational one common to many domed structures," wrote Saarinen.[39] Long narrow skylights sliced through the shell of the roof, bringing natural light to the inner recesses and articulating the different roof sections.

Everything inside the terminal—flight information board, lights, staircase, railings—was designed to be part of a total environment in which each part was the natural consequence of the other, all belonging to what Saarinen called the same "form-world." Even the heating ducts ("air fountains") looked like free-form sculptures rising off the floor. The semicircular waiting

TWA terminal, Idlewild/Kennedy.
Eero Saarinen, architect, 1962.

lounge was a softly cushioned environment, a bit like the conversation pits that were popular in the 1960s—with deep red carpeting and a convex window that slanted out toward the airplanes and the drama of flight. Few other architects could have convinced their client to risk building such an unconventional piece of architecture, but the airline business had become so competitive that this level of bravura was actively encouraged.

Saarinen was seeking a modern kind of monumentality, one that acknowledged the dynamism of the jet age. "Our architecture," he said, "is too humble. It should be prouder, much richer and larger than we see it today," and, to a degree, he succeeded.[40] When his bird terminal opened on May 28, 1962, it was hailed by many as a major work of art. (Not since Tempelhof had an air terminal made such an impact.) But Saarinen himself missed the tributes to his success. In August 1961, he had been diagnosed with a brain tumor and died shortly after at the age of fifty-one.

Saarinen's triumph at Idlewild spawned a whole school of acrobatic airport design. The most distinctive feature of Atlanta's new jetport was a barrel-vaulted roofline that projected out from the terminal like the path of a bouncing ball. Inside the main concourse was a metallic mobile that spun and jangled in the downdrafts from the ventilation system. (Designed by sculptor Julian Harris, it was meant to represent a phoenix rising from the ashes of the Old South.)

Every device was employed to draw attention to the new terminals. Ferro-cement mushrooms sprouted at Newark's new jet terminal, while a forest of treelike columns supported the crystalline forms of a hyperbolic paraboloid roof at the terminal in Memphis, Tennessee. Pointed beaks of concrete swept up from the ground to greet the planeloads of gamblers who arrived at Las Vegas's new terminal. Inside, there were rows of slot machines and a cocktail lounge with a forty-four-foot mural depicting the history of gambling.

Jet-Doric

The press as well as the general public loved the soaring airport style. It made air travel more fun, and even nonflying sightseers came out to look and soak up the atmosphere. But while many applauded Saarinen and his imitators, others thought their terminals were little more than overblown advertisements for the airline business, what one journalist called "three-dimensional billboards."

Purists were offended by the flamboyance and impracticality of such excess. Not only were these structures expensive and difficult to build, but they were usually inflexible to the changing needs of aviation. Peter Blake, editor of the *Architectural Record,* compared Saarinen's TWA terminal to an enlarged Danish modern salad bowl. Ada Louise Huxtable, architecture critic for the *New York Times,* thought it represented all that was demeaning about the jet age: "The modern traveler, fed on frozen flight dinners, enters the city, not in Roman splendor, but through the bowels of a streamlined concrete bird," she wrote.[41] If the dynamic styles of TWA and Las Vegas constituted a kind of jet baroque, there was sure to be a countermovement and a return to classical forms.

One final piece of the Idlewild/JFK puzzle remained to be filled in. It was an open lot at the northeast end of the loop, just to the left of the TWA terminal. The Port Authority considered building a multiuse facility for several domestic airlines and a design competition was announced. Most of the entries were, predictably, of the soaring/Saarinen school, including an undulating pavilion by Philip Johnson and a splayed concrete octopus by B. Sumner Gruzen. An unlikely entry by I. M. Pei, however, impressed the jury with its elegant restraint and it was chosen as the winner.

Pei's concept was to complement, not compete with, the expressive character of neighboring buildings—in particular Saarinen's terminal. "This was not a time to add to the chaos of the airport experience, but rather to try to alleviate it," said Pei, who vowed to create an "island of conspicuous serenity."[42] Presentation renderings showed a transparent pavilion that appeared to have no walls at all, just a flat roof suspended by sixteen flaring, bonelike columns, while a pair of glass tubes led to the planes. As the design evolved, the columns grew less organic and became minimal, jet-Doric cylinders, made from cast concrete. The final version of the slablike roof was composed of steel tetrahedrons hovering atop stainless steel bearings that were set in the top of each column to permit thermal expansion.

Pei believed that the skinlike effect of curtain walls was ultimately ruined by steel mullions, so a system of vertical glass stabilizers was used instead. These finlike attachments were glued to the outside surface with clear epoxy to provide the necessary bracing. All opaque surfaces, including the columns and the broad fascia, were either white or off-white in color. Travertine marble was used on the floors, and white-coated aluminum was used for interior partitions. It made for a pale, soothing pause in the cluttered skyline of the Idlewild loop. Automotive approaches to the building were kept on a single level to retain architectural integrity. A "split" roadway brought cars to both sides of the terminal, with departures in front and arrivals at the back. The multiairline concept was eventually scrapped and the "Sundrome," as it was soon known, became the jumping-off point for National Airline's economy flights to Florida.

Similarly classical themes were adopted at other airports. Newark Airport, which had been allowed to fall behind Idlewild, reopened with two pseudoclassical terminals. Parabolic umbrellas were cast in concrete and supported by sixteen tapered columns, the same number as the Parthenon.43 "Our technology today has brought chaos," wrote Minoru Yamasaki, who designed a temple-like terminal for Eastern Airlines at Logan/Boston (1969). "We have speed, traffic, fear, congestion, and restlessness. We need a place to put our lives in balance."44 Precast columns were spaced at sixty-foot intervals to create the feeling of airy suspension amid the airport clutter. Like Pei, Yamasaki wanted his terminal to be free of ungainly ramps, so he placed the parking on the upper floors and disguised it behind a screen of plastic grill work. Cars entered at basement level and ascended to the roof on spiraling ramps concealed within the body of the building.45 (While he went on to design other airport projects, Yamasaki would be remembered best for designing the doomed towers of the World Trade Center in New York.)

The most compelling and ironic shift away from jet-baroque tendencies may have been by Eero Saarinen himself. After considering several options, the federal government, in the form of the

National Airline Sundrome, Idlewild/Kennedy. I. M. Pei, architect, 1960. *(top)* Rendering of interior. *(bottom)* Exterior view as built.

Federal Aviation Administration (FAA), decided to build its own airport in Fairfax County, Virginia. When Saarinen won the job, he promised a "great entrance to the United States, not just another airport," and set out to improve on what he had accomplished in New York. At Idlewild/Kennedy he had been forced to work in a cluttered arena of competing architectural styles, but in Virginia the canvas was empty. The site was ninety-eight hundred bucolic acres buffered from urban sprawl by a forest, twenty-seven miles west of Washington, D.C.[46] It would be called Dulles International, after John Foster Dulles, Eisenhower's secretary of state, who had flown abroad on so many diplomatic missions during the cold war.

Saarinen wanted to make a freestanding object, without any of the parasitic attachments that ruined so many other terminals. There would be no ugly fingers or boarding satellites, just a pavilion of white concrete rising from the plain of Chantilly, a concept made possible through the invention of a vehicle called the "mobile lounge"—"a cross between a bus and a waiting room"—which could carry eighty passengers from the terminal out to the planes. While it had its own problems, the mobile lounge allowed the building to remain a single, pristine entity.

"Architecture consists of placing something between earth and sky," said Saarinen, and at Dulles he made the sky itself his medium, inviting it into sensual union with the earth. Walter McQuade, writing in *Fortune,* called the finished terminal "a gigantic oriental dreadnought riding the swells of a sea of land," but most saw it as a jet-age interpretation of classicism.[47] If TWA had been "birdlike," the terminal at Dulles was, according to *Time* magazine, "templelike" with its columns, Medusa-white concrete, and handsome proportions. The 150-foot-span roof was shaped like an inverted shield, slung between sixteen sloping columns that penetrated its surface through grommet openings. There were no right angles anywhere except for a central downspout that drained water from the great sky-roof. The breathless effect was further enhanced by the bucolic setting and the distant backdrop of the Blue Ridge Mountains. As counterpoint to the lateral stroke of the roof, Saarinen gave the 193-foot control tower an exotic and mysterious pagoda form.

World Way

When finished, Idlewild was hailed by some as the prototype for future airport planning— a "technological primer of jet age

Dulles Airport. Eero Saarinen, architect, 1962.

forethought," pronounced *Time* in 1960. Airport authorities around the world were expected to follow its lead, but there was widespread criticism of Idlewild's theme park approach. So many competing styles made for an "architectural zoo," wrote one critic, while another dismissed it as a "great big playground."[48]

While hardly any of the new jetports would copy its eclectic hodgepodge, virtually all would imitate Idlewild's allegiance to the automobile.

Seen from the air, the great complex of O'Hare looked like a giant spermatozoa, its hexagonal head made up of terminals and parking lots, with the long swirling tail of Interstate 90 squirming its way out from the heart of Chicago. This looping kind of access road was something born of the jet and would become the standard connection between the highway and skyway, the axis of entry for airport cities around the world. Chicago's airport development mirrored that of New York's. Midway, the out-of-date, inner-city airport, gave way to a larger, more remote facility fif-

Aerial view of O'Hare Airport, Chicago, circa 1964.

teen miles from the Loop.[49] O'Hare was completed in 1963 at a cost of $120 million and, like Idlewild, was a self-contained city. But unlike New York, there would be no one-of-a-kind terminals. The firm of Landrum and Brown, airport specialists, advised against such excess and pressed their theory of the Three C's—concentration, consolidation, and connection—through all stages of O'Hare's development. There were no flashy gestures or soaring vaults, only a cool symmetry. Modular repetition provided flexibility and ease of expansion. O'Hare's architecture, interior furnishings, and signage would all be consistent with the spare and calculated modernism of Mies van der Rohe. The former director of the Bauhaus had emigrated from Germany in 1938 and moved to Chicago to act as director of architecture at the Illinois Institute of Technology. His less-is-more approach cast a spell over many architects including Stanislav Gladych, the chief designer of O'Hare.

The architecture for Chicago's new airport was as restrained as the narrow lapels and skinny black ties that Gladych himself wore to work every day. Two terminals for domestic flights were connected by narrow glass walkways. The seventy-seven-foot-long pavilions were framed in cast concrete and encased in a curtain wall of gray tinted glass that was held in place by aluminum mullions. At night, the buildings resembled crystalline space stations, with boarding fingers extending onto the apron like spiky antennae. The heart of the complex was taken up by a sprawling parking lot for fifty-five hundred cars and an elevated roadway. The Y-shaped columns supporting the roadway lent a barely perceptible note of contrast to the Cartesian geometry. About the only other ornament in the entire scheme was the application of vertical I beams on the facade of the Heating and Air-Conditioning Plant. These had no functional purpose other than to emphasize the vertical lines of the composition, just as Mies van der Rohe had done at the Seagrams Building in New York.

The problem with Gladych's scheme, however, was that one glass terminal looked exactly like the other, which would be con-

LaGuardia Airport rebuilt for the jet age. Wallace Harrison, architect, 1964. *(top)* Aerial view. *(bottom)* New control tower.

fusing, so a Rotunda Building was placed as a kind of knee joint between the buildings. This circular structure was designed by Gertrude Kerbis as a counterpoint to the rectilinear uniformity of the terminals. It contained a restaurant and cocktail lounge with 360-degree views of the airport grounds. Its precast concrete roof was suspended like a circus tent with steel cables and a central steel ring. While nothing as giddy as Idlewild's wonders, it provided the only moment of frolic in the entire scheme.[50] "O'Hare looks like a giant, sprawling gray factory for processing people instead of things," wrote architect and critic George Nelson soon after the new complex opened.[51]

Airport planners in San Francisco also rejected the helter-skelter style of Idlewild but copied its circulation plan. Welton Becket designed a master plan that would unite all services into a single "cartilaginous" gesture that stretched to the east and west. At the center of the complex was a multistory parking structure and a two-level "belt driveway" that received traffic from the Bayshore Freeway. But the most unified transition between highway and jetway must have been the new terminal that Wallace Harrison designed for LaGuardia's 1960s conversion. An overpass was built off the Grand Central Parkway and Harrison chose to echo its shape in the sweeping curve of the 1,300-foot-long terminal. The tilted roof rose at a winglike 30-degree angle. By marrying the off-ramp to the aileron roof, Harrison suggested a continuity between the turning radius of the car and the glide path of a plane.

In keeping with the automobile-centric nature of Los Angeles, the planners for Los Angeles International (LAX) wanted to keep the cars parked as close to the boarding points as possible. This dictated the overall concept for the new airport. Cars would stream off Century or Sepulveda boulevards, through a four-leaf clover, and enter a U-shaped access road called the World Way, which led to the terminals and then looped back to the east. Cars would be able to park in an area closest to the designated terminal. Each of the major airlines got its own terminal, but unlike Idlewild's smorgasbord,

Valium-shaped boarding pod at LAX.

the architecture was all of a kind: low, long, and consistent with the prefab, strip architecture of Orange County. The seven terminals were connected to Valium-shaped boarding pods through underground passageways. As at O'Hare, everything looked the same. Airline buildings, boarding pods, and multilevel parking structures all blended into the smoggy surroundings. While the concept of "center" may have seemed anachronistic in the sprawl of southern California, a Theme Building was built so people could orient themselves and remember where they had parked their cars. This oddly shaped building had a space-age dome and gangling spider legs to stand out from other structures. Ironically, it became one of the few architectural landmarks in a city devoid of memorable buildings.

Stewardesses and pilots waiting at LAX, 1964.

Automobile traffic and aviation were similarly merged in the large new airports of Europe. The new Leonardo da Vinci Airport (1960) was built on the Tyrrhenian coast of Italy and connected to Rome by a high-speed highway. The $50 million complex was roughly the size of Florence. Orly, the new jetport for Paris, was built twelve miles to the north of the city and also connected by a multilane highway. "[Orly], with its gleaming high steel-blue outline, pure and clean, stands alone at the end of the motorway rushing towards it, into it, under it," wrote one enthusiastic journalist.[52] The main terminal was designed by Henri Vicariot as a sleek, 660-foot-long box, with curtain walls of tinted glass and a reflecting pool in front. "The facades [at Orly] do not have a beginning, middle, or end," noted one critic, "but consist of repetitive elements which could be continued to infinity without any fundamental design change."[53]

In place of Orly's uniform plan, Heathrow evolved over the years in a piecemeal fashion, mirroring the way London itself had grown from a constellation of small villages into a seething metropolis. "Despite some fine buildings," complained one critic in 1962, "Heathrow is still a hopeless jungle."[54] Buildings by Frederick Gibberd and Partners were clustered in a fifty-four-acre island at the heart of the star-shaped runway system, and this central terminal area was connected to the Bath Road by tunnels passing beneath the runways.

By the late 1960s more than 4 million Americans were traveling overseas annually. While mass-market air travel allowed for an unprecedented level of mobility, it also brought an unsettling sense of sameness. George Nelson wrote of the "almost unbelievable synthetic landscape spawned by the jet age," but he wasn't referring just to the immediate environs of the airport, with their "mass modernist" terminals and sprawling support systems. He was describing a broader phenomenon—a synthetic landscape of American-style hotels, restaurants, conference centers, highways—whole new cities, in fact, that were being built in service of the jet. "[There] is now the possibility of moving all over the world without ever, in a sense, leaving home," wrote Nelson. "The Fly-Now-Pay-Later crowd . . . are nervous about the water, food, germs, 'natives', tipping, and all the rest of it," he wrote. "For these queasy multitudes the familiar look of a Hilton in Rome, Cairo, or anywhere else provides reassurance and the guarantee of a sanitary, English-speaking refuge with corn flakes for breakfast."[55]

Sociologist Alvin Toffler called those queasy multitudes the "new nomads" and they were certainly less glamorous than the jet-setters of the early 1960s: "Never in history has distance meant less," wrote Toffler. "Never has man's relationships with place been more numerous, fragile and temporary . . . We are breeding a new race of nomads."56 At the same time, the *Wall Street Journal* chronicled the phenomenon of "corporate gypsies" who jetted restlessly around the globe. The newspaper cited the case of one peripatetic CEO who moved location twenty-eight times in a period of twenty-six years. "I almost feel like we're just camping," confessed his jet-lagged wife.57

CHAPTER 6

The Sterile Concourse: 1970–2000

"As the last gateway to the State, the airport came to resemble the fort."
—*Paul Virilio*

Anti-Airport

It would be nice to imagine a brief period, a golden moment, somewhere between, say, 1958 and 1963, between Pan Am's first jet flight to Europe and the assassination of John F. Kennedy, when advanced technology and American-style marketing produced a perfect, jet-setting age of travel. More airports were built during this period. More money was spent. More fantastic forms of architecture were erected. And more people flew the friendly skies. But if such a period ever really existed, it was over in a nanosecond, and the subsequent fall from grace was swift and merciless.

Airports would reach an almost supernatural level of temporality, leaving little lag time between conception and demolition. When Atlanta's jetport opened in the early 1960s, planners were confident that it would meet airline needs well into the 1980s. But during the opening-day ceremonies Jack Gray, airport manager, told the mayor that the multimillion-dollar facility was already out-of-date. In the brief interval between planning and completion, before the first plane landed, before the first passenger alighted, Atlanta's gleaming new airport had slipped into obsolescence. Conceived for an annual peak of 6 million passengers, it processed more than 9 million in the first year of operations. Like many other airports of the period, Atlanta Hartsfield would spend the next twenty years struggling to catch up.[1]

By 1968, American airports had reached their "bursting point," according to FAA administrator General William F. McKee.[2] The soaring jet terminals of the early 1960s were already too small, and the skies they served were dangerously crowded. Between 1955 and 1972, U.S. passenger traffic rose from 7 million to 32 million, exceeding any other industry in growth during the same period. People who had never flown were queuing up for economy tickets to Europe and beyond. (In 1967, 132 million tickets were sold in the United States. In 1968, 154 million were sold.) "Air transportation is rapidly strangling on its own success," reported *Time* in 1969.[3]

By 1970, O'Hare had become the busiest airport in the world, processing more than 14 million passengers a year. LAX was close behind, and the New York airports were almost reaching their limit. "Within four years we were handling a volume of passengers [at Kennedy] larger than we expected for fifteen years," said Thomas Sullivan, chief planner for all of New York's airports.[4] When the first Soviet airliner flew to New York in the summer of 1968, this symbolic moment of cold war thaw became a national embarrassment when the Ilyushin jet had to circle Kennedy for an hour and a half before being able to land. By the end of the decade, things had gotten so bad that traffic actually decreased. "Air travelers by the thousands are bypassing New York because of the harrowing traffic jams and congestion . . ." reported the *New York Times* in 1970.[5]

To make matters worse, the jumbo jet entered the scene in 1970, demanding a whole new set of standards. Determined to stay ahead of the competition, Juan Trippe ordered twenty-five of the giant 747s and Pan Am was the first to fly jumbo. The inaugural flight left Kennedy on January 22, 1970, and the airline's new chairman, Najeeb Halaby, stood with First Lady Pat Nixon on the dais. Halaby spoke a few words, and then the first lady, wearing a double-breasted wool coat, launched the age of aerial discomfort by pulling the lever on a plastic podium that released a gush of pressurized champagne onto the bulbous nose of the aircraft.

Just when airport architects and engineers had begun to understand the needs of the first generation of jets, they were required to accommodate a machine that was twice as big: 231 feet long, 63 feet high, and with a wingspan of 196 feet. The 747 changed the scale of everything on the field and in the terminals. Runways had to be widened and reinforced to support the Boeing monsters, which weighed in at a concrete-busting seven hundred thousand pounds. Parking aprons also had to be expanded. "Trying to unload a 747 through one of today's airports is like trying to unload the *Queen Elizabeth* through a porthole," wrote one critic.[6] The planes could carry four hundred passengers, so departure lounges and concourses needed to be twice as big. Docking systems, parking structures, hotels, and ground transportation systems also had to be enlarged. The stylish restaurants and cocktail lounges of the 1960s gave way to self-service food courts and fast-food franchises, where herds of rumpled travelers waited in line to buy processed snacks.

The impact of the 747 was particularly felt at Kennedy. Only a few years after completing the first phase of development, New York's Port Authority was forced to spend more than $150 million to upgrade. Taxiway bridges over the Van Wyck Expressway had to be rebuilt to support the jumbos' extra weight. Twelve new loading bridges were added to the international arrivals building. Pan Am's terminal was expanded with additional boarding gates and a 655,000-square-foot wing called the Worldport. When it opened in December 1973, the sprawling extrusion made Walther Prokosch's original jet-set terminal seem minuscule.

Astroway

In time, the free standing terminal lost its architectural identity. The martini-modern aesthetic of the 1960s gave way to an ad hoc

The jumbo jet arrived in 1970 and demanded a new set of standards.

style of hyperextended breezeways: narrow prosthetic piers, flyways, jetways, all devised as schematic solutions to one intermodal dilemma or another. Terminal floor plans began to mirror the complex geometries of air traffic itself—those aerial corridors and approach vectors that filled radar screens. Described as the "leanest structure in history," the finger, or variations thereof, became the panacea for all forms of airport chaos. Some were Erector Set steel and glass; others were sheathed in concrete or ribbed aluminum and stretched between terminals and boarding satellites on the apron. There were straight ones in New York at Kennedy and in Dallas at Love Field, T-shaped fingers in Boston, sprocket-shaped fingers at San Francisco, and "split-finger" piers at Atlanta and Memphis.

Like an architectonic form of kudzu, fingers sprouted everywhere. They connected with ground transportation centers, and straddled highways to reach waffle-stacked parking structures and hotels. Indeed, the finger was the airport's gift to architectural history and would spread beyond the immediate context to shopping malls, multiplex cinemas, and convention centers—all places that demanded seamless enclosure and retail flexibility.

But many found these passageways unnerving and the aerophobic's fear of flying was magnified by such elongated mutations.[7] John Updike described one airport as being a "long rats'-passage of corridors." Others compared the finger to a cattle chute or a "hallway without end." One writer described it as an "above-ground tunnel," but there were below-ground versions, too, like the 420-foot-long sensory-deprivation tubes that burrowed between terminal and satellite at LAX.

A sense of compressed linearity was further extended by automated boarding ramps that provided direct connection between building and aircraft. There would be no more passengers running across rain-smeared tarmacs; no more geriatrics breaking hips on slippery steps; no more skirts blown up in sudden gusts of wind, but something was lost. In the jumbo era passengers became oblivious to the outside world, moving through concourses that were double-glazed and super-insulated to muffle the roar of jet engines. Conventional points of entry and transition disappeared. Glass doors opened automatically at the command of seeing-eye photoelectric cells. Moving sidewalks, escalators, and baggage conveyors whispered hydraulically. Departure lounges became shadowless holding tanks, saturated with Muzak and fluorescent lighting. Video screens, first introduced in the 1970s, glowed dimly with arrival and departure times. The experience was ersatz and vacuum-sealed from beginning to end. It was as if one entered a tube that narrowed in diameter as one passed through concourse, finger, and boarding ramp, and finally entered the body of the plane itself. At the destination end, the process would be repeated, but in reverse. One air terminal of the 1970s was described by its architect as being "a funnel leading from its parking garages and drop-off curb, through a linear concourse directly to its [boarding] pavilion."[8] There was no break or sense of threshold, certainly nothing gatelike in this funneling process, and it started to feel more like simulation than actual travel. "Encapsulation is a good part of the price paid for speed," lamented George Nelson.[9]

As early as 1958, United Airlines had introduced its "aero gangplank," a cantilevered ramp enclosed with stainless steel panels and propelled by a small motorized dolly. It could swivel around in a 180-degree arc and telescope out to meet the planes with a rubberized weather seal that conformed to the shape of the aircraft like the lips of a sucker fish.

There was an ironic side effect to extended encapsulation. While able to fly anywhere in the world in a matter of hours, passengers were now forced to walk longer distances on the ground. "[The fingers] are sheer hell for the traveler, as anyone knows who has hiked what seems miles along these noisy, confusing, crowded, hard-paved, and slippery corridors, baggage in hand and/or babe in arm, anxious to catch a connecting plane," wrote critic Wolf Von Eckardt.[10] By the end of the early 1970s, passengers were walking an average of 650 feet from parking lot to check-in. From check-in to plane was another 950 feet, which made for an average walk of 1,600 feet, five times the length of a football field.[11] In this pre-aerobic era, that was more than some Americans walked in a week. The Everest of airport trekking, however, was O'Hare, which became known in the trade as "cardiac alley." In-transit passengers had to walk, in some cases, over a mile and a half through endless glass tentacles. "I was halfway to Michigan before I got on the plane," complained one weary travel.[12] Internal pedestrian traffic at Atlanta's Hartsfield became so congested that yellow traffic lines were painted on the floors to separate in-transit crowds.

Moving sidewalks helped to accelerate the process, but they added further to an out-of-body sense of dislocation. To help passengers traverse the thousand-foot-long passageways at Love Field in Dallas, engineers devised a system of moving sidewalks that were said to have been the first in airport history. The walkways moved in two directions at the granny-friendly speed of one and a half miles per hour, but they seemed futuristic at the time. Rubes from outlying communities made pilgrimages to Love Field just to ride back and forth.[13]

American Airlines inaugurated a campaign to "take the walking out of flying." At LAX, where passengers had to march 1,250 feet from check-in to plane, the company installed a moving sidewalk in the underground concourse that ran between terminal and boarding satellite. The automated rubber sidewalk was similar to the kind used at Love Field, but it was faster and could make the 420-foot trip in three minutes flat. It was officially called the Astroway—"astro" being the space-age prefix of the day. Public relations were concerned that customers might be frightened away. Conveyor belts were used in assembly-line production for dumb, inanimate objects, not for people. So they invited TV comedienne Lucille Ball to inaugurate the device and show how moving sidewalks were not only safe but fun. (The publicity event was supposed to remind people of the famous episode of *I Love Lucy* in which Lucy, working at a chocolate factory, had to sort a stream of bonbons rushing along the conveyor belt.) She rode the Astroway cracking jokes to a group of reporters who ran along beside her. At first she was unsure of her balance on the moving rubber mat and clutched on to the handrail, but then she gained confidence, raised her arms, and cried to the reporters: "Look, Mom, no hands. . . ."

Mutation

As terminals expanded, passengers became increasingly disoriented. Elaborate information systems were devised to guide them from point to point through the perplexing maze of deregulated space. California architect William Pereira wrote a treatise on motion theory, *A Journey to the Airport,* in which he discussed such aspects as "attraction factors," "desired motion," and "trip analy-

Lucille Ball inaugurates the Astroway moving sidewalk at LAX, 1964.

sis." Continuity could be established by many different means, explained Pereira, not just by signs and pictographs, but by the use of contrasting shapes, shifts in scale, wall textures, bands of color, and repetitive patterns that could be scientifically keyed to a traveler's speed of motion.[14]

Architectural Graphics Associates and other firms specialized in providing clear and consistent signage to help establish continuity in the terminal flow. Lettering and pictograms were simple and bold, easy to read by non-English speakers or someone running to catch a plane. Objects were reduced to simplified icons: the silhouette of a plane to designate a boarding gate; a suitcase for baggage claim; a coffee cup for a restaurant. More abstract symbols were sometimes used in place of words or recognizable icons. The airport in Shreveport, Louisiana, adopted a signage system of hanging metal balls decorated with op-art stripes. Upward swirling lines (in sky blue) pointed to departure gates, while downward swirling lines (in earth tones) pointed to arrival and ground facilities. But airport signs, however universal they were intended to be, assumed a degree of cultural bias that made them unintelligible to many foreign travelers. "This latest mutation in space—postmodern hyperspace—has finally succeeded in transcending the capacities of the individual human body to locate itself," wrote Frederic Jameson. "Color coding and directional signals have been added in a pitiful, rather desperate and revealing attempt to restore the coordinates of an older space."[15]

English critic Reyner Banham compared the airport to a "demented amoeba" grown recklessly out of control, beyond its own confines.[16] Residential and industrial areas alike were invaded by the techno-furniture of approach lights, glide-slope transmitters, and Doppler VOR installations. Towers and flashing strobes appeared unexpectedly in the middle of quiet neighborhoods, while other areas suffered the intrusion of long-term parking lots, freight depots, discount hotels, gas stations, and other outgrowths of airport sprawl.

Harking back to the utopian days of airport design, architects proposed extreme remedies for controlling the demented amoeba. "The airport is that place where things don't seem able to stay put together," wrote Paolo Soleri, who saw the problem as systemic. "To say that this is a sign of dynamism just obscures the issue." Soleri believed that it wasn't just the airport but the mode of transportation that was at fault and compared commercial airplanes to

"Color coding and directional signals have been added . . . to restore the coordinates of an older space." *(top)* Terminal signage designed by William Pereira for his study *A Journey to the Airport*, 1967. *(bottom)* International pictographs for airports, 1970.

"awkward animals."[17] Throwing the "awkward animal" out of the equation, Soleri tried to rethink the paradigm. His "arcological" airport was to be a self-contained ecosystem resting on an insect-like tripod that straddled an artificial lake. Lush gardens would be planted on canisters that floated in the lake. In place of conventional aircraft, Soleri's alternative airport was designed to serve a new kind of Aquarian aircraft, about which Soleri remained characteristically vague. He made reference only to a "saucerlike craft" and left the rest to the imagination—one thinks of Frank Lloyd Wright's "aerotors" and the UFO sightings that were endemic in the Southwest. These mystery aircraft would hover gracefully for a moment before making their descent through a series of shafts that penetrated the megastructure. In the event of an accident, they would fall safely onto a cushioned platform.

Soleri's airport was visionary speculation, but similarly grand schemes were seriously considered during the 1970s. One of the most popular themes was the offshore, island airport, a throwback to Geddes's rotary airport of 1930. The concept provided a neat if naive solution to the nightmare of overcrowded airports. Push the problem offshore, where there was unlimited room for expansion and no litigious neighbors. C. F. Murphy Associates, the architects of O'Hare, proposed an eight-thousand-acre island in Lake Michigan that would serve as Chicago's much-needed third airport. Cleveland considered building a $1.2 billion jetport a mile offshore in Lake Erie, while New Orleans, a city that built its first airport on a man-made peninsula in 1934, now considered building one on concrete pilings in the middle of Lake Pontchartrain.

Engineer Paul Weidlinger designed a universal floating airport system called "FLAIR" in which bubble units made from concrete would support a landing surface. The whole structure would be anchored to the ocean floor by cables.[18] In 1973, the Eggers Partnership developed another island concept called the "Systemodule." A circular dike, two miles in diameter, would be built offshore and connected to the mainland by a tunnel. The Systemodule would solve several urban problems at the same time: providing a major jetport, a waste-processing and landfill area, nuclear power plants, and a harbor and pumping station for superships.

Airport Sublime

The breathless enthusiasm of early jet travelers quickly dissipated. An anti-airport sentiment developed in the 1970s, and the whole industry came under attack. Reports began to appear about faulty, out-of-date equipment. Public trust in the airline business was eroding. George Johnson's book *The Abominable Airlines: An Alarming Report* revealed the truth of midair collisions, shoddy maintenance, and incidents of "laxity in the cockpit."[19] (In one instance, a stewardess was caught cavorting on a pilot's lap midflight.) Outlying communities mobilized against the noise, pollution, and excessive traffic coming into airports. They held rallies, hired lawyers, and sued airline companies and aviation authorities. After being bumped from a flight in 1972, activist Ralph Nader founded a watchdog group called the Aviation Consumer Action Project, which targeted the airlines for unfair practices and lax safety standards. In 1974, the industry got its own version of Watergate when Ted Kennedy chaired Senate hearings on airline corruption that eventually led to the Airline Deregulation Act of 1978. The younger generation of travelers rebelled against high fares and found alternative means of escape by taking cheap charter flights, going standby, or flying Freddy Laker's Skytrain service, which cost less than $100 one way between New York and London.

In the popular imagination, air travel was now equated with boredom and disaster. "On a transcontinental flight by a jet plane," wrote Lewis Mumford, "the actual trip is so cramped, so dull, so vacuous, that the only attraction the airlines dare to offer are those vulgar experiences one can have by walking to the nearest cabaret, restaurant, or cinema: liquor, food, motion pictures, luscious stewardesses. Only a lurking sense of fear and the possibility of a grisly death help restore the sense of reality."[20]

Indeed, the airport was now seen as an allegory for all that was dehumanizing in modern life. It made the perfect background for a tale of youthful alienation, as in the opening scene of *The Graduate* when Dustin Hoffman rides the Astroway at LAX in the fluorescent glow of airport lighting. A robotic voice drones across the loudspeaker system, repeating its message over and over again: "Please hold the handrail and stand to the right. . . ."

The disillusionment with air travel paralleled attitudes in the broader culture. The idealism of the 1960s was slipping into jaded realism, apathy, and paranoia. In 1970, Lieutenant William L. Calley was court-martialed for premeditated murder in the My Lai massacre; Charles Manson was tried for the Tate-LaBianca murders; the Beatles broke up, all in the same year. Jimi Hendrix, Janis Joplin, and Jim Morrison died of drug overdoses. Richard Nixon resigned in 1974 after the revelations of the Watergate scandal. Architecture and fashion took on a more defensive posture, a bulky, insulated look. It was a time of synthetic fabrics, double knits, polyester stretch pants, platform shoes, and wide lapels.

If an earlier generation of fiction had helped to glamorize air travel, a new type of novel explored the dark side of the airport boom. The undisputed *Moby-Dick* of the genre was Arthur Hailey's *Airport,* published in 1968. The story takes place at Lincoln International, a fictional airport based on the first generation of jetports like Kennedy and LAX. The opening pages reveal a dysfunctional airport on the verge of collapse, crippled by a blizzard and labor unrest. "The wind howled across the deserted runway," wrote Hailey. "In the main passenger terminal, chaos predominated."[21] Gwen Meighen, stewardess slut, enters the narrative fully naked, taking a shower. "Her filmy underthings were laid out on the bed," wrote Hailey, "panties, sheer nylons, and transparent bra, flesh colored." Her "pert" body is the only talisman of redemption amid the corruption and mechanical failure of the airport. Even the air traffic controllers, those "celestial rulers" of early aviation literature, had become all too human—prone to nervous breakdown ("going down the pipes"), heart attack, and suicide, like Keith, the manic-depressive controller in *Airport*: "In this darkened, tightly packed radar room," wrote Hailey, "other controllers, as well as Keith, were sweating."[22]

Hailey's best-seller generated a school of trashy airport prose that followed the same formula of crippled airliners and sex-starved stewardesses. In the screen adaptation of *Airport* (1970), a bleary-eyed Dean Martin starred as Captain Vernon Demerest and Jacqueline Bisset as Gwen. This, in turn, inspired a series of spin-offs, including *Airport 1975, Airport '77, The Concorde: Airport '79,* and even a short-lived television series called *International Airport* that aired in 1984.

In high-brow literature, the airport was depicted as a place of sinister brightness.[23] In Max Frisch's *Homo Faber,* the in-transit narrator enters a bathroom at a Houston airport and notices his waxy pallor in the mirror, "like the face of a corpse," before passing out. He reboards his southbound plane only to crash in a Mexican desert. The English poet Stephen Spender characterizes Heathrow as a "landscape of hysteria." Shirley Hazzard describes the "white light, thin air" of an air terminal in *The Transit of Venus* and its "total absence of morning, climate, and substance." Jonathan Raban squints in the glare of airport lighting that burns so "violently white in the surrounding murk" that it hurts his eyes to look at it.[24]

Excessive lighting creates the reverse of Gothic gloom and makes the airport an overlit House of Usher. The apparati of the horror story are replaced by moving sidewalks, jetways, baggage carousels, and X-ray portals. In John Updike's novel *Marry Me,* an air terminal is the setting for a doomed romance. The floor of the boarding gate tips "as if to drain blood," and a steel door is shut tight, "like a gas chamber."[25] In *Fear of Flying,* Erica Jong describes the "gleaming newness" of the lounge at the Frankfurt airport and how it makes her think of "death camps and deportations." Neil Simon's odyssey of urban angst, *The Out of Towners,* opens with a purgatorial airport sequence in which a naive couple are forced to circle Kennedy International for hours before diverting to Logan, where angry passengers storm the baggage carousel. In *The Rings of Saturn,* W. G. Sebald imagines the airport as an antechamber to the hereafter: "The atmosphere at Schiphol airport was so strangely muted that one might have thought one was already a good way beyond this world," he writes. "Every now and then the announcers' voices, disembodied and intoning their messages like angels, would call someone's name."[26]

The Exploding Airport

An increased level of anxiety would pervade the departure lounges of the 1970s as aerial hijackings became more common. The trend not only changed the mood of travel but had a profound effect on airport design. Between 1969 and 1978, there were more than four hundred international hijackings involving over seventy-five thousand passengers. The first wave in America was comparatively benign. Between 1968 and 1972, there were 154 attempted hijackings to Cuba. As one of the hijackers explained, it was the easiest way to get there.[27] But in most of these incidents, the passengers were released unharmed. The next wave, however, was much more bloody and saw a series of Bonnie and Clyde–style abductions. In July 1972, there was a four-hour standoff between FBI agents and two armed men who pirated a commercial airliner. The men wanted $800,000 in ransom, two parachutes, and safe conduct to the Soviet Union; but they were both killed when FBI agents rushed aboard the airliner in San Francisco. Three months later, a group of fugitives shot their way aboard an Eastern Airlines 727 at Houston Intercontinental and managed to reach Cuba. Shortly after that, an escaped convict and two accomplices hijacked a Southern Airways DC-9 and forced the pilot to land at several different airports while demanding $10 million in ransom and threatening to crash the plane into a nuclear reactor at Oak Ridge, Tennessee.

Airline terror became the fastest way for extremists to gain global attention and advertise their cause. The Palestine Liberation Organization (PLO) and other guerrilla factions made airports into the new front line. The evening news showed nightmare footage of terrorists wielding guns out of cockpit windows, passengers and crew being executed, blood-smeared stewardesses running out onto the tarmac. Most dramatic of all was the sight of commercial jetliners being blown to smithereens, as happened in September 1970, when four hijacked planes—a Pan Am 747, a TWA 707, a Swissair DC-8, and a BOAC VC-10—were destroyed in Jordan.

On July 23, 1968, two terrorists armed with automatic weapons and hand grenades attacked an El-Al plane in Athens. Two months later, members of the Popular Front for the Liberation of Palestine ran from behind a snowbank and attacked an El-Al plane on the tarmac at Zurich. On May 9, 1972, two PLO terrorists took over a Sabena 707 at Lod Airport in Israel, demanding the release of three hundred Arab prisoners. A few weeks later, three

The exploding airport: a BOAC airliner, Jordan, September 1970.

unassuming-looking Japanese tourists arrived at Lod and opened fire in the terminal, indiscriminately killing twenty-six and wounding seventy. One of the most audaciously planned actions happened on December 17, 1973, when a band of Palestinian terrorists opened fire inside the terminal at Leonardo da Vinci Airport in Rome. They took ten hostages, ran onto the tarmac, and set fire to a Pan Am jetliner, killing thirty passengers. They then commandeered a Lufthansa plane and threatened to crash it into the ancient center of Athens.

In response to these assaults, airports adopted strict security measures. Special forces were armed with machine guns and stationed inside high-risk terminals. Passengers who had once been treated like royalty were now assumed guilty until proven innocent. They were questioned before boarding. Individuals who looked suspicious or seemed nervous were singled out for interrogation. Bags were inspected by hand, while bomb-sniffing dogs searched cargo bays. Some airports, like London's Heathrow, installed screening devices—"electronic gallows," as they were called—through which departing passengers were required to walk. But the new equipment was expensive, and most airports continued to use old-fashioned methods of visual inspection.

The FAA adopted similar measures for American airports. Anti-hijacking legislation was officially put into effect on January 5, 1973, and all passengers and luggage would be searched before leaving any airport. Narrow points of control were established at the "throat" of each concourse. By the end of January 1973, the first screening devices had been installed at New York airports in compliance with FAA requirements. The contents of carry-on luggage were freeze-framed and magnified on X-ray screens. Lipstick cases, shaving cream cans, and transistor radios all appeared sinister in the low-dosage twilight of the new monitors. Elliptically shaped magnometers were also installed. These portals were made from molded plastic and were just big enough for a single person to walk through. Bells rang and lights blinked when the machines sensed a metallic object. Male passengers were required to empty their pockets of loose change, keys, cigarette lighters. Women removed jewelry before walking through the portals, but metal stays were still being used in girdles and bras, and these often set off alarms. Short of conducting strip searches, security agents were obliged to allow some women to pass through regardless. "There's not much you can do about it, unless we can get the Federal Government to ban metal from all women's foundation garments," explained an airline official.[28]

Interior spaces no longer flowed together but choked to a standstill at security throats, causing backups and short tempers. Moments of departure anxiety were aggravated by the sense of being funneled up another chute like a herd of cattle. In many cases, the screening devices were manned by poorly trained personnel, adding further to a sense of violation.

Despite some complaints, most air travelers accepted the inconvenience as a necessary part of the airport experience. The press managed to downplay the assault on personal privacy and turn it into something lighthearted. The *New York Times* ran a story on January 27, 1973, called "Air Riders Take Search in Stride" that was accompanied by photographs of fashionably dressed young people striding through the new lotus-shaped magnometers at LaGuardia. There was a woman in a miniskirt and high heels; a man with striped bell-bottoms who raised his hands as if being frisked; an African-American woman in sunglasses: "Each passenger going through the TWA security tunnel . . . has his—or her— own style," reported the *Times*.[29]

The electromagnetic gateway became the new point of transition, providing the missing sense of "gateway" that airports had lost in the jumbo-jet age. Departure was no longer determined by distance but rather by clearance. "I never passed through security for a flight to Miami without experiencing a certain weightlessness," wrote Joan Didion.[30] The security checkpoint replaced the boarding gate where lovers and relatives once embraced. Wellwishers now lurked on one side of the machines, straining to watch their loved ones disappear down long corridors. The moment of farewell was strangely deferred by the knowledge that the departee

SATURDAY, JANUARY 27, 1973

The New York Times

"Air Riders Take Search in Stride." Metal detectors go into service at LaGuardia, 1973.

would remain isolated in a sterile lounge for some time before take-off, the poignancy of parting displaced by technology.

The severity of hijackings abated somewhat after security measures were adopted, but magnometers were unable to detect plastic explosives, and determined individuals could still penetrate the system. As if to prove the point, a crazed gunman stormed newly installed security devices at Friendship in Baltimore on February 22, 1974. He killed the guard on duty and proceeded into the departure lounge of Concourse B, wielding his gun and an incendiary bomb. Passengers screamed and ran for their lives. The man boarded a Delta DC-9 and ordered the pilot to take off, but when he refused, the assailant killed him. The public learned later that the man had been incensed over the Watergate scandal and wanted to crash the jetliner into the White House.

A defensive new style of architecture came along to match the anxious mood of the day. Lobbies and concourses designed to be open and flowing were now segregated into "sterile" or "nonsterile" zones, as prescribed by federal regulations: "The perimeter of the sterile concourse must be secured by physical barriers."[31] Exits were sealed, temporary partitions erected, views obscured. Once inside the sterile area, an individual was not permitted to leave without being reexamined. Passengers arriving from foreign destinations were not allowed into any other part of the airport until they had cleared immigration and customs. Preexisting terminals were retrofitted with windowless additions. A seven-hundred-foot-long passageway that resembled oversized ductwork was added to the back of American's terminal at Kennedy so as to isolate arriving passengers.[32]

Posthijack terminals were heavy and grounded, whereas earlier ones had been light and soaring. The sleek and sexy envelopes of the 1960s gave way to blocky concrete and bunkerlike shapes: no more of the seductive curves of Saarinen or Yamasaki. Open-style planning gave way to partitions, narrow corridors, single-entry points, and artificial lighting.

Transparency had suddenly become a liability at the airport. The freely flowing terminals of the 1960s were blindered or mirrored to thwart terrorism and international smuggling. There were unbroken expanses of wall space where once there had been expanses of glass. Transparency was now limited to the X-ray devices that scanned passengers and their personal effects, reversing and internalizing the "view." The famous glass "fishbowl" gallery at JFK's arrivals hall was boarded over in the spring of 1972, fifteen years after it opened. The U.S. Bureau of Customs discovered that smugglers were signaling their confederates from the upper observation level, making it difficult for the authorities to apprehend them.[33]

The architectural style of the day became, as one critic described it, a "beefy concrete idiom," fashioned by security codes and characterized by slabs of cast concrete, massive roofs, and roughly finished surfaces.[34] A variation on Brutalism, it was adapted in part from the late work of Le Corbusier, in particular his monastery at La Tourette, which had thick cloistered walls and small openings. Horizontally splayed structures were surrounded by helical car ramps and megalithic towers that concealed ventilation systems. Multilevel parking structures dominated the landscape and blocked views.

For its terminal at Kennedy, the British airline BOAC (British Overseas Airways Corporation) built a terminal with sloping, tomblike walls that pressed downward in stark contrast to the neighboring TWA terminal.[35] Hellmuth, Obata and Kassabaum designed a Brutalist terminal for Lubbock, Texas, with precast slabs of concrete heaved on top of one another like overscaled building blocks. Curving crossbeams and tapered columns supported the roof of the new North Terminal at Detroit's Metropolitan Airport, conveying a plunging, sacrificial movement—into the earth—like a plane losing altitude.[36] Even the FAA's standardized control tower had the impregnable look of an updated siege tower, isolated and forbidding, precisely the image the agency wanted to convey. Access to the tower was restricted to an underground passageway, so there was no visible point of entry.[37]

Similar trends were followed in Europe, where fortified megastructures were built of bulky concrete, as at the Cologne-Bonn Airport and the Otto Lilienthal Airport in Berlin, both of which looked as if they had been designed to withstand nuclear attack.[38] "As the last gateway to the State, the airport came to resemble the fort," observed French critic Paul Virilio, who may have had in mind the bomb-proof exterior of Terminal 1 at Charles de Gaulle in Roissy-en-France.[39] But inside the circular terminal, architect Paul Andreu had at least attempted to reinsert a sense of visual connection and "center" that had been lost to terrorism.[40] Plexiglas tubes crisscrossed obliquely through the open core so that passengers (riding on escalators) could glimpse people in other transparent tubes arriving from other flights. A feeling of procession and arrival—however vacuum-sealed—was reconstituted within an otherwise blinded sequence.

Roissy was an exception to the rule, however, and the task of humanizing terminals usually fell to interior designers who made valiant attempts to soften hard edges and abrasive surfaces with thick carpeting, fabric art, or contoured couches. Departure lounges were decorated with bright-colored patterns to fill the empty walls and offset the doomsday palette of precast concrete. Circles and rainbow stripes ran the entire length of a concourse at Friendship Airport, Baltimore. For a cheerless lounge at Lubbock, Texas, designers hung cloth banners with oversize numerals that corresponded to the different boarding gates.[41] Instead of lifting spirits, however, these token gestures were reminders of all that had been lost.

Antiterrorist measures turned the airport into an electronically controlled environment rivaled only by the maximum security prison. It was more than mere coincidence that the architects responsible for some of these fortified terminals had also designed penitentiaries.[42] Both the airport concourse and the cell block used similar kinds of logic. Interior and exterior spaces were under twenty-four-hour surveillance from electronic eyes, motion detectors, and video cameras. Both inmates and passengers moved through a similar series of sealed passageways, automatic doors, and narrow checkpoints, where personal screenings were administered with metal detectors and body searches. Only the duration of incarceration differed.

Miami International suffered more aerial abductions than any other airport in the United States and its new arrivals building was designed accordingly. Boarding bridges jutted out from each corner like the redoubts of a medieval fortress, while thick stucco walls and flat roofs added further to a tough, impenetrable look. In keeping with FAA guidelines, there were no windows on the arrivals level except the kind of vertical slits used at prisons. Here was the fortified gateway to the promised land, through which hopeful immigrants would pass, blinded to the outside world until clearing immigration and making their way into the sunny parking lots of Miami.[43]

(opposite) Modern siege tower: the FAA's standardized control tower. I. M. Pei, architect.

Attempting to restore a sense of arrival that was lost to terrorism. Transparent tubes carry arriving passengers to customs at Charles de Gaulle International Airport, Paris. Terminal 1. Paul Andreu, architect, 1974.

Park and Fly

"The design of the master plan," wrote one airport analyst of the 1970s, "has become a problem of such complexity that an intuitive design approach can no longer serve to obtain appropriate solutions."[44] The role of the independent designer would be usurped by analysts who scrutinized the airport as if it were a purely mechanical system. Philadelphia's new airport plan resembled the cross section of a complex filtration device with symmetrical brackets, blocks, and nozzles.[45] Given the scale of their task, planners sought diagrammatic solutions in which everything was simplified in a sequence of interconnected "nodes," interfaces, and modes of transport.

In the arcane parlance of the day, the airport was referred to as the Passenger Processing System, the main components of which were outlined as: (a) "The *access interface* where the passenger transfers from the access mode of travel to the passenger-processing component . . ." i.e., the curb; (b) "The *processing component* where the passenger is processed in preparation for starting or ending an air trip . . ." i.e., the terminal; and (c) "The *flight interface* where the passenger transfers from the processing component to the aircraft . . ." i.e., the boarding gate.[46] Of course, this numbing kind of analysis precluded good architecture as much as it overlooked basic human needs.

Final plans mimicked the look of schematic diagrams and gave rise to an awkward style that came to be known as "intermodal." Square, blockish terminals were attached to doughnut-shaped satellites by narrow ligaments as at Tampa International where a central structure was connected to distant satellites by electric-powered transit cars that whisked travelers back and forth on elevated rails.[47] With starkly bland buildings, massive parking structures, and drive-through access, Houston Intercontinental was another example. But the ultimate expression of the intermodal school was being built in another part of Texas.

J. Erik Jonsson, the mayor of Dallas, believed that Texas—a state that was at the forefront of the oil and aerospace industries—should build an airport that would set new standards for the future. A 17,500-acre site of prairie scrubland was chosen midway between Dallas and Forth Worth. Such a vast tract of real estate would allow for infinite expansion and insulate the airport from the kind of residential encroachment that was plaguing older sites.[48]

Intermodal style at Tampa International Airport. Boarding satellites were connected to the main terminal by electric-powered trams. Reynolds, Smith, and Hills, architects, 1970.

Thomas Sullivan, mastermind of Kennedy, was hired to manage the monumental undertaking. "I made a list of all the things that went wrong in the New York airports and set out to change them," said Sullivan.[49] In an early plan by Walther Prokosch, long fingers projected out from a drive-through terminal like the nerves of a spinal column. Sullivan sensed trouble with Prokosch's under-lying concept and scrapped the plan. "It was another megastruc-ture and I wanted decentralization," said Sullivan. "We did not set out to build a monument." Instead, he explained, the airport would function as an "efficient tool."

The inspiration for Dallas/Fort Worth's park-and-fly concept was a television commercial for Hertz Rent-a-Car, which showed a businessman flying into an airport and literally floating from the plane into the seat of a convertible car. Sullivan loved the commer-cial and kept reminding his new architect, Gyo Obata, that this was what he wanted: an airport in which there was no transition between plane and car.

Obata's plan began with a line in the desert: a central "spine" called the International Parkway that would feed thousands of cars directly into the heart of the complex. Sprouting from this spine would be a series of semicircular terminals, each measuring more than a mile in circumference. "I used a semicircle so I could get more perimeter, so I could put more planes around it," said Obata. There would be no token gestures, no extravagant pavilions. "The Grand Central Terminal approach to airports is outmoded," explained Obata. "Our idea is to have a parking space and out of the parking space you can go directly to the gate. No crowds, no confusion, no pain."

The terminals were connected by a people-moving system called Airtrans. Each of the uniform structures contained its own parking area within a semicircular corral. The plan was open-ended, had no real beginning or end, and could be infinitely expanded. Building units were prefabricated for easy assembly with what one critic described as "clip-on potential."[50] Concrete sections were cast in nearby factories, then assembled on site like parts of a kit.

Dallas/Fort Worth stretched across the Texas landscape like a four-mile-long wagon train, three times the size of Kennedy Interna-tional, larger in total land area than the island of Manhattan.[51] "As far as a man can look (which is barely into the next loop) he sees the

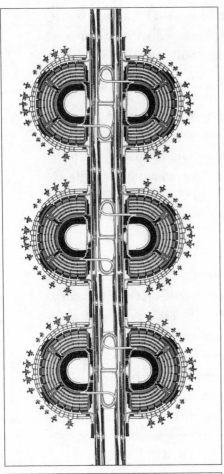

same geometry of forms, the same columns and doors and windows, the same roadways, the same honey-brown concrete," wrote critic Douglas Davis in *Newsweek*. "Both the promise and the threat of Dallas–Fort Worth is summed up in that image."[52] While attempting to push beyond conventional thinking, Obata and Sullivan had conjured up a hybrid structure that was somehow monumental and frighteningly mundane at the same time. Its numbingly repetitive architecture captured the essence of modern jet space, while fostering a new kind of megacity that would mutate around its periphery. Before it was even finished, the outer fringes of the two cities—Dallas and Fort Worth—began to creep toward each other, eventually morphing around the airport into a sprawling blob that came to be known as the Metroplex.

The moment of truth came when Dallas/Fort Worth was ready to open but administrators couldn't decide where to hold the dedication. In all of the airport's 17,500 acres, there was no ceremonial point of entry or convergence, no

(left) The master plan for Dallas/Fort Worth Regional Airport was inspired by a television commercial for Hertz car rental. Gyo Obata, architect, 1973.

distinguishing feature that stood out from the uniform circuitry of honey-brown concrete. Kennedy had Liberty Plaza, O'Hare had the Rotunda Building, Los Angeles had the spacy Theme Building, but Dallas/Fort Worth, airport of the future, was all circumference and no center. This might have been interpreted by some as a mark of success—after all, the original intent was to create complete decentralization—but humans are creatures of habit and continue to need places for gathering and celebrating. At one point Sullivan considered adding something called the Spiritual Center, just for such occasions, but it never materialized. "We will have a dedication," promised Sullivan, "but I don't know where."

Hubs and Spokes

President Jimmy Carter signed the Airline Deregulation Act into being on October 24, 1978, thereby removing federal controls over commercial fares and routes. Deregulation became the dividing line between the modern and postmodern periods of commercial aviation—between the golden days of the jet age and the transportation agonies of today. The passage of the act had an immediate effect on the running of airports. It unleashed an avalanche of competitive bidding, and it brought lower fares, more scheduled flights, and, in turn, more people. Airlines could now choose their airport routes based on market conditions. Service at profitable airports increased, while less popular destinations languished. At the time it seemed like the fair, democratic thing to do, and deregulation had widespread support. It would encourage competition, break the monopoly of the major airlines, and bring affordable airfares. (The number of airlines would increase fourfold.) But deregulation also brought a new level of uncertainty. Before deregulation, no major airline had gone bankrupt, but in its aftermath, several leading companies, including Eastern, Pan Am, and Braniff, went out of business.

Airlines centralized their operations and inaugurated the concept of "hubbing," which was seen as the most cost-effective way to link a network of remote destinations, or "spokes." Since it was impossible to make every route profitable, flights would make one-stop connections via a central point known as the "hub." Delta Airline established its hub in Atlanta, American in Dallas, United in Chicago. To maximize profits, hub airports adopted carefully coordinated patterns of arriving and departing flights at peak business hours. Referred to as "waves" or "banks," these high-density periods brought a sudden glut of passengers rushing through terminals to reach connecting flights.

The problem for airport authorities was no longer how to move passengers from their cars to the planes but, rather, from gate to gate as quickly as possible. The park-and-fly concept of Dallas/Fort Worth was suddenly outmoded. Hubbing demanded "transfer-friendly" configurations. It also increased the pressure on baggage-sorting systems that were obliged to handle much higher volumes of transfer luggage. Circulation patterns changed, and even the most flexible arrangements proved inadequate. "There used to be formulas for the design of airports," complained one architect, "but since deregulation, the formulas simply don't apply."[53] Facilities that were already overcrowded were pushed to greater levels of confusion.

After considering several new locations, the city of Atlanta decided to expand the original Hartsfield site. The 1960s terminal was demolished, and a new complex was built just to the south. The airline companies themselves underwrote the construction, so everything was built as cheaply as possible and without frills.[54] It was estimated that three out of four passengers using the airport would be transferring from one airline to another, so the entire docking complex was designed as a sterile zone so that passengers wouldn't need to go through additional security checks while in transit.

Instead of many security throats, there was a single centralized checkpoint with twelve magnetometers operating simultaneously to avoid delays. The four concourses were separated from one another by a thousand feet of apron, wide enough for two jumbo jets to pass each other. This helped to speed up taxiing and docking times. Each concourse had thirty-four to thirty-six gates and was connected to the main terminal by an underground passageway called the "transit mall." People could either walk, ride a moving sidewalk, or take the people-moving subway. Getting from the terminal to the most distant concourse was supposed to take less than five minutes, in theory.

When completed, the Midfield Complex was the largest civilian air facility in the world, with its cavernous 378-acre main terminal and four concourse buildings. President Carter came to baptize the facility on September 16, 1980—a fitting gesture since it was the first true offspring of his deregulation act.[55] He was on a hectic reelection swing, so he made only a brief speech praising the

By-product of deregulation: Midfield Complex, Atlanta Hartsfield International Airport, 1980.

new complex before turning to more pressing political issues like the Iran hostage crisis.

While hailed as a hubbing success, Hartsfield raised the Brutalist aesthetic to a new level. (Here the story comes full circle to that moment when Lindbergh found himself confused by the lights of Bourget. Was it a factory or an airport?) The Midfield Complex was a 2.2-million-square-foot warren. Its megalithic concrete slabs—vaguely sacrificial in character—were relieved only by the occasional monitor skylight or venting duct. Dallas/Fort Worth seemed intimate in comparison. An effort was made to humanize the bland interiors with half a million dollars' worth of public art, but the effect was hardly perceptible.

The Postmodern Airport

Airport building slowed to a trickle in the 1980s as American and European cities ran out of available real estate. "We're not going to build any big new airports in the foreseeable future," announced Brock Adams of the Airport Operators Council International.[56] But meanwhile, other parts of the world—countries considered Third World or "undeveloped"—were not only catching up with the West but, in some ways, surpassing it. Petro dollars paid the way for sparkling new airports in the Persian Gulf that helped to soften the impact of modern technology by evoking indigenous forms of building. Skidmore, Owings, and Merrill designed the King Abdul Aziz Airport in Jeddah, Saudi Arabia, to handle millions of Islamic pilgrims on their way to Mecca. The terminal had more than a hundred acres of floor space and was the world's largest-roofed structure with a tentlike canopy made from Teflon-coated fiberglass. Three mosquelike terminals were built at the Sharjah Airport in the United Arab Emirates, and a quarter of a million trees were planted at the King Khalid Airport in Riyadh to create a literal oasis within the harsh Saudi climate. Skylights and clerestory windows shed indirect light into the air-conditioned

Pilgrims to Mecca await their flights at the Haj Terminal, King Abdul Aziz Airport, Jeddah, Saudi Arabia. Skidmore, Owings, and Merrill, architects, 1980.

interior of the King Khalid terminal to minimize the effects of desert light and create the feeling of a safe, sheltered refuge.[57] Walls were hung with Saudi tapestries, and a fountain shot jets of water thirty feet into the air. However artificial they may have seemed these exotic terminals offered the illusion of "place" and suggested alternatives to the impersonal nature of deregulated airports.

In the expanding network of global investment, business travelers were in need of places to ground themselves within the desertlike expanse of a borderless economy. The postmodern concourse would become the oasis (or village green) for that restless, floating class of airport nomads and "departure lounge lizards," as Pico Iyer called them.[58]

Architecture with a capital "A" made a sudden return to the airport environment in the 1990s, with monumental gestures and signature design. The trend moved away from factory-style processing and toward "symbolism, imagery, and the creation of memorable spaces within terminals," as the editors of one journal put it.[59] Despite all the limitations brought by terrorism and deregulation, architects found ways to repackage air travel and restore what Frederic Jameson called the "coordinates of an older space."[60] A more personal and gestural style was reintroduced in reaction to the alienating indignities of Dallas/Fort Worth and Atlanta's Midfield. The grand and soaring departure hall, lost in the numbing days of intermodal planning, would return as a unifying concept. In the postmodern airport, the idea of "view" was also reclaimed and crystal mountains of tempered glass once again rose above the runway landscape. Airport architects, evoking the thrill of flight, made sentimental references to the golden era of Lindbergh. They took their cues from the kind of retail complexes in which sun-drenched atriums and splashing fountains were employed to soothe and otherwise seduce the consumer into making a purchase. Theories of commercial developers like Victor Gruen and John Portman became more important than those of Gropius or Le Corbusier.

Marketing analysts recognized that the most profitable resource was a traveler locked in transit limbo. By the mid-1990s, the average wait for an international flight was as long as two hours and twenty-three minutes and the airport atrium became an anchor for high-end stores, fast-food stands, and other concessions. "I just wonder how many people will miss their planes because they are busy shopping," said one retailer.[61] Harrods of London opened branches at Gatwick and Heathrow and earned more revenue for those airports than any other income-producing service. Pittsburgh International opened the Air Mall in 1992, with more than thirty stores, including Victoria's Secret, Starbucks, and the Body Shop, and served more than sixty thousand customers a day. Denver opened over a hundred different shops and restaurants in its 1.5-million-square-foot terminal. Sales per square foot at airport malls were reported to be three to four times higher than those at normal shopping malls. As one airport manager put it, the terminal was becoming a "shopping mall with planes leaving from it."[62] Ryan Bingham, frequent-flying protagonist of Walter Kirn's novel *Up in the Air* (2001), feels at home in the transient realm of Air World: "I love the Compass Club lounges in the terminals," says Bingham, "especially the flagship Denver club, with its digital juice dispenser and deep suede sofas and floor-to-ceiling views of taxiing aircraft. I love the restaurants and snack nooks near the gates, stacked to their heat lamps with whole wheat mini-pizzas and gourmet caramel rolls."[63]

Commercialization went far beyond the air malls, however. Airports were now seen as international trade centers with corporate parks and conference centers colonizing their outskirts. Atlanta established a commercial zone adjacent to its airport called Tradeport. Las Colinas grew up beside Dallas/Fort Worth with several corporate headquarters, including GTE and Exxon. Denver built a 450-acre International Business Center beside its new airport with hotels, office complexes, and conference centers. Developers had more leeway since these areas were usually outside city limits, removed from strict zoning and inner-city problems. Good highways were already in place, and real estate was, initially, less expensive. Businessmen could fly in, have meetings, and leave without ever venturing away from the airport vicinity. "In fifteen minutes these guys can get on a plane and go any place in the world," said one planner.[64] The airport was becoming a model for the ideal corporate city.

Kennedy International had been losing passengers at an alarming rate, so in 1984, New York's Port Authority inaugurated its "Kennedy 2000" rehabilitation program to turn the twenty-seven-year-old dinosaur back into New York's leading airport. Henry

Cobb of I. M. Pei and Partners recognized that there was no way to expand outward, so the idea was to reach inward and somehow centralize the paragon of decentralization. A soaring structure would be built at the center of the old Idlewild loop and consolidate the movement of passengers and baggage through a high-tech circulation system of people movers and automated baggage handling. Such a building would provide, as Cobb put it, "the heart this airport needs," uniting its disparate parts and correcting the errors of the original plan. The focal point was the "Great Space," a sphere that measured two hundred feet in diameter and hovered within a cone-shaped spire of glass and metal truss work. Nine arteries would branch out from this allegorical heart and convey passengers via shuttle train to the old terminal units—TWA, Pan Am, United, etc.—which would now serve as glorified satellites. "The hall would have been a space of both majesty and drama," wrote Paul Goldberger in the *New York Times,* "Soanian in spirit, and perhaps

Postmodern heart: a soaring glass atrium was designed to provide the ceremonial center that Kennedy International Airport never had. The "Great Space" was part of the ill-fated Kennedy 2000 renewal program.

the closest our age has come to the grand and uplifting public space of the great railways terminals."[65] But the days for such grand schemes were past, at least in New York. Instead, Kennedy would be rebuilt in an agonizingly piecemeal fashion.

When it opened in 1987, United's Terminal for Tomorrow at O'Hare was also compared to a train station. Its "exhilarating form" was praised for the way it embraced the past while acknowledging the age of supersonic travel. The main hall was designed by Helmut Jahn to evoke Proust's "marvelous but tragic" sheds of the nineteenth century. The glass walls and ceiling were supported by steel I beams. Jahn hoped to reintroduce the romance of travel, in contrast to the cool functionalism of O'Hare's original scheme. The United terminal had fourteen gates, while a second, more distant concourse had twenty-eight gates that were connected by an underground passage. Here Jahn saw his chance to reinvent the long, sensory-deprived passageways of airport vernacular and stimulate the transfer experience with undulating walls of color. "The device of the translucent wall expands the sense of space," explained Jahn, "extending the 'horizon' beyond the literal limits of the architecture." The ceilings were backlit with a rainbow palette of color. A neon sculpture by Michael Hayden stretched the eight-hundred-foot length of the concourse and flushed alternating pulses of light that were synchronized to the rhythms of an original score by William Kraft.

The rat-in-the-maze effect of windowless fingers and underground passageways could also be neutralized by extending visibility back out toward the airfield. English architect Sir Norman Foster introduced a kind of open clarity that hearkened back to the early days of aviation. For Stansted, London's third airport, which opened in 1991, Foster designed a terminal that rose above the gentle Essex landscape like a pavilion in a garden setting. Its form was simple and easy to read from afar. The modular roof was made from a grid of shallow domes hovering above a forest of slender, treelike columns. Mechanical systems were hidden beneath the floor (as Saarinen had done at Dulles), thereby liberating the roof to become a single architectural gesture. Foster believed that the most dramatic element in the airport's scenography, the aircraft, had been kept conspicuously out of sight—an "invisible offstage presence"—and set out to reclaim Le Corbusier's "naked airport" theme.[66] Airplanes on the tarmac were clearly visible through walls of floor-to-ceiling glass. Interior space was kept as open and flexible as possible. Shops, banks, bathrooms, and cafés were designed to be freestanding structures that could be dismantled and moved to other parts of the terminal without major remodeling. Circulation patterns were simplified so that passengers could move through the building in a straight line instead of snaking through a series of blind turns.

When Denver's new airport was finished in 1995, it was the first major American airport built from the ground up since Dallas/Fort Worth twenty-two years earlier.[67] The snowy white roofline of the terminal became an instant logo, not just for the airport, but for the mile-high city itself: "At night, lit from within, the roof will be a spectacular beacon that is expected to become Denver's architectural signature." The Teflon-coated roof echoed the shape of the Rocky Mountains that rose behind it.

Similarly overscaled allegories from nature were suggested at other airports like Renzo Piano's design for Kansai International in Osaka, Japan, which was a tsunami of glass and steel breaking over its artificial island. The terminal was said to be the only man-made object, other than the Great Wall, visible from the moon. Kansai was just one of many Pacific Rim airports built in the booming economy of the 1990s. Other epic projects were begun at Narita, Fukuoka, and Sendai, Japan, while China announced plans to build twenty-five new airports by the end of 2002, including one for Pudong, Shanghai's free-market trade zone. A 2.33-million-square-foot terminal is being built for the capital city of Beijing, and a new complex is also planned for Guangzhou, China's third-

(opposite) The Teflon-coated roofs of Denver's airport terminal echo the snowcapped peaks of the Rockies, 1995.

busiest airport. A futuristic terminal with sweeping glass walls opened in Kuala Lumpur, Malaysia, and there were major plans in the works for Singapore, Taipei, Manila, and Bangkok.[68] A new airport for Seoul, South Korea, was planned to include an entire city for international commerce laid out like a vast formal garden with office blocks and tree-lined avenues leading to a central mall of reflecting pools and parks.

All of these Asian extravaganzas were planned during a period of unbridled confidence. Kansai cost $14 billion; Kuala Lumpur cost $2.5 billion, but Hong Kong broke the bank. Chek Lap Kok Airport was built to replace the dangerous old Kai Tak, with its suicide approaches, but, more important, as a token of faith in the city-state's continued prosperity: a $20 billion "vote of confidence in Hong Kong's future," which would form a symbolic bridge between British and Chinese rule. This "mother of all airports" turned into one of the world's largest engineering projects with $13.7 billion spent on infrastructure alone, including the building of a seven-square-mile island in the South China Sea. A new highway, railway line, suspension bridge, and harbor tunnel were built to connect the airport to downtown Hong Kong. The master plan also included a self-contained city and economic development zone called Tung Chung, with a population of twenty thousand.

In contrast to the simple pavilion that Foster had designed for Stansted, the terminal at Chek Lap Kok was a gargantuan pterodactyl of glass and steel, impossible to grasp in a single glance. Its central spine was almost a mile in length. "I think of it as one building under a 45-acre roof," said Foster. As at Stansted, air-conditioning ducts, pipes, and electrical wiring were concealed beneath the floor, so the scalloped roof could act as a unifying presence. Foster's terminal could also be seen as a kind of feng shui charm for redirecting the movement of international capital. "When money begins flowing," reported one local newspaper, "Hong Kong International will scoop up as much of it as it can."[69]

By the end of the 1990s, air traffic into the area began to decline. Hong Kong slipped into its worst recession since World

City of glass. All is revealed at Hong Kong's new Chek Lap Kok airport. Sir Norman Foster, architect, 1998.

War II, with 24 percent fewer tourists. Osaka's new airport island started to sink soon after opening. Even before the first planes landed at Chek Lap Kok in July 1998, rumors spread about misappropriated funds, imported slave labor, and shoddy construction. During the first months of operation, there were massive delays, lost baggage, backed-up toilets, and crates of perishable food left to rot on the tarmac. Things got so bad at one point that an embargo was imposed on all imports and exports, except for food and medical supplies. "This was meant to be a first-class project," lamented Lau Kong-way, a Hong Kong politician, "but it has turned into a ninth-class airport and a disgrace. Our airport has become the laughing stock of the world."[70]

Air Rage

By the end of the century, an odd new phenomenon was starting to occur with alarming regularity. "This has been the season of discontent for enraged passengers and the various carriers who brand, herd and ship them from point to point," reported the *New York Times* on September 24, 2000.[71] With so many delays and overcrowded flights, passengers were venting their frustrations with a violence never before seen. The press was quick to call it "air rage." "People's attitudes have changed," said one airline employee. "They lash out, scream at ticket agents. I'm concerned for my personal safety."[72] A passenger on a flight from Anchorage, Alaska, maliciously poured his beer over a flight attendant and bit the pilot when he came to the rescue. Two drunken rowdies on a flight to Amsterdam urinated on the seats as well as on their fellow passengers. A woman on a flight from Paris to Toronto got down on all fours and growled like a dog before biting three flight attendants. A woman on another transatlantic flight head-butted the flight attendant and broke her nose when asked to stop smoking in the lavatory. Similar incidents were taking place on the ground in airport terminals. Angelo Sottie, a gate agent at Newark International, was almost killed when an angry passenger picked him up and hurled him to the floor, fracturing his spine and skull. The assailant had been waiting impatiently with his family for a delayed flight to Orlando, Florida.[73]

Airport planners began to plot ways to reduce the kind of stress factors that precipitated air rage and reinstate a clear sense of orientation within overcrowded concourses. Terminal 4 at JFK was planned so that passengers would be led intuitively to the boarding gates without having to follow signs. "The architecture provides clues as to how the visitor should move from curb to plane," said the architect Anthony Vacchione. "When you walk in the front entrance, you immediately see the tails of the planes and know which direction to go."[74]

A desire for clear orientation was also a priority in the recent renewal of San Francisco International Airport. "We tried to design the entire terminal so there was a sense of human dignity," said architect Craig Hartman, believing that agoraphobic anxiety was primarily caused by a lack of clarity. "People have a territorial sense of space that they carry with them and the problem with air terminals is that you have to secede that sense of space as soon as you enter the building."[75]

The terminal's wing-shaped roof is supported by ribbon bow trusses that undulate above the concourse like gently rolling waves. Unlike the synthetic interiors of most terminals, San Francisco has natural, tactile surfaces. An enormous wall of cherrywood rises in the main concourse, and a forest of eighty-foot-high bamboo grows in the departure lounge.

Other air terminals have also gone "green," with fern gardens, forests, and computerized waterfalls to help reduce terminal angst. Kuala Lumpur has a tropical rain forest inside the airport's central atrium. Sendai Airport in Japan echoes the local landscape, complete with terraced plantings and cascading streams. Denver has a cactus garden, and a new terminal for Cologne-Bonn Airport was designed to sustain an entire ecosystem of healing plant life beneath a glass bubble roof.

Some airports have added health spas and massage parlors to calm the nerves of stressed-out travelers. Psychotherapists at San Francisco's Fear of Flying Clinic use desensitization techniques while other airports offer aerophobia workshops with names like Thairapy and Aeroanxiety Relief. Pittsburgh International built a thousand-square-foot meditation room, with images of puffy clouds and soft trance music. British Airways installed a computer-controlled system of aroma therapy at Heathrow's Terminal 4. Heated capsules concealed at floor level suffuse the arrivals lounge with the tranquil scents of sea mist and mowed grass. Singapore Changi Airport has a swimming pool and hot tubs. Calgary International offers OraOxygen treatments in which clients take hits of pure oxygen to relieve their preflight stress.

Ironically, this transitory realm has to be remarketed as a place of "downtime." Terminals shaped for speed now attempt to evoke the quality of slowness. The sterile oasis of the transit lounge becomes a refuge of unexpected tranquillity.

Epilogue:
From Lindbergh to bin Laden

The trajectory that began with Lindbergh's landing at Bourget in 1927 culminated when the first plane struck the north tower of the World Trade Center on September 11, 2001. Two icons of the machine age—airliner and skyscraper—came into collision and the tragic result was simulcast around the world. Our faith in technology and unfettered mobility was shaken to the core. Television pundits described the ingenuity of the terrorists and how they had used unconventional, low-tech methods to operate "below the radar"—a commonly heard phrase at the time. Considering the aeronautical associations of radar, it seemed an odd choice. Surely the terrorists were very much on the radar. Their assault began within the fluorescent passageways of Logan, Dulles, and Newark. There was no flag-waving or fanfare: they were simply exploiting the shoddy banality of the airport system. Minicams at ATM machines and twenty-four-hour surveillance cameras recorded their movements before they boarded. X-ray machines scanned their belongings. A barely perceptible line was crossed and nineteen hijackers were waved past the security checkpoints.

The FAA tracked deviations in flight patterns. The North American Aerospace Defense Command (NORAD) and the National Security Agency (NSA) plotted threat scenarios. Fighter

September 11, 2001. The jetliner and the skyscraper.

jets scrambled and locked on to jetliners that were still in the air. Onboard devices recorded cockpit conversations. Cell phones connected doomed passengers with loved ones on the ground. Network and amateur video cameras documented impact from a variety of angles. Still, the metaphor stuck—below the radar—implying an act that was, somehow, pretechnological and therefore unpreventable.

In response, airport security was tightened and President Bush appeared at O'Hare to tell Americans that the skies were safe.[1] Television carried scenes of National Guardsmen marching through terminals dressed in camouflage fatigues and carrying M-16s. "I noticed a big rifle while I was eating my Big Mac," said one passenger at Newark Airport where ninety of the soldiers were stationed.[2]

If it weren't already obvious, these images conveyed the inescapable truth: airports would play a frontline role in the coming global showdown. The newly formed Transportation Security

Administration announced Orwellian plans for CAPPS II (Computer-Assisted Passenger Prescreening System) to provide instant preflight profiles of passengers based on information drawn from FBI and CIA files, as well as bank and credit records. The anonymity travelers once enjoyed has been replaced by full electronic disclosure: a personalized "threat index" that threatens to erode the line between security and insecurity. (Iris-scanning devices, the kind anticipated by science fiction, have already been installed.)

Once again, the future beckons and the airport becomes a gauge of human tolerance as it continues to provide a testing ground for new technology—a place where the underlying forces and anxieties of modern living are revealed. Roland Barthes wrote that architecture is, simultaneously, an "expression of a utopia and instrument of a convenience."3 This has been particularly true at the airport, where dream and function have been intertwined from the start. The airport is still the threshold of change, as it was in Lindbergh's day, but at this point in the twenty-first century all vestiges of utopia have been lost.

Notes

1. PROTOTYPES: 1924–1930

1. Charles A. Lindbergh, *The Spirit of St. Louis* (New York: Charles Scribner's Sons, 1953), 489.
2. Rudyard Kipling, "With the Night Mail," *McClure's Magazine*, November 1905, 23–25.
3. Claude Grahame-White and Harry Harper, *The Aeroplane* (London: T. C. and E. C. Jack, Ltd., 1914), 217.
4. François Peyrey, "Les Premiers Hommes-Oiseaux." In Robert Wohl, *A Passion for Wings: Aviation and the Western Imagination, 1908–1918* (New Haven, Conn.: Yale University Press, 1994), 40.
5. Erich Mendelsohn's drawing was called *Skizze für einen Flughafen für Luftschiffe und Aeroplane*. See George Collins, *Visionary Drawings of Architecture and Planning: 20th Century Through the 1960s* (Cambridge, Mass.: MIT Press, 1979).
6. Ulrich Conrads and Hans G. Sperlich, *The Architecture of Fantasy, Utopian Building and Planning in Modern Times* (New York: Frederick A. Praeger, 1962), 128.
7. *Metropolis* was released in 1926, *Just Imagine* in 1930, and *Things to Come* in 1936. See Donald Albrecht, *Designing Dreams* (New York: Harper and Row, 1986), 153–65.
8. *Aerial Age Weekly*, 14 February 1921.
9. John Stroud, "The Birth of Air Transport," *The Putnam Aeronautical Review*, 164–76.
10. Carl Solberg, *Conquest of the Skies: A History of Commercial Aviation in America* (Boston: Little, Brown, 1979), 63.

11. Lowell Thomas, *European Skyways: The Story of a Tour of Europe by Airplane* (Boston: Houghton Mifflin Company, 1927).

12. Ibid., 21.

13. Joseph F. Hood, *Skyway Round the World: The Story of the First Global Airway* (New York: Scribner, 1968), 55.

14. Captain Norman Macmillan, *The Air-Tourist's Guide to Europe* (New York: n.p., 1930), 33–34. Croydon's new terminal was dedicated in January 1928.

15. Thomas, *European Skyways*, 47.

16. Ibid., 56–57.

17. Peter Schmidt, *A Nation of Fliers: German Aviation and the Popular Imagination* (Cambridge, Mass.: Harvard University Press, 1992).

18. Steadman S. Hanks, *International Airports* (New York: Ronald Press Company, 1929).

19. This building was one of the first freestanding passenger terminals in the world. See John Zukowsky, ed., *Building for Air Travel: Architecture and Design for Commercial Aviation* (New York: Prestel, USA, 1996), 33.

20. The English architectural historian Reyner Banham referred to this as the "yacht-basin approach." See "The Obsolescent Airport," *Architectural Review* 132 (October 1962), 250–60.

21. Built as early as 1923, these two runways are considered the world's first. See Wood Lockhart, "A Pilot's Perspective on Airport Design," in Zukowsky, *Building for Air Travel,* 215.

22. *Contact*, 16 July 1938.

23. William E. Arthur, "How Shall We Design Our Airports," *Scientific American* (October 1929), 298–301.

24. "An Airport and Recreation Center Combined," *The Architectural Record* (March 1934).

25. "Flashbacks—Sixty Years Ago in *Forbes*," *Forbes* (15 June 1987), 279. As cited in A. Scott Berg, *Lindbergh* (New York: Putnam, 1998), 171.

26. The company was a subsidiary of the Curtiss Aeroplane and Engine Company. See *Curtiss-Wright Airports: A Nation-Wide Chain of Strategically Located Ports* (New York: Curtiss-Wright Airports Corporation, 1930).

27. The Ford airport opened in 1925. Timothy J. O'Callaghan, *Henry Ford's Airport, and Other Aviation Interests, 1909–1951* (Ann Arbor, Mich.: Proctor Publications, 1993), 7.

28. As quoted in Donald Duke, *Airports and Airways: Cost, Operation and Maintenance* (New York: Ronald Press Company, 1927), 86.

29. *The Literary Digest*, 7 April 1928.

30. Thomas, *European Skyways,* 33.

31. Advertisement for Ford Airplanes in *The Literary Digest*, 21 July 1928.
32. W. E. Larned, *NAPA Journal* 2 (March 1929), 24–25. As cited in William M. Leary, *From Airships to Airbus: The History of Civil and Commercial Aviation* (Washington D.C.: Smithsonian Institution Press, 1995), 107.
33. Sinclair Lewis, *Dodsworth* (New York: Harcourt, Brace and Company, 1929), 283.
34. During eight years of manufacturing, testing, and running Ford Air Transport, there were only eight fatalities.
35. Eastern Air Transport merged with Colonial Airways to become Colonial Air Transport.
36. See Sanford B. Kauffman, *Pan Am Pioneer: A Manager's Memoir from Seaplane Clippers to Jumbo Jets* (Lubbock, Tex.: Texas Tech University Press, 1995) 30–42.
37. Matthew Josephson, *Empire of the Air: Juan Trippe and the Struggle for World Airways* (New York: Harcourt, Brace, 1943), 33.
38. PAA's foreign agents began to expand the company's network into Latin America in March of 1928.
39. David Grant Mason was PAA's main negotiator in Latin America.
40. Kauffman, *Pan Am Pioneer,* 18.
41. Ibid., 17.
42. Josephson, *Empire of the Air,* 64.
43. Kauffman, *Pan Am Pioneer,* 53.
44. Ibid., 21.
45. Ibid., 22.
46. William E. Arthur, "How Shall We Design Our Airports?" *Scientific American*, October 1929, 300.
47. Thomas, *European Skyways,* 22.
48. "Airport Architecture," *New York Times,* 10 February 1929, sec. 12, p. 18.
49. Francis Keally, "Architectural Treatment of the Airport," *The Architect and Engineer,* Airport Number, November 1930, 43–51.
50. Ernest Herminghaus, "Landscape Art in Airport Design," *American Landscape Architect,* July 1930, 17–18.
51. Dominick A. Pisano, *American Airport Designs* (New York: Taylor, Rogers, and Bliss, 1930; reprint, Washington, D.C.: American Institute of Architects, 1990).
52. Author's emphasis. Sterling Wagner, *The Modern Airport* (Syracuse, N.Y.: Syracuse University Press, 1931), 73.
53. Ibid.
54. Swan Island was designed by DeYoung and Roald Architects. *The Architect and Engineer,* Airport Number, November 1930, 60.
55. Wyatt Brummitt, "Contact!" *American Architect* 135 (5 April

1929), 431–32. As cited in David Brodherson, "What Can't Go Up Can't Come Down: The History of American Airport Policy, Planning and Design," Ph.D. dissertation, 1993, Cornell University, 328.

56. Talbot F. Hamlin, "Airports as Architecture," *Pencil Points* 21 (October 1940), 636–46.

57. Wagner, *The Modern Airport.*

58. See the Lloyd Wright collection at the Canadian Centre for Architecture, Montreal.

59. "What Is Art?" *Los Angeles Evening Herald,* 7 March 1929.

60. Thomas, *European Skyways,* 222, 311.

61. Lindbergh, *The Spirit of St. Louis.*

62. C. B. Allen and Lauren D. Lyman, *The Wonder Book of the Air* (Chicago: John C. Winston, 1936), 20.

63. F. Scott Fitzgerald, *The Last Tycoon* (New York: Charles Scribner's Sons, 1941).

64. Ibid.

65. Antoine de Saint-Exupéry, *Wind, Sand and Stars* (New York: Reynal and Hitchcock, 1939).

66. A string of "aërial lighthouses" was built along the route, including one, near Dijon, that had a billion-candlepower beacon.

67. Allen and Lyman, *The Wonder Book of the Air,* 24.

68. Hanks, *International Airports,* 100.

69. Ibid., 104.

70. Fitzgerald, *The Last Tycoon,* 8.

71. O'Callaghan, *Henry Ford's Airport,* 67.

72. *Hell's Angels* starred Jean Harlow. It was released in 1930 at a cost of $3.8 million.

73. This was the case with Norman Bel Geddes, K. Franzheim, and Vilhelm Lauritzen, all of whom were known for theater design.

74. Fitzgerald, *The Last Tycoon,* 20.

75. Ibid., 136 (Fitzgerald's notes).

76. Betsy Braden and Paul Hagan, *A Dream Takes Flight: Hartfield Atlanta International Airport and Aviation in Atlanta* (Athens, Ga.: University of Georgia Press, 1989), 115–18.

77. Lewis, *Dodsworth,* 1224.

78. Allen and Lyman, *The Wonder Book of the Air.*

79. Fitzgerald, *The Last Tycoon,* 4–5.

2. NAKED AIRPORT: 1930–1940

1. Charles Owen, *The Grand Days of Travel* (New York: Smithmark Publishers, 1980), 120.

2. Macmillan, *The Air-Tourist's Guide to Europe,* 35; Thomas, *European Skyways,* 56–57.

3. Saint-Exupéry, *Wind, Sand and Stars.*

4. Macmillan, *The Air-Tourist's Guide to Europe,* 35.

5. Virgilio Marchi, *Architettura Futurista* (1924).

6. Francis Keally, "Architectural Treatment of the Airport."

7. Walter Gropius, *The New Architecture and the Bauhuas* (Cambridge, Mass.: MIT Press, 1965), 30.

8. Ibid.

9. Le Corbusier founded the review *L'Esprit Nouveau* in 1922 with Amédée Ozenfant and Paul Dermée.

10. Le Corbusier, *Aircraft* (London: The Studio Ltd., 1935).

11. Ibid.

12. Ibid.

13. The Orly hangars were designed by the engineer Eugène Freyssinet. Le Corbusier, *Towards a New Architecture* (New York: n.p., 1960), 264–66.

14. Contemporary city for 3 million people, 1922.

15. "Les Aéroports," *L'Architecture d'Aujourd'hui,* 1931.

16. Antonio Sant'Elia, "Manifesto of Futurist Architecture 1914," in *The Documents of 20th Century Art: Futurist Manifestos,* ed., Umbro Apollonio (New York: Viking Press, 1973), 160–72.

17. Marinetti took his first flight in 1912.

18. Dennis P. Doordan, *Building Modern Italy* (New York: Princeton Architectural Press, 1988), 23–25.

19. "Pilot's House," 1924: collection of the Museum of Modern Art, New York; "Design for an Airfield," 1924: collection of the Sammlung Museum Ludwig, Cologne, Germany.

20. Conrads and Sperlich, *The Architecture of Fantasy,* 108.

21. Howard Mansfield, *Cosmopolis: Yesterday's Cities of the Future* (New Brunswick, N.J.: Center for Urban Policy Research, 1990).

22. "Airport for London Opened at Gatwick," *New York Times,* 7 June 1936.

23. As quoted in Thomas, *European Skyways,* 90.

24. Chief of Britain's Air Staff, Sir Hugh Trenchard, proposed the idea in 1920.

25. Kenneth Hudson and Julian Pettifer, *Diamonds in the Sky: A Social History of Air Travel* (London: Bodley Head, 1979), 80.

26. Ibid., 67.

27. Ibid.

28. Owen, *The Grand Days of Travel,* 138.

29. Hudson and Pettifer, *Diamonds in the Sky,* 80.

30. Le Corbusier was on his way to Moscow to work on the *Centrosoyuz,* the Central Union of Consumer Co-Operatives. It would be the first

of many such air trips during his long, globe-trotting career. Le Corbusier, *Aircraft,* 10.

31. Deborah Douglas, *Aviation Engineering,* January 1932. As cited in "Airports as Systems and Systems of Airports" in Leary, *From Airships to Airbus.*

32. The FW.200 Condor took twenty-four hours, fifty-six minutes to reach New York and nineteen hours, fifty-five minutes to fly back to Berlin in August 1938.

33. Hudnut was dean of the School of Design at Harvard. He may be best remembered for the role he played in importing the Bauhaus to America. He invited Walter Gropius to come teach at Harvard, in 1937. See *Architectural Forum,* September 1941, 100.

34. Graham Greene, *England Made Me* (London: Heinemann, 1935; reprint, London: Penguin Books, 1970), 161–62.

35. Croydon preserved its all-grass field until it finally closed in 1959.

36. Dawbarn went on to specialize in aviation architecture. Nigel Norman, "Aerodrome Design," *Architectural Association Journal* 48, no. 555 (May 1933): 359–74. The information that Norman and Dawbarn gathered was used in an exhibition mounted by the RIBA in 1937 called Airports and Airways.

37. John King, *Gatwick: The Evolution of an Airport* (Gatwick Airport Ltd./Sussex Industrial Archaeological Society, 1986). Jackaman may have been influenced by Sven Markelius's circular plan for Bromma Airport, Stockholm, which had been published in 1934.

38. *"La beauté d'un aéroport, c'est la splendeur de l'espace!"*

39. "The Sky Line, Millions for Mausoleums," *The New Yorker,* 30 December 1939, 49–50.

40. Hanks, *International Airports,* 141–42.

41. Linate was the first Italian airport built solely for civilian use. See John Walter Wood, *Airports: Some Elements of Design and Future Development* (New York: Coward-McCann, 1940).

42. Ibid., 257.

43. Lisbet Balslev Jørgensen, Vilhelm Lauritzen, Jørgen Sestoft, Morten Lund, eds., *Vilhelm Lauritzen: A Modern Architect* (Corte Madera, Calif.: Gingko Press, 1995), 190.

3. NEW DEAL: 1933–1941

1. *New York Times,* 2 July 1932, p. 1.

2. "Family Flies to Chicago." *New York Times,* 2 July 1932, p. 1.

3. James M. Kiernan Jr., "Message Written on Way," *New York Times,* 3 July 1932.

4. "Family Flies to Chicago."

5. The Ford Airport in Dearborn would be closed in 1947.

6. Josephson, *Empire of the Air,* 81.

7. As PAA's chief engineer, André Priester, put it: "A seaplane carries its own airport on its bottom."

8. An improved version, the S-42, was produced by Sikorsky in 1934 and allowed even longer flights.

9. "The Miami Airport," *Architecture,* April 1935, 202.

10. The Honorable W. R. D. Perkins, a Conservative Member of British Parliament, in a speech December 1942. As cited in Josephson, *Empire of the Air,* 14.

11. Alice Dalgliesh, *Wings Around South America* (New York: Charles Scribner's Sons, 1941).

12. Ibid.

13. Braden and Hagan, *A Dream Takes Flight,* 92.

14. "Red Propaganda in WPA Murals at Floyd Bennett Charged," *New York Times,* 8 July 1940.

15. Geoffrey Arend, *Great Airports: Kennedy International* (New York: Air Cargo News, Inc., 1987), 26–31.

16. The Army Air Force took control of Newark's terminal during World War II and Gorky's murals were painted over and forgotten. Some of the panels were rediscovered in 1972 covered in fourteen layers of enamel paint. They were restored and are now in the permanent collection of the Newark Museum of Art. "Murals Without Walls," *Skyline,* January 1979, 8–9.

17. Frederick A. Gutheim, "Seven Years of Public Buildings," *The Magazine of Art* 33 (July 1940), 433.

18. Wood, *Airports,* 103.

19. Construction on the Pulaski Skyway began in March 1930. The original bridge section opened in 1932.

20. Reginald M. Cleveland, "Contact," *New York Times,* 3 July 1932.

21. Allen and Lyman, *The Wonder Book of the Air,* 4.

22. Joseph Hudnut, "Washington National Airport," *Architectural Forum,* September 1941, 171.

23. Richard Neutra, "Terminals?—Transfer!," *Architectural Record* 68 no. 2 (August 1930), 99–104. Throughout the 1930s, Neutra developed ideas for a modern, high-speed metropolis called Rush City, which would be designed "in a scientific manner," with a multilevel air station at its center. See Thomas S. Hines, *Richard Neutra and the Search for Modern Architecture* (New York: Berkeley, 1982), 61.

24. In 1940, Wood published his findings in a methodically researched, 364-page book. Wood, *Airports.*

25. Wood, *Airports,* 326.
26. Norman Bel Geddes, *Horizons* (Boston: Little, Brown 1932), 24.
27. Ibid., 83.
28. John R. Tunis, *Million-Miler: The Story of an Air Pilot* (New York: n.p., 1942).
29. La Guardia served in Foggia, Italy, with the rank of major. He was awarded the Flying Cross by King Victor Emmanuel III.
30. David Gelernter, *1939: The Lost World of the Fair* (New York: Free Press, 1995), 2.
31. Thomas Kessner, *Fiorello H. La Guardia and the Making of Modern New York* (New York: McGraw-Hill, 1989), 433.
32. New York City archives are filled with an odd assortment of schemes from this period. The seaplane station for the East River was called the "Central Air Terminal" (1936), a WPA-sponsored project designed by Gordon Reel in collaboration with New York's Department of Engineering. See the La Guardia Papers in the New York Municipal Archives.
33. Kessner, *Fiorello H. La Guardia and the Making of Modern New York,* 433.
34. Before Curtiss-Wright, North Beach had been the site of the Gala Amusement Park.
35. The airport cost approximately $40 million. Archibald Black, *The Story of Flying* (New York: McGraw-Hill, 1940), 180.
36. *Contact,* 16 July 1938, 5.
37. Robert A. Caro, *The Power Broker* (New York: Alfred A. Knopf, 1974), 758.
38. *New York Times,* 16 October 1939, 1.
39. Geoffrey Arend, *Air World's Great Airports: La Guardia, 1939–1979* (Newark, N.J.: Air Cargo News, 1979), 21.
40. Lewis Mumford, "The Sky Line, Millions for Mausoleums," *The New Yorker,* 30 December 1939, 49–50.
41. David Leigh, "Aerial Floorshow," *Airlanes,* December 1940, 4–5.
42. *New York Times,* 15 October 1939.
43. *The New Yorker,* 13 May 1939, 85.
44. Leigh, "Aerial Floorshow."
45. Tunis, *Million-Miler,* 141.
46. Guggenheim was addressing a Senate committee, 1936. "Guggenheim Urges New Plane Rules," *New York Times,* 15 February 1936.
47. *Washington Herald,* 20 January 1938.
48. Work on National Airport was supervised by Colonel Sumpter Smith, head of the CAA. The consulting architect was Howard Lovewell Cheney and the supervising architect was Louis A. Simon,

who worked with a team of architects and engineers from the Public Buildings Administration. The actual hands-on designer of the terminal building was probably a government architect named Charles M. Goodman.

49. National Airport, brochure published by the U.S. Department of Commerce, Civil Aeronautics Administration, 1941.

50. John Crider, "A National Airport," *New York Times Magazine,* 15 June, 1941, 9.

51. Joseph Hudnut, "Washington National Airport," *Architectural Forum,* September 1941, 100.

4. AIR POWER: 1939–1957

1. Albion Ross, "Reich Bids for Place in Skies," *New York Times,* 12 December 1937, IV, 5:3.

2. "Reich Leads in Air, Tomlinson Asserts," *New York Times,* 29 November 1938, 2:7.

3. In a letter of thanks to Göring, August 20, 1936, as quoted in Berg, *Lindbergh,* 361. In 1938, Lindbergh was awarded the Order of the German Eagle, much to detriment of his golden boy image.

4. In September 1936, the flying ship *Zephir,* flown by Captain Joachim von Blankenburg, completed the first of a series of survey flights from the Azores to Port Washington, Long Island. The flight took twenty-two hours, ten minutes.

5. Albert Speer, *Inside the Third Reich* (New York: Macmillan, 1970), 26.

6. William L. Shirer, *The Rise and Fall of the Third Reich: A History of Nazi Germany* (New York: Simon and Schuster, 1959), 281–82.

7. In fact, Tempelhof was a bit out of alignment with Berlin's main axis.

8. When the Nazis came to power in 1933, Hermann Göring was given responsibility over all aviation matters. He had been a flying ace in World War I and then served as an adviser to Lufthansa airlines during the 1920s.

9. Besides Tempelhof, Sagebiel also developed plans for Munich-Reim and Stuttgart airports.

10. From a speech by Hitler as quoted in Elaine S. Hochman, *Architects of Fortune: Mies van der Rohe and the Third Reich* (New York: Weidenfeld and Nicolson, 1989), 191.

11. Hitler was especially fond of Paul Ludwig Troost, the Munich-based architect who specialized in a spare neoclassical style in his designs for the Temple of Honor, the Führer Building, and the House of German Art (all built in Munich). Troost also developed plans for a giant classical arena at the old Zeppelin Field in

Nuremberg. When Troost died in 1934, his role as the füher's favorite architect passed on to Albert Speer. See Hochman, *Architects of Fortune*, 191.

12. Speer, *Inside the Third Reich.*

13. Professor Gerdy Troost, widow of the architect Paul Ludwig Troost: Peter Adam, *Art of the Third Reich* (New York: H. N. Abrams, 1992), 248.

14. Johann Wolfgang von Goethe, *Italian Journey, 1786–1788,* trans. W. H. Auden and Elizabeth Mayer (San Francisco: North Point Press, 1982).

15. Goebbels made the speech in 1933. See Hochman, *Architects of Fortune,* 316.

16. Graham Greene, *Journey Without Maps* (London: William Heinemann, 1936).

17. See Norman Bel Geddes Collection, Harry Ransom Humanities Research Center, University of Texas at Austin.

18. "Air Transport Command Port Features, Charles M. Goodman, Principal Architect," *Architectural Record,* April 1945, 94.

19. Robert Daley, *An American Saga: Juan Trippe and His Pan Am Empire* (New York: Random House, 1980), 306.

20. Ibid., 302–9.

21. Cited in Robert Friedel, "Scarcity and Promise," *World War II and the American Dream,* ed., Donal Albrecht (Cambridge, Mass.: MIT Press, 1995).

22. Collins, *Visionary Drawings of Architecture and Planning.*

23. Advertisement in *New Pencil Points,* June 1943, 2.

24. "58 Feared Lost in Crash of Airliner," *New York Times,* 25 June 1950.

25. W. G. Sebald, *On the Natural History of Destruction* (New York: Random House, 2003), 34.

26. "What's Wrong with Our Air Terminals?" *Architectural Forum,* January 1946, 123–32.

27. "U.S. Air Has a Busy 24 Hours," *Life,* 18 June 1956, 39–44.

28. CAB Chairman Ross Rizley, quoted in Solberg, *Conquest of the Skies,* 363.

29. "What's Wrong with the Airlines," *Fortune,* August 1946; "Why Air Passengers Get Mad," *Saturday Evening Post,* 19 October 1946, 12–13; "The Airline Squeeze," *Fortune,* May 1947; David Bernstein, "Our Airsick Airlines," *Harper's,* May 1947; Bernard De Voto, "Transcontinental Flight," *Harper's,* July 1952.

30. "What's Wrong with the Airlines."

31. "Cities of U.S. Get Airport Nerves," *Life,* 25 February 1952, 17–19.

32. Ibid.

33. "Aids for Airports," *Newsweek,* 15 September 1952, 35.

34. Lewis Mumford, "An American Introduction to Sir Ebenezer Howard's 'Garden Cities of Tomorrow,'" *New Pencil Points*, March 1945, 73.

35. Quoted in press release from the Office of the Mayor, New York City, 6 February 1945, from Municipal Archives, New York City.

36. *Architectural Record*, April 1945, 79.

37. Ibid.

38. See Greg Hise, "The Airplane and the Garden City: Regional Transformations during World War II," *World War II and the American Dream*, ed., Albrecht, 144–83.

39. "Toledo: A Model of Proposed Changes in the Transportation Pattern Arouses Citizen Interest in Planning the City's Future," *Architectural Forum*, August 1945.

40. Charles Froesch and Walther Prokosch, *Airport Planning* (New York: John Wiley and Sons, 1946).

41. Ibid., 6.

42. Frank Lloyd Wright, *The Living City* (New York: Horizon Press, 1958), 148.

43. During World War II, Orchard Place was the site of the Douglas assembly plant.

44. Press release dated 6 February 1945 from the Office of the Mayor, Municipal Archives, New York.

45. Fiorello H. La Guardia, "Finest Airport in the World," *New York Times Magazine*, 21 January 1945, 43.

46. Ibid.

47. Harrison was married to Ellen Milton, sister-in-law of Abby Aldrich Rockefeller. During the war he worked in the Washington offices of the CIAA (Coordination of Inter-American Affairs), under the directorship of Nelson Rockefeller.

48. See Downer, Green and Carrillo; Clarke, Rapuano and Holleran; Harrison and Abromovitz, *The New York Municipal Airport at Idlewild*, (New York: n.p., 1946).

49. "Airport Honky-Tonk," *Fortune*, September 1947, 120.

50. Downer, Green and Carrillo; Clarke, Rapuano and Holleran; Harrison and Abromovitz, *The New York Municipal Airport at Idlewild*.

51. Harrison soon moved on to bigger and better commissions, however, including the United Nations Headquarters and Lincoln Center. He would return to work on Idlewild at a later stage of development.

52. Anthony Sampson, *Empires of the Sky* (New York: Random House, 1984), 77.

53. Wendell Willkie, 1943, as quoted in Sampson, *Empires of the Sky*, 57.

54. Foreword to Froesch and Prokosch, *Airport Planning*, 183.

55. Noel Barber, "I Flew 14,000 Miles for Dinner," *Saturday Evening Post*, 9 November 1957.

56. As cited in Roger E. Bilstein, *Flight in America* (Baltimore: Johns Hopkins University Press, 1984), 170.
57. "New Gateways to the Wide World: Artist Views Life of the Airports," *Life*, 18 June 1956, 86–95.
58. Joseph J. Corn, *The Winged Gospel* (New York: Oxford University Press, 1983), 68.
59. Trippe said this at a meeting of airline executives in 1955. As quoted in Josephson, *Empire of the Air*, 111.
60. "Air Age," *Life*, Special Issue, 18 June 1956.
61. Ibid.
62. As quoted in Stephen Ambrose and Douglas Brinkley, "Like Music to Our Ears," *Newsweek*, 25 May 1998.
63. "Traffic Jam in the Sky," *U.S. News and World Report*, 7 January 1955, 40–41.
64. "New Gateways to the Wide World."
65. "Europe Here They Come," *Life*, 27 June 1955, 34.
66. Christopher Isherwood, "Coming to London," *Exhumations* (New York: Simon and Schuster, 1966).
67. The DC-7C and the Starliner were also used for one-stop service to Tokyo from New York and other cities.
68. Ernest K. Gann, *The High and the Mighty* (New York: Sloane, 1953), 35.
69. "Airports," *Architectural Forum*, August 1940.
70. Three years after it opened, the name of Chicago's new municipal airport was changed to "Midway" in honor of the World War II battle.
71. Albert F. Heino, "Designing the Large Terminal," *Architectural Record*, April 1945, 82.
72. Ibid., 83.
73. Walther Prokosch, "Airport Design: Its Architectural Aspects," *Architectural Record*, January 1951, 112.
74. Ansel E. Talbert, *Famous Airports of the World* (New York: Random House, 1953), 5.
75. The Sheraton chain opened its first airport hotel on the grounds of Cleveland Hopkins in 1958. Idlewild got a wing-shaped International Hotel the same year. "Stranded and Bushed," *The New Yorker*, 4 June 1955, 24–26.
76. For Greater Pittsburgh Airport, see Talbert, *Famous Airports of the World*, 10–12; Frank Kingston Smith and James P. Harrington, *Aviation and Pennsylvania* (Philadelphia: Franklin Institute Press, 1981), 89–90.
77. "Baltimore's Lonely Big Airport," *Life*, 19 November 1951.
78. Solberg, *Conquest of the Skies*, 361.

79. *Business Week*, 1 May 1954, 92–94.
80. *Airport Reference,* 5th Annual (1945–1946 edition) (Los Angeles: R. Borrows, Occidental Publishing Company, 1945), 93.
81. G. L. Christian, "Loadair Dock Goes into Operation," *Aviation Weekly* 62 (17 January 1955), 63–64; "Future Uncertain for Idlewild Loadair," *Aviation Weekly* 65 (August 1956), 434.
82. Heino, "Designing the Large Terminal."
83. Ibid.
84. Ibid.
85. Joseph Hudnut, "Washington National Airport," *Architectural Forum,* September 1941.
86. Geddes pitched the Gate Unit System to James C. Buckley, chief of planning for New York's Port Authority, who expressed interest in the concept but ultimately declined. See Geddes's correspondence and proposals for this and other airport schemes in the Harry Ransom Humanities Research Center at the University of Texas, Austin.
87. "New Terminal Under Way for Newark Airport," *Architectural Record,* November 1952, 26.
88. The new terminal at Gatwick was designed by Yorke, Rosenberg, and Mardall architects. G. E. Kidder-Smith, *The New Architecture of Europe* (Cleveland: World Publishing Company, 1961), 56.

5. JET-LAND: 1957–1970

1. Sampson, *Empires of the Sky.*
2. John Betjeman, *A Nip in the Air* (New York: Norton, 1974).
3. As cited in Solberg, *Conquest of the Skies,* 405.
4. Daniel J. Boorstin, *The Image: A Guide to Pseudo-Events in America* (1961; reprint, New York: Atheneum, 1971).
5. Roland Barthes, *Mythologies* (Paris: Éditions du Sevil, 1957).
6. Boorstin, *The Image.*
7. Paul Virilio, *The Art of the Motor,* trans. Julie Rose (Minneapolis: University of Minnesota Press, 1995).
8. George Scullin, *International Airport* (Boston: Little, Brown, 1968), 154.
9. "The Word Is Soar," *Time,* 29 March 1963, 67; United Air Lines Press Release, 8 June 1959.
10. Buford L. Pickens, "Proud Architecture and the Spirit of St. Louis," *Architectural Record,* April 1956.
11. Ibid., 199.
12. "Airport City, U.S.A.," *Newsweek,* 5 April 1965, 90.
13. Trudy Baker and Rachel Jones, *Coffee, Tea or Me?* (New York: Bartholomew House, 1967).

14. Mary Wells Lawrence, *A Big Life in Advertising* (New York: Touchstone, 2002), 37.

15. From a Braniff magazine advertisement, 1965. See Ibid., 41.

16. Gann, *The High and the Mighty,* 32.

17. Ian Fleming, *Diamonds Are Forever* (New York: Macmillan, 1956), 91.

18. J. G. Ballard, *Crash* (London: Jonathan Cape, 1973).

19. "Airport City, U.S.A.," *Newsweek,* 5 April 1965, 90.

20. Ibid.

21. See Joel Garreau, *Edge City: Life on the New Frontier* (New York: Anchor Books, 1988).

22. For early history of Idlewild, see Fiorello H. La Guardia, "Finest Airport in the World," *New York Times Magazine,* 21 January 1945; *Municipal Airport at Idlewild* (New York: Department of Marine and Aviation, 1945); "Gateway for Overseas Travelers," *Progressive Architecture,* December 1957, 86–95; "New Aerial Gateway to America," *Architectural Forum,* February 1958, 78–86; Scullin, *International Airport;* Geoffrey Arend, *Air World's Great Airports: Kennedy International* (New York: Air Cargo News, 1987).

23. Edward Hudson, "Aviation: Showplace, Idlewild Projects Designed to Please Sight-Seer as Well as Traveler," *New York Times,* 18 August 1957.

24. "Idlewild Dedicates Central Unit of Mammoth Jet-Age Terminal City," *New York Times,* 6 December 1957.

25. Robert Wagner, New York's new mayor, blamed Tobin for the delays and told reporters that the authority's handling of the airport was a "disgrace." Tobin fired back, accusing Wagner of trying to sabotage his efforts.

26. *New York Herald Tribune,* 31 January 1956, 1.

27. From an editorial in the *New York Herald Tribune,* c. 1955 (unmarked, undated clipping from SOM archives, New York).

28. Caro, *The Power Broker.*

29. Harrison would serve in that capacity until 1960, at which point he went on to design the new terminal at LaGuardia.

30. Harrison's Trylon and Perisphere at the 1939 New York World's Fair used a similar kind of elevated walkway, the 950-foot-long "Helicline," which also passed through a freestanding building and curved around a circular reflecting pool. See "NYIA," *Progressive Architecture,* December 1957, 77.

31. *Architectural Record,* September 1961, 186.

32. Severinghaus had joined Skidmore, Owings, and Merrill in the late 1930s to work on the 1939 New York World's Fair.

33. "New Aerial Gateway to America," *Architectural Forum,* February 1958, 78–86.

34. Froesch and Prokosch, *Airport Planning.* Prokosch was a partner at Tippets-Abbett-McCarthy-Stratton and had formerly worked for Eastern Airlines. He helped to design the Puerto Rico International Airport in San Juan (1955) and had also served as an adviser on the development of Friendship Airport in Baltimore. See Walther Prokosch, *Detailed Design* (Cambridge, Mass.: Chimera Press, 1983).

35. Prokosch, "Airport Design: Its Architectural Aspects," 115.

36. "Umbrella for Airplanes," *Time*, 13 June 1960, 103.

37. For Saarinen's airport studies, see the Eero Saarinen papers, Manuscripts and Archives, Yale University Library.

38. This may be yet another piece of Saarinen mythology borrowed from Sydney. Jørn Utzon was also said to have been inspired during breakfast, discovering the forms of his opera house in the curving sections of an orange.

39. Eero Saarinen, quoted in Allan Temko, *Eero Saarinen* (New York: G. Braziller, 1962).

40. Cranston Jones, *Architecture Today and Tomorrow* (New York: McGraw-Hill, 1961).

41. Peter Blake, *No Place Like Utopia: Modern Architecture and the Company We Keep* (New York: Alfred A. Knopf, 1993), 259; Ada Louise Huxtable, "A Vision of Rome Dies," *Will They Ever Finish Bruckner Boulevard?* (New York: Macmillan, 1970), 214.

42. "Simplicity Picked for Air Terminal," *New York Times*, 19 August 1960; "I. M. Pei Wins Idlewild Terminal Competition," *Progressive Architecture*, October 1960, 72–73; "Multi-Airline Terminal," *Architectural Record*, September 1961, 168–69.

43. Designed by John Veerling, the Port of New York Authority's project director for Newark Airport.

44. Jones, *Architecture Today and Tomorrow*, 148.

45. See Minoru Yamasaki, *A Life in Architecture* (New York: Weatherhill, 1979), 33–34; *Architectural Record*, August 1970.

46. "Airport Cities: Gateways to the Jet Age," *Time*, 15 August 1960. Eighty thousand new trees were planted to help absorb the noise of jet engines.

47. Walter McQuade, "The Birth of an Airport," *Fortune*, March 1962, 92–97.

48. "Airports: The Dark Side of the Travel Boom," *Fortune*, 4 December 1978, 103; George Nelson: "Architecture for the New Itinerants," *Saturday Review*, April 22, 1967.

49. Ralph Burke, a civil engineer who had formerly worked in the city's sanitation department, was in charge of planning.

50. By 1970, O'Hare was the busiest airport in the world, capable of handling more than 14 million passengers a year.

51. Nelson, "Architecture for the New Itinerants," 31.

52. François Maspero, *Roissy Express: A Journey through the Paris Suburbs* (New York: Verso, 1994), 6.

53. Nelson, "Architecture for the New Itinerants," 30–32.

54. Raymond Spurrier, "The Landscape of Hysteria: Towards a Clarified Aesthetic," *Architectural Review* 132 (October 1962), 250–60.

55. Nelson, "Architecture for the New Itinerants," 31.

56. Alvin Toffler, *Future Shock* (New York: Random House, 1970), 69.

57. *Wall Street Journal*, 26 April 1966, as cited in *Future Shock*, 75.

6. THE STERILE CONCOURSE: 1970–2000

1. Braden and Hagan, *A Dream Takes Flight*, 137.

2. "Terminal Illness," *Newsweek*, 29 July 1968.

3. "The Future: Airports at Sea," *Time*, 30 May 1969, 61.

4. Douglas Davis, "2001: The Ultimate Airport," *Newsweek*, 28 August 1972, 77–78.

5. *New York Times*, 25 August 1970.

6. Unattributed quote from HOK files.

7. John Updike, *Marry Me* (New York: Alfred A. Knopf, 1976).

8. "Philadelphia International Airport," *Architectural Record*, August 1968.

9. Nelson, "Architecture for the New Itinerants," 66.

10. Wolf Von Eckardt, "Redesigning American Airports," *Harper's*, March 1967.

11. *Architectural Record*, March 1960, 176.

12. "Airports: The Dark Side of the Travel Boom," 102.

13. "Terminal Building, Love Field Airport, Dallas, Texas," *Architectural Record*, September 1960, 180–81.

14. William Pereira, *A Journey to the Airport*, in-house publication (Los Angeles: Pereira Associates, 1967).

15. Jameson was writing specifically about a hotel lobby in Los Angeles. Frederic Jameson, "Postmodernism and Consumer Society," *The Cultural Turn: Selected Writings on the Postmodern, 1983–1998* (London: Verso, 1998).

16. *Architectural Review* 132 (October 1962): 250–60.

17. *The Sketchbooks of Paolo Soleri* (Cambridge, Mass.: MIT Press, 1971), 308–14.

18. "The Future: Airports at Sea," *Time*, 30 May 1969, 61.

19. George Johnson, *The Abominable Airlines: An Alarming Report* (New York: Macmillan, 1964).

20. Lewis Mumford, *The Pentagon of Power* (New York: Harcourt Brace Jovanovich, 1970), 309.

21. Arthur Hailey, *Airport* (Garden City, N.Y.: Doubleday, 1968).

22. Ibid.

23. In 1909, Franz Kafka described the airfield at Brescia as "an artificial desert." (Franz Kafka, "The Aeroplanes at Brescia," 1909.) When Marcel Proust visited an aerodrome outside of Paris, he was reminded, oddly, of the seashore. Marcel Proust, *Remembrance of Things Past,* vol. III, trans. C. K. Scott-Montcrieff and Terence Kilmartin (New York: Random House, 1981), 100–101.

24. Jonathan Raban, *Hunting Mister Heartbreak: A Discovery of America* (London: Collins Harvill, 1990), 219–23.

25. Updike, *Marry Me.*

26. W. G. Sebald, *The Rings of Saturn* (London: Harvill Press, 1998), 89.

27. For a grisly inventory of aerial hijacking, see David Gero, *Flights of Terror, Aerial Hijack and Sabotage Since 1930* (Somerset, U.K.: Patrick Stephens, 1997).

28. Kenneth E. Cotcamp, an executive of Eastern Airlines, as quoted in "Air Riders Take Search in Stride," *New York Times*, 27 January 1973, 31.

29. Ibid.

30. Joan Didion, *Miami* (New York: Simon and Schuster, 1987), 23.

31. Kenneth C. Moore, *Airport, Aircraft, and Airline Security* (Boston: Butterworth-Heinemann, 1991), 66.

32. "Superimposed Functions: American at Kennedy," *Architectural Record*, October 1976, 136.

33. "Customs Area at Airport Screened to Foil Smuggling," *New York Times*, 26 April 1972.

34. *Architectural Record,* October 1966, 182–83.

35. BOAC's was the first terminal built in the United States by a foreign carrier. The British firm of Gollins Melvin Ward and Partners designed it.

36. The architects were Smith, Hinchman and Grylls.

37. I. M. Pei, architect of National's Sundrome at JFK, designed the tower with a slender, pentagonal base that flared near the top to support the air controllers' "cab," a prefabricated unit that was lowered into place by helicopter. The FAA tower, which came in several sizes, would be built at different airports around the country, including O'Hare, Houston, St. Louis, and El Paso.

38. Cologne-Bonn (1970) was designed by Paul Schneider-Esleben, architect. Otto Lilienthal Airport, Berlin/Tegel (1974), was designed by Meinhard von Gerkan, with Volkwin Marg and Klaus Nickels, architects.

39. Paul Virilio, *The Lost Dimension,* trans. Daniel Mashanberg (New York: Semiotext, 1991), 10.

40. Terminal 1, Charles de Gaulle International Airport, Roissy-en-France (1967–1974), Paul Andreu, chief architect for the Aéroports de Paris.
41. Interiors at Lubbock were by the firm InterArc. "New Airport with a Big Commitment," *Architectural Record,* October 1976.
42. Hellmuth, Obata and Kassabaum designed a penitentiary in Marion, Illinois, and the Illinois Maximum Security Psychiatric Center.
43. Between 1968 and 1972, 85 percent of all U.S. hijackings ended up in Cuba. Harry, Openheimer, Ross and Associates designed Miami's new international arrivals satellite in 1975. See "Airports," *Architectural Record,* October 1976, 127–31, 132–33.
44. H. P. Daniel van Ginkel, "Airports, The Systems Approach: A Working Tool for Airport Design," *Architectural Record,* August 1968.
45. Designed by Vincent G. Kling and Associates, opened in 1970. "Philadelphia International Airport," *Architectural Record,* August 1968.
46. Robert Horonjeff and Francis X. McKelvey, *Planning and Design of Airports* (New York: McGraw-Hill, 1983). As Richard de Neufville, a systems expert himself, confessed, the airport was not so much a "system" as it was a series of improvisations. George McCue, "Airport Architecture: The Dallas–Fort Worth Solution," *Art in America,* January–February 1974.
47. Reynolds, Smith and Hills were the architects. The cars were manufactured by Westinghouse Electric and could each carry a hundred people.
48. See "Airport Architecture: The Dallas–Fort Worth Solution."
49. Douglas Davis, "2001: The Ultimate Airport," *Newsweek,* 28 August 1972, 77–78.
50. Ibid. D/FW's park-and-fly configuration became a model for other airports, and crescent-shaped terminals were built in Kansas City, Rio de Janeiro, and elsewhere.
51. Ibid.
52. Ibid.
53. Geoffrey Egginton of the airport planning firm of Thompson Consultants, as quoted in "P/A Inquiry: Airport Terminals," *Progressive Architecture,* March 1987.
54. Stevens and Wilkinson along with Smith, Hinchman and Grylls designed the terminal.
55. For a comprehensive history of Atlanta Hartsfield, see Braden and Hagan, *A Dream Takes Flight.*
56. "Airports: The Dark Side of the Travel Boom," 106.

57. Gyo Obata designed the central hall at King Khalid.

58. Pico Iyer, *The Global Soul* (New York: Vintage Books, 2000).

59. "P/A Inquiry: Airport Terminals," *Progressive Architecture,* March 1987, 96–103.

60. "Postmodernism and Consumer Society," *The Cultural Turn.*

61. "Airport Offers Flights of Meditation," *New York Times,* 2 October 1992.

62. Ibid.; "It's a Mall . . . It's an Airport," *New York Times,* 10 June 1998; "shopping mall with planes leaving from it" was said by Jan Jansen, general manager of Terminal 4, Kennedy Airport, New York. See Alastair Gordon, "Lifting the Curse," *Condé Nast Traveler,* April 1999, 142; Chek Lap Kok in Hong Kong had the "Sky Mart" with more than 140 concessions, including Gucci, Ferragamo, Christian Dior, and an Irish pub. At Ronald Reagan National, sales averaged $950 per square foot, compared with $250 to $300 at regular malls.

63. Walter Kirn, *Up in the Air* (New York: Doubleday, 2001), 5.

64. Gyo Obata in interview with author.

65. Paul Goldberger, "Blueprint for an Airport That Might Have Been," *New York Times,* 17 June 1990.

66. *Norman Foster, 1964–1987* (Tokyo: A + U Publishing Company, 1988).

67. Atlanta's Midfield Complex, which opened fifteen years earlier, was an expansion of an older airport.

68. Kuala Lumpur opened in June 1998: "Bad Timing for Some Epic Projects," *New York Times,* 2 July 1998.

69. Ibid.

70. "Latest Letdown: Airport's Nosedive," *New York Times,* 11 July 1998.

71. Jeff MacGregor, "Fly the Angry Skies," *New York Times Magazine,* 24 September 2000, 21–22.

72. Timothy Peterson, a Continental Airlines baggage handler, as quoted in "Airport Attack at Newark Raises Fears," *New York Times,* 25 July 1999, 21.

73. John C. Davis Jr. was the assailant.

74. Gordon, "Lifting the Curse," 141.

75. Phone interview with author, 12 August 2000.

EPILOGUE: FROM LINDBERGH TO BIN LADEN

1. "[We will] provide security measures—visible security measures—so the traveling public will know that we are serious about airline safety in America," said the president. Elisabeth Bumiller, "Bush to

Increase Federal Role in Security at Airports," *New York Times,* 28 September 2001, 1.

2. Ethan Eyer, as quoted in "Guardsmen Take Positions at Terminals," Randy Kennedy, *New York Times,* 6 October 2001, B9.
3. Roland Barthes, *The Eiffel Tower and Other Mythologies* (New York: Hill and Wang, 1979).

Selected Bibliography

Airport Buildings. Washington D.C.: Civil Aeronautics Administration, U.S. Department of Commerce, 1946.

Airport and Airways. The Royal Institute of British Architects, London, 1937.

Allen, C. B. and Lauren D. Lyman. *The Wonder Book of the Air.* Chicago: John C. Winston Co., 1936.

American Airport Designs (reprint of 1930 edition). Washington D.C.: The American Institute of Architects Press, 1990.

Arend, Geoffrey. *Great Airports: Kennedy International.* New York: Air Cargo News, Inc., 1987.

———. *Air World's Great Airports: La Guardia.* New York: Air Cargo News, Inc., 1979.

———. *Air World's Great Airports: Newark 1928–1952.* New York: Air Cargo News, Inc., 1978.

Arthur, William E. "How Shall We Design Our Airports." *Scientific American,* October 1929, 298–301.

Baker, Trudy and Rachel Jones. *Coffee, Tea or Me?* New York: Bartholomew House Ltd., 1967.

Banham, Reyner. "The Obsolescent Airport." *Architectural Review,* October 1962, 250–60.

Berg, A. Scott. *Lindbergh.* New York: G.P. Putnam's Sons, 1998.

Bilstein, Roger E. *Flight in America: From the Wrights to the Astronauts.* Baltimore: Johns Hopkins University Press, 1984.

Black, Archibald. *Civil Airports and Airways.* New York: Simmons-Boardman Publishing Company, 1929.

Blow, Christopher J. *Airport Terminals.* Oxford: Butterworth-Heinemann Ltd., 1991.

Braden, Betsy and Paul Hagan. *A Dream Takes Flight: Hartsfield Atlanta International Airport and Aviation in Atlanta.* Athens, Georgia: The Atlanta Historical Society / University of Georgia Press, 1989.

Brodherson, David. "What Can't Go Up Can't Come Down: The History of American Airport Policy, Planning and Design." Ph.D. dissertation, Cornell University, 1993.

Corn, Joseph J. *The Winged Gospel: America's Romance with Aviation, 1900–1950.* New York: Oxford University Press, 1983.

Crider, John. "A National Airport." *New York Times Magazine,* 15 June 1941.

Curtiss-Wright Airports Corporation. *Curtiss-Wright Airports: A Nation-Wide Chain of Strategically Located Ports.* New York: Curtiss-Wright Airports, 1930.

Dempsey, Paul Stephen. *Denver International Airport: Lessons Learned.* New York: McGraw-Hill, 1997.

Duke, Donald. *Airports and Airways: Cost, Operation and Maintenance.* New York: The Ronald Press Company, 1927.

Frater, Alexander. *Beyond the Blue Horizon: On the Track of Imperial Airways.* London: William Heinemann Ltd., 1986.

Fritzsche, Peter. *A Nation of Fliers: German Aviation and the Popular Imagination.* Cambridge, Mass.: Harvard University Press, 1992.

Froesch, Charles and Walther Prokosch. *Airport Planning.* New York: John Wiley and Sons, 1946.

Geddes, Norman Bel. *Horizons.* Boston: Little, Brown and Company, 1932.

Gero, David. *Flights of Terror, Aerial Hijack and Sabotage since 1930.* Somerset (UK): Patrick Stephens Ltd., 1997.

Gordon, Alastair. "Lifting the Curse." *Condé Nast Traveler,* April 1999.

Greif, Martin. *The Airport Book: From Landing Field to Modern Terminal.* New York: Mayflower Books, Inc., 1979.

Hailey, Arthur. *Airport.* New York: Doubleday & Co., Inc., 1968.

Hamlin, Talbot F. "Airports as Architecture." *Pencil Points* 21, October 1940, 636–46.

Hanks, Steadman S. *International Airports.* New York: The Ronald Press Company, 1929.

Hayter, George. *Heathrow: The Story of the World's Greatest International Airport.* London: Pan Books Ltd., 1989.

Heino, Albert F. "Designing the Large Terminal." *Architectural Record,* April 1945.

Hood, Joseph F. *Skyway Round the World: The Story of the First Global Airway.* New York: Charles Scribner's Sons, 1968.

Horonjeff, Robert and Francis X. McKelvey. *Planning and Design of Airports.* New York: McGraw-Hill, 1983.

Hubbard, Henry V., Miller McClintok, and Frank B. Williams. *Airports: Their Location, Administration and Legal Basis.* Cambridge, Mass.: Harvard University Press, 1930.

Hudson, Kenneth. *Air Travel: A Social History.* Bath, UK: Adams & Dart, 1972.

Hudson, Kenneth and Julian Pettifer. *Diamonds in the Sky: A Social History of Air Travel.* London: The Bodley Head, 1979.

Iyer, Pico. *The Global Soul: Jet Lag, Shopping Malls, and the Search for Home.* New York: Vintage Books, 2000.

Jeanneret-Gris, Charles Édouard. *Aircraft.* London: The Studio Publications, 1935.

Johnson, George. *The Abominable Airlines: An Alarming Report.* New York: Macmillan, 1964.

Josephson, Matthew. *Empire of the Air: Juan Trippe and the Struggle for World Airways.* New York: Harcourt, Brace and Company, 1943.

Kaplan, James. *The Airport: Terminal Nights and Runway Days at John F. Kennedy International.* New York: William Morrow and Company, Inc., 1994.

Kauffman, Sanford B. *Pan Am Pioneer: A Manager's Memoir.* Lubbock, Tex.: Texas Tech University Press, 1995.

Keally, Francis. "Architectural Treatment of the Airport." *The Architect and Engineer* (Airport Number), November 1930, 43–51.

Kirn, Walter. *Up in the Air.* New York: Doubleday, 2001.

Komons, Nick A. *Bonfires to Beacons: Federal Civil Aviation Policy Under the Air Commerce Act, 1926–1938.* Washington, D.C.: Smithsonian Institution Press, 1989.

La Guardia, Fiorello H. "Finest Airport in the World." *New York Times Magazine,* 21 January 1945.

Lewis-Dale, H. Angley. *Aviation and the Aerodrome.* Philadelphia: J.B. Lippincott Company, 1932.

Lindbergh, Charles A. *The Spirit of St. Louis.* New York: Charles Scribner's Sons, 1953.

Lovegrove, Keith. *Airline: Identity, Design and Culture.* London: Laurence King Publishing, 2000.

McCue, George. "Airport Architecture: The Dallas–Fort Worth Solution." *Art in America,* January–February 1974.

McQuade, Walter. "The Birth of an Airport." *Fortune,* March 1962, 92–97.

Milhous, Katherine. *Wings Around South America.* New York: Charles Scribner's Sons, 1941.

Moran, Tom. *LAX, Los Angeles International Airport: From Lindbergh's Landing Strip to World Air Center.* Los Angeles: Los Angeles Department of Airports, 1993.

Mumford, Lewis. "The Sky Line: Millions for Mausoleums." *New Yorker,* 30 December 1939, 49–50.

Nelson, George. "Architecture for the New Itinerants." *Saturday Review,* 22 April 1967.

Neutra, Richard. "Terminals?—Transfer!" *Architectural Record,* August 1930, 99–104.

Norman, Nigel. "Aerodrome Design." *The Architectural Association Journal* 48, May 1933.

O'Callaghan, Timothy J. *Henry Ford's Airport and Other Aviation Interests.* Ann Arbor, Mich.: Proctor Publications, 1993.

Palmer, Henry R., Jr. *This Was Air Travel.* New York: Bonanza Books, 1960.

Pereira, William. *A Journey to the Airport.* Los Angeles: Pereira Associates (in-house publication), 1967.

Powell, Kenneth. *Stansted: Norman Foster and the Architecture of Flight.* London: Fourth Estate Ltd., 1992.

Prokosch, Walther. "Airport Design: Its Architectural Aspects." *Architectural Record,* January 1951.

————. *Detailed Design.* Cambridge, Mass: Chimera Press, 1983.

Román, Antonio. *Eero Saarinen: An Architecture of Multiplicity.* New York: Princeton Architectural Press, 2003.

Sampson, Anthony. *Empires of the Sky: The Politics, Contests and Cartels of World Airlines.* New York: Random House, 1984.

Schoneberger, William A. *California Wings: A History of Aviation in the Golden State.* Woodland Hills, Calif.: Windsor Publications, 1984.

Scullin, George. *International Airport: The Story of Kennedy Airport and U.S. Commercial Aviation.* Boston: Little, Brown and Company, 1968.

Solberg, Carl. *Conquest of the Skies: A History of Commercial Aviation in America.* Boston: Little, Brown and Company, 1979.

Spurrier, Raymond. "The Landscape of Hysteria: Towards a Clarified Aesthetic." *Architectural Review,* October 1962, 250–60.

Stratford, Alan. *Airports and the Environment.* New York: St. Martin's Press, 1974.

Stroud, John. *The World's Airports.* London: The Bodley Head, 1973.

Temko, Allan. *Eero Saarinen.* New York: Simon and Schuster, 1962.

Thomas, Lowell. *European Skyways: The Story of a Tour of Europe by Airplane.* Boston: Houghton Mifflin Company, 1927.

Von Eckardt, Wolf. "Redesigning American Airports." *Harper's Magazine,* March 1967.

Wagner, Sterling. "The Modern Airport." Bulletin of the New York State College of Forestry at Syracuse University, June 1931.

Wohl, Robert. *A Passion for Wings: Aviation and the Western Imagination, 1908–1918*. New Haven: Yale University Press, 1994.

Wood, John Walter. *Airports: Some Elements of Design and Future Development*. New York: Coward-McCann Inc., 1940.

Zukowsky, John, ed. *Building for Air Travel: Architecture and Design for Commercial Aviation*. Chicago: The Art Institute of Chicago, 1996.

Illustration Credits

Frontispiece: Rendering by Hugh Ferriss of a 1945 proposal for New York's Municipal Airport at Idlewild by Delano and Aldrich, architects. Avery Architectural and Fine Arts Library, Columbia University

Page xiv: TWA Terminal, Idlewild/Kennedy Airport, 1961, ESTO

Page 3: ESTO

Page 9: Cradle of Aviation Museum

Page 10: *Aerial Age Weekly*, June 7, 1920

Page 12: *Aerial Age Weekly*, February 14, 1921

Page 15: H. A. Lewis-Dale, *Aviation and the Aerodrome*, 1932

Page 16: Stedman Hanks, *International Airports*, 1929

Page 20: Lowell Thomas, *European Skyways*, 1927

Page 27: Air and Space Museum Archives, Smithsonian Institution

Page 35: Henry Ford Museum

Page 37: Air and Space Museum Archives, Smithsonian Institution

Page 42: *Scientific American*, October 1929

Page 45: Greater Buffalo International Airport

Page 46 (top): Avery Architectural and Fine Arts Library, Columbia University

Page 46 (bottom): Pan Am Archives, University of Miami

Page 49 (top): Henry V. Hubbard, Miller McClintok, and Frank B. Williams, *Airports: Their Location, Administration and Legal Basis*, 1930

Page 49 (bottom): American Airport Designs, 1930

Page 51 (top): Metropolitan Washington Airports Authority, Washington, D.C.

Page 51 (bottom): Port of Portland, Oregon

Page 53: Canadian Centre for Architecture, Montreal

Page 57: Martin Greif, *The Airport Book*, 1979

Page 58: Carnegie Library, Pittsburgh

Page 61: Los Angeles Department of Airports

Page 63: Los Angeles Department of Airports

Page 66: Virgilio Marchi, *Architettura Futurista*, 1924

Page 68: Le Corbusier, *Urbanisme*

Page 71 (top and bottom): No credit

Page 72 (top and bottom): No credit

Page 74: The Museum of Modern Art, New York

Page 78: John Stroud, *The World's Airports*, 1973

Page 80: *The Architectural Forum*, July 1930

Page 82: *Architectural Review*, July 1937

Page 84: Le Corbusier, *Oeuvres Complètes*, volume V, 1946–52

Page 86 (top): Air and Space Museum Archives, Smithsonian Institution

Page 86 (bottom): Jørgen Sestoft, *Vilhelm Lauritzen: A Modern Architect*, 1994

Page 95: Pan Am Archives, University of Miami

Pages 100–101: Newark Museum

Page 103: Author's collection

Page 105: Harry Ransom Humanities Research Center

Page 106: Harry Ransom Humanities Research Center

Page 110: *Contact*, July 16, 1938

Page 113: John Walter Wood, *Airports*, 1940

Page 115: Air and Space Museum Archives, Smithsonian Institution

Page 118: Cartoon by Sparling, *The Washington Herald*, January 20, 1938

Page 120 (top): Rendering by Hugh Ferriss. Drawings and Archives, Avery Architectural and Fine Arts Library, Columbia University

Page 120 (bottom): Metropolitan Washington Airports Authority

Page 125: Air and Space Museum Archives, Smithsonian Institution

Page 130: United Artists

Page 131: Geoffrey Arend, *Air World's Great Airports: La Guardia*, 1979

Page 133: Douglas Aircraft Company/McDonnell Douglas Corporation

Page 136: Advertisement, *The New Pencil Points*, June 1943

Pages 138–39: Vasari, Rome

Page 143: Photograph by Jacques Lowe

Page 148: *Architectural Record*, April 1945

Page 153 (top and bottom): Rendering by Hugh Ferriss. Avery Architectural and Fine Arts Library, Columbia University

Page 155: Downer, Green, and Carrillo; Clarke, Rapuano, and Holleran; Harrison and Abromovitz, *The New York Municipal Airport at Idlewild*, 1946

Page 160: No credit
Page 163 (top): Chicago Historical Society
Page 163 (bottom): No credit
Page 165 (top): Greater Pittsburgh Airport
Page 165 (bottom): Author's collection
Page 169 (top): *Architectural Record*, January 1951
Page 169 (bottom): *Architectural Record*, January 1951
Page 171 (top and bottom): No credit
Page 175: San Francisco International Airport
Pages 178–79: Ezra Stoller, ESTO
Page 181: United Airlines Archives
Page 182: Trudy Baker and Rachel Jones, *Coffee, Tea or Me?*, 1967
Page 183: No credit
Page 185: Hank Searls, *The Crowded Sky*, 1960
Page 191: Skidmore, Owings, and Merrill
Page 192: Skidmore, Owings, and Merrill
Page 194: Skidmore, Owings, and Merrill
Page 195: Skidmore, Owings, and Merrill
Page 197 (top): ESTO
Page 197 (bottom): Hugh Ferriss rendering. Avery Architectural and Fine Arts Library, Columbia University
Page 200 (top): Ezra Stoller, ESTO
Page 200 (bottom): Magazine advertisement
Page 201: Ezra Stoller
Page 205 (top and bottom): Pei, Cobb, Fried, and Partners
Page 207: Skidmore, Owings, and Merrill
Page 208: Murphy/Jahn
Page 210 (top and bottom): Harrison Abromowitz Architects
Page 212: Los Angeles Department of Airports
Page 213: Gary Winogrand
Page 220: Gary Winogrand
Page 224: Los Angeles Department of Airports
Page 226 (top): William Pereira, *A Journey to the Airport*, 1967
Page 226 (bottom): Edward G. Blankenship, *The Airport*, 1974
Page 232: No credit
Page 235: *The New York Times*, January 27, 1973
Page 239: Pei, Cobb, Fried, and Partners
Page 240: ESTO
Page 242: Tampa International Airport
Page 244 (top and bottom): Dallas/Fort Worth Airport
Page 247: Atlanta Hartsfield Airport
Page 249: *Progressive Architecture*, February 1982

Page 252: Pei, Cobb, Fried, and Partners
Page 255: Denver International Airport
Page 257: Sir Norman Foster and Partners
Page 262: William D. Nunez

Acknowledgments

In 1989 I organized a design competition for an airport and learned how little had been written on this enigmatic subject. Existing texts were either technical and unreadable or written for children. A notable exception was John Walter Wood's *Airports,* an insightful study of forty-eight airports around the world and a model of its kind. But even Wood's comprehensive analysis was out of date by the time it was published in 1940.

Every effort has been made in the present volume to provide accurate dates, descriptions, and proper names of those who designed or otherwise shaped the airport environment. Given the constant changes in aviation, however, authorship has not always been verifiable and my apologies are given in advance for any mistakes or misattributions.

I wish to acknowledge the thoughful guidance of my editor Riva Hocherman at Metropolitan Books as well as the encouragement of Heather Schroder at ICM and Peter Frank at *Condé Nast Traveler* for publishing an early excerpt. I am indebted to many individuals and institutions who either made invaluable suggestions or helped with research. I wish to thank the National Air and Space Museum; Avery Architectural and Fine Arts Library, Columbia University; Baltimore/Washington International Airport; Bregman + Hamann Architects; David Brohederson; the Greater Buffalo International

Airport; the Canadian Centre for Architecture; the Carnegie Library of Pittsburgh; the Chicago Historical Society; Cleveland Hopkins International Airport; Alan Colquhoun; the Cradle of Aviation Museum; Dallas/Fort Worth International Airport; Detroit Metropolitan Wayne County Airport; the Geraldine R. Dodge Foundation; Kate Evarts; the Henry Ford Museum; Sir Norman Foster and Partners; James E. Foy; Frontiers of Flight Museum, Dallas; Jordan Gruzen; Charles Gwathmey; Craig Hartman; Helen Harrison; William B. Hartsfield Atlanta International Airport; Hellmuth, Obata + Kassabaum, Inc.; Kansas Aviation Museum; Balthazar Korab; Lambert–St. Louis International Airport; Roland Legiardi-Laura; the Los Angeles Department of Airports; Maryland Aviation Administration; Massport/Logan Airport; McCarran International Airport, Las Vegas; the McDowell Colony; the Museum of Modern Art, New York City; the New York State Council on the Arts; Murphy/Jahn Architects; the Newark Museum; Gyo Obata; Tim O'Callaghan; the Princeton University Library; the Harry Ransom Humanities Research Center; the Archives of the City of New York; the Museum of the City of New York; Pei Cobb Fried & Partners; the Port Authority of New York; Port of Portland, Oregon; the Otto G. Richter Library at the University of Miami; the San Diego Aerospace Museum; San Francisco International Airport; Howard Shubert; Skidmore, Owings, and Merrill; Philip Smith; Ezra Stoller; Tampa International Airport; Marilyn Taylor; Doug Thompson; Wichita Airport Authority; the Yale University Library; the New York Public Library; United Airlines Archives; U.S. Library of Congress; Anthony Vacchione; Metropolitan Washington Airports Authority; and Minoru Yamasaki Associates.

I especially want to thank my four children: Iain, Iona, Kiki, and Leila who provide a constant source of inspiration and my wife, Barbara, for her loving support and editorial advice. It is to her that this book is dedicated.

Index

United Airlines, 164, 181, 222, 246
  boarding satellite, 175*f*
  terminal at Idlewild/Kennedy, 177,
    193, 195, 252
  terminal at Newark, 47
  Terminal for Tomorrow (O'Hare), 253
United Airport, Burbank, 63*f*
United Fruit Company, 41
United States, 135
  see also America
Updike, John, 221, 230
U.S. Airmail Service, 22
U.S. Department of Commerce, 115,
    117–18
  Aeronautics Branch, 57
U.S. Postal Service, 102–4, 117
U.S. State Department, 38, 40, 134
Utzon, Jørn, 198, 199

Vacchione, Anthony, 258
Vail Field, Los Angeles, 24
Vanderbilt, William H., 36
Versailles, 190–91
Vicariot, Henri, 213
Vienna, 17, 19, 20
Virilio, Paul, 177, 237

W. R. Grace and Company, 40
Wagner, Robert, 188
Wagner, Sterling, 50
Walker, James J., 107, 108
Washington, D.C., terminals in, 50

Washington-Hoover Air Terminal, 23,
    28, 50, 51*f*, 117
Washington National, 119–21, 120*f*,
    123, 137–40, 143, 145, 166, 173
Wayne Airport, Detroit, 28
Weidlinger, Paul, 227
Wells, Mary, 182
Western Air Express, 30, 31, 92
Whiting Corporation, 168
Whitney, Cornelius Vanderbilt, 36
Whittemore, Herbert, 135
Willkie, Wendell, 155
Willow Run Airport, Ypsilanti, 144
Wittwer, Hans, 85
Wood, John Walter, 104
Work Projects Administration (WPA),
    109, 111
  airports, 98–107
  Division of Airways and Airports, 98
World Trade Center, 204, 261–62
World War I, 13, 19, 23, 36, 65
World War II, 129–37, 142
WPA Modern, 102
Wright, Frank Lloyd, 52, 149, 227
Wright, Lloyd, 52–54, 131
Wright, Orville, 22, 157
Wright, Wilbur, 11, 22, 157

Yamasaki, Minoru, 177, 199, 204, 236
Yonge, James, 93

Zimmerman, A. C., 48

About the Author

Author, critic, curator, ALASTAIR GORDON is a contributing editor to *House & Garden* and *Dwell* magazines. He writes regularly for *The New York Times* and his articles have been published in *Architectural Digest, Condé Nast Traveler, Vanity Fair, Town & Country,* and *The New York Observer.* He is the author of several books including *Weekend Utopia: Modern Living in the Hamptons* and *Beach Houses: Andrew Geller.* He lives in Pennsylvania.